ALSO BY JAY GALE

A Young Man's Guide to Sex

A YOUNG WOMAN'S GUIDE TO SEX

Jacqueline Voss, Ph.D.
Jay Gale, Ph.D.

Henry Holt and Company   New York

613.955
V932y
1987

First published in January 1987 by
Henry Holt and Company, Inc., 521 Fifth Avenue,
New York, New York 10175.
Distributed in Canada by Fitzhenry & Whiteside Limited,
195 Allstate Parkway, Markham,
Ontario L3R 4T8.

86-1462

Library of Congress Cataloging in Publication Data
Voss, Jacqueline.
A young woman's guide to sex.
Bibliography: p.
Includes index.
Summary: A comprehensive guide to sex and sexuality,
especially for young women, with discussions of the
male and female bodies, making decisions, pregnancy,
masturbation, diseases, sexual responsibilities, desire,
sexual problems, helpful organizations, homosexuality,
and much more.
1. Sex instruction for girls. [1. Sex instruction
for girls] I. Gale, Jay. II. Title. [DNLM: 1. Sex—
in popular works. 2. Sex Behavior—in adolescence—
popular works. 3. Women—popular works. WS 462 V969y]
HQ51.V67   1986   613.9'55   86–4786
ISBN: 0-8050-0082-8

First Edition

Illustrations by Scott E. Carroll
Printed in the United States of America
1 3 5 7 9 10 8 6 4 2

ISBN 0-8050-0082-8

To my parents, Ila and Les, and my sister Kathy, for being my first family and for teaching me to believe in myself. To Janet Loxley and Joe White for nurturing that belief. And to Roy Campbell for his critique, computer, and caring.

—J.R.V.

To Mom and Dad

With love and appreciation for all that you have given and for all your support has meant.

—J.G.

CONTENTS

ILLUSTRATIONS

ACKNOWLEDGMENTS

The authors would like to thank Grant LeRoy Campbell, M.D., for his conscientious help in the preparation of the medical and biological information in this book.

A YOUNG WOMAN'S
GUIDE TO SEX

INTRODUCTION

This book is designed to educate you about the facts of sex, to dispel as many of the myths and exaggerations as possible, and at the same time to try to address many of the confusing emotional issues that teenage girls commonly face while adjusting to their new sexuality. It is *not* designed to influence you to be more sexual or less sexual. Nor is it designed to preach to you about how you ought to behave. That is a value you will have to determine for yourself. It is a book that will deal realistically with the facts about sex, the joyful part as well as the serious responsibilities, so that you can make up your own mind. It will attempt to guide you so that you may clarify your own feelings and attitudes in a way that will enable you to feel more confident of yourself as a sexual human being.

You may think that it is a huge assumption to refer to you as a "sexual human being," but actually it is not an assumption at all. Sexuality is merely one aspect of all humans. Being sexual does not necessarily mean hopping into bed with a boy. Flirting, kissing, petting, self-pleasuring, and intercourse are all different types of sexual activity. Even the presence of sexual thoughts, feelings, and values is a clear demonstration of the existence of your sexuality.

Although many other teenagers, including some of your

friends, may experience similar emotional and physical reactions, your pattern of sexual growth is as unique as the pattern on a snowflake. That is why in reading this book you may relate to many situations that are very similar to your own and yet find others that do not seem relevant at all. You are a unique individual, and consequently your experiences will differ somewhat from those of other adolescents. That does not make you weird, nor does it make them weird. It simply means that you are not identical to your friends, so your feelings, beliefs, values, and relationships will be somewhat different. I hope that after reading this book you will find that you are the only true expert on your body and feelings.

When reading a book on sex, you probably will want to look ahead to the "good" parts where I discuss more about making love, or to a chapter that discusses a problem you are presently experiencing. If you want to do that, fine, but don't forget to come back to the chapters you've skipped. It is helpful to have a thorough understanding of what you have already gone through and of what you are currently facing if you are to meet your sexual future with a minimum of hang-ups. The order of these chapters was based on the way I felt they could be most beneficial to you, but you might have a different order in mind. It may be good to note which chapters you've read, so you don't forget to return to the ones you've skipped.

The book is designed so that you can keep it and go back to it throughout your teenage years. It provides an opportunity for you to become aware of who you are sexually, and to understand what you are going through. You cannot read this book just once and expect to understand everything there is to know about sex. I hope that reading through it a single time will help you in clearing up much of the confusion that most adolescents (and adults) experience about sex. However, to take full advantage of this book, try lightly reading through the entire book once from cover to cover to become familiar with the information it contains. Then, put it away until you enter a different stage of your sexuality or until you think of some more questions you want answered. For instance, although chapter 9, about making sexual decisions, may not seem very relevant to you now, as you become romantically or sexually involved with someone this chapter may seem more pertinent.

As you are reading through this book you may wonder why when the two authors talk about personal feelings or experiences they use the word *I* instead of *we*. This is a book for and about young women. Therefore, although the factual information here came from both authors, the personal point of view reflects mainly the experiences and feelings of the female author, Jacqueline Voss.

Each chapter will open up new aspects of sexuality you might want to think about so that you can make more educated choices about the direction you want to move toward in the future. As a sexual being, you will be growing and changing for the rest of your life. You will have both positive and negative experiences, and I hope you will be able to learn from both.

1

BECOMING A SEXUAL PERSON

I really wanted a decent book on sex when I was a teenager. To say that I felt curious and confused does not at all describe the extreme fascination and bewilderment I experienced. My body was rapidly developing, but it still didn't look as spectacular as those of the stars in the movie magazines or even like those of some of the other girls in my classes. I daydreamed about boys and was captivated by romantic movies. I'd remember some beautiful love scene and try to picture what it would be like for me. It was fun and exciting, and even a bit scary.

My friends and I talked constantly about boys, giggling about who was cute and whispering about who was fast. We swapped information we had picked up about love and sex, all the time trying to sound sophisticated and worldly. I developed a series of heartbreaking crushes: George Harrison of the Beatles, the student teacher in my math class, and several guys at my school. Later, I fell in love "for real." Then my confusion, insecurities, and excitement only intensified.

Throughout my adolescence I was curious about sex, but in no way did I want anyone to know how curious I was. I sometimes spent hours skimming through novels from my parents' bookcase, looking for a few steamy scenes. Once I stayed up all night reading a boring novel, because when I asked my dad if it was a good book he yelled *"No!"* From the tone of his voice I was sure it had some "hot" passages.

Another book I found on my parents' shelf was a *Reader's Digest* medical guide. The book was huge, literally weighing about five pounds, and had a bright-green cover. I smuggled this thing up to my room (which is not easy to do with a five-pound, bright-green book) and hid in my closet with it. When I opened the book, most of the words were Latin and beyond figuring out anyway. For years I pretty much alternated between feeling like a nerd for not knowing much about sex and feeling like a pervert for trying to find out about it.

At this point in your life you are undoubtedly being bombarded with "facts," opinions, feelings, and messages about sexuality. Sex is all around you. Friends and parents are talking, joking, and whispering about it. Teachers and clergymen are lecturing about it. And sex is in nearly every movie and a good share of magazines, novels, and TV programs.

With all these potential sex education resources, you might expect that you should be very knowledgeable about sex and confident of your own sexuality. However, I have *never* known a teenage girl who didn't experience some confusion about sex: about the facts, her feelings, how she wanted to behave, and about her femininity.

The reason that you and other girls get confused is that most of the different sources of information about sex offer contradictory opinions, unrealistic views, and often just plain inaccurate information. It will not be easy for you to sort through all the conflicting information that will confront you during your **adolescence**, and figure out what is true, what isn't, and what is simply personal opinion.

One prime source of inaccurate information is other adolescents. When I was a teenager, a friend told me that because she now wore a bra, she was also producing milk and had nursed a baby. I believed her. I even read something similar in one of my parents' novels, which confirmed it in my mind. Only years later did I find out that producing milk is very much tied to chemical changes that occur in a woman's body during pregnancy. Just buying a bra won't do the trick.

That's the problem with sex information. It's hard to know who has their facts correct and who doesn't. Maybe if my friend had purposely lied about the information or had just tried to fool me, I might have been able to tell that the information was incorrect. However, often when friends talk about the "facts" of life, they don't even know that they don't have their facts straight. This is illustrated in the following excerpt from *Fast Times at Ridgemont High*, a novel by Cameron Crowe.

There had been a guy in the seventh grade whose mother told him women had teeth in their vagina. The boy must have believed it. He stood up in sex-ed class one day—Stacy was there—and asked, "Do very many men get their penises cut off?"

The kid quickly got himself the nickname Jaws, and didn't come back to Paul Revere Junior High the next year. Someone called his home and was referred to a number in Alabama.[1]

Parents and adults are not certified sex experts either. A girl in one of my classes wrote to me,

My mother was very embarrassed by her lack of knowledge as she grew up.

Because of this my mother had to learn everything from outside the family. She said she would make sure if she had kids, she would tell them as much as she could. She is always open with us, but when we had our talk, I found out later that there was a lot of information that she didn't know or that she was not accurate about. I felt embarrassed at times when my girlfriends were talking about something and I didn't know what it was.

When I got into high school, part of my health class was devoted to an open discussion about sex. We all wrote ten questions down and all of them were answered. *It was great because my mother and I learned a lot.*

Even more confusing than the facts are the opinions about sex. Everyone seems to feel strongly about it, one way or another. Some people insist that sex is sinful, dirty, ugly, and that only bad girls engage in it. Others swear that it is fun, exciting, warm, beautiful, and that it makes you a "real" woman. There are even a lot of people who will avoid mentioning it and will act uncomfortable and change the subject when the topic of sex is brought up. People will lie about sex, whisper about it, laugh and joke, lecture and brag, but few people will appear neutral about it.

At the same time movies, television, and many novels make it seem as if anyone who is not "frigid" has sex eight or ten times a day. From many of the soap operas, it appears that sex is the only important thing people do. Being a "real woman" is equated with being a sexual athlete or a seductive "fox." This is not at all the way sex is in the real world. Trying to live up to this fantasy view of sex portrayed in the media is a sure way to end up feeling inadequate and disappointed.

At this point it might make sense to stop and think about what you already have been taught about sex. While doing this, you can try to sort out accurate information from myth, and fact from opinion. Here are some questions you can ask yourself:

What are some facts I have been taught about sex?
Where did I learn them?
Do I think each "fact" is true? Am I sure?

What are some feelings and attitudes I have been taught about sex?
How did I learn them?
Do I accept them as my own?

What are some things I have been taught about how I should behave?
Who taught me these?
Would I really feel comfortable behaving that way?

Answering these questions can give you an idea of which areas are confusing to you and those for which you may need further information. It will also help make more obvious some of the conflicting messages you have been told about how to feel and how to behave.

2

LEARNING ABOUT SEX

One thing is certain. Whether you read this book or not, you will learn about sex. That doesn't mean that you should put this book up on a shelf and forget about it. It means that there is no way you can live in any society without accumulating all sorts of facts, attitudes, and misconceptions about sex. I guarantee that you already have some strong feelings about sex. If you don't believe me, think about the following: When you first saw the name of this book, what was your reaction to the word *sex*? Was there a feeling of embarrassment, excitement, strong curiosity, or a feeling that you wanted nothing to do with it? Did you laugh uncomfortably, make a joke, or blush? My guess is that in some way or other you had some sort of strong feeling. If this book were *A Young Woman's Guide to Computers*, your reaction would probably have been quite different. Simply seeing or hearing the word *sex* seems to create very strong feelings among people in our society— adults as well as teenagers. As you well know, when you are highly emotional about an issue, the facts easily become distorted.

Learning about sex will mean sorting through these highly charged feelings and separating the facts from the myths. This process can be confusing, difficult, and exciting, but there are ways to approach it that make hassles less likely. Important goals are: first, to learn some factual information about the human body and how it functions sexually; second, to get a chance to talk and think about your feelings with regard to sex; and third, to make some tentative decisions about how you want to behave sexually at this point in your life. Let's look at your potential sources of help and talk about how you might use them. Possible places to turn are friends, parents, brothers and sisters, teachers, counselors, and books.

Talking with Friends

Talking with friends is the most common way teenagers learn about sex, but sometimes those discussions are not as enlightening as we would like them to be. I learned some classic myths from my friends. One girl authoritatively announced that it had been proven that breast size is related to intelligence—the larger the breasts, the dumber the woman. At a slumber party a friend whispered that you could tell if a girl was a virgin by the way she walked. (The following day we checked out all the other girls as they unsuspectingly walked down the school halls.)

In addition, friends can often communicate contradictory attitudes about sex. Peers have a funny way of telling you to "go for it" and to "save yourself" practically in the same conversation. One of my students talked about this double message:

> I was encouraged not to be old-fashioned and a prude, but at the same time told not to ruin my reputation or be a "slut." We all wanted to be popular, to look sexy, and to be pursued by the boys. At the same time we didn't want to be "cheap" or "easy." We compared notes on when and how to kiss, how far to go, and which boys had fast hands. Some of my friends bragged about things they'd done with boys; some bragged about things they wanted me to think they'd done; and almost all of them gossiped.

Again, it helps to remember that your friends have been exposed to the same contradictory messages that you have. Most of them are probably not any more sure about what is going on than you are. They, too, are apt to have mixed and changing feelings.

If you do choose to be open with friends, I would suggest one important caution. No matter what your friends tell you, reserve some doubt about the information they offer. Not only might they share myths rather than facts, but also, many of them will find it difficult to be completely honest about sexual feelings and experiences. Often, teenagers (as well as some adults) feel a need to pretend that they are more comfortable and experienced than they actually are. In other cases, some teenage girls refuse to admit to any sexual feelings or behavior because they have been taught that sexuality is shameful or wrong. I was completely surprised to find out years later that girls among my friends whom we all teased about being too "square" were probably the first to "go all the way."

On the other hand, because your friends are more than likely going through similar emotional and physical experiences, they can be an important resource in checking out your sexual feelings and helping to resolve your conflicts. As you proceed on your adventure through the physical and emotional changes of **puberty**, they will share many of the same concerns.

One consideration for getting the most out of discussions with friends is to be careful about who you choose to be open with. You will probably feel more comfortable if you choose to talk to someone you like and trust—someone who is not a teaser, a gossip, or a person who constantly brags. Sometimes the people who appear to be the most experienced and "cool" about sex are not the most honest or supportive.

Talking privately with only one person or with a very small group of friends may make it quite a bit easier to ask uncomfortable questions. Usually it is easier for girls to talk to other girls about sex. Again the body changes, pressures, and emotions are more alike. Occasionally, however, you might have a close male friend to whom you can talk about sensitive matters. If you are lucky enough to have such a friend, he may be able to help you to understand what boys are going through and how they look at things.

A last thing to consider is that even with close friends your feelings and experiences will not be identical to theirs. Each of you gets turned on or off by different things. A person whom you find attractive may not at all appeal to your friends. I've never been able to understand why everyone goes wild when Billy Idol jumps onto the stage, while many of my students chuckle at my continued adoration of Jackson Browne. Share your feelings with your friends and listen to what they have to say, but try not to harshly judge either them or yourself. Each of you will have different values, different standards, different feelings, different relationships, and different backgrounds. Sexual feelings are not correct or incorrect, they are personal.

When Will My Parents Teach Me About Sex?

Actually your parents have been teaching you about sexuality, relationships, and what it means to be a woman from the day you were born. The name they chose for you, the pink blanket they wrapped you in, the toys they bought for you all came with certain expectations of you as a female. It is impossible for parents not to have expectations for a child.

As girls are growing up, they are often raised with the expectations that they should take care of others, that being popular is important, and that anger and assertiveness are unacceptable. Even in our modern times, most girls are hesitant to be the one to make the first move to initiate a romantic relationship. Girls are often encouraged to be sweet and appealing, but not aggressive. Certainly this can be confusing if you are beginning to feel attracted to a person and yet won't give yourself permission to approach him for fear of being perceived as "unfeminine" or "pushy." It is also confusing when you feel that you have been treated badly, but are afraid of expressing anger; or when you feel someone is pushing you too fast, but are scared that standing up for yourself will make you risk losing the relationship.

Some parents are uncomfortable with physical contact and expressions of caring, and so they rarely hug or come out and say that they love their children. Unfortunately, instead of realizing that the parents have a problem in this area, a child is likely to perceive it as rejection and conclude that she is not very lovable or appealing. This can affect her self-image in later years and make relationships more difficult.

The relationship your parents have with each other serves as a model that you will use to compare future relationships of your own. If your parents are affectionate and loving to each other, it will probably make it easier for you to communicate these feelings because they have been modeled for you. If your parents are comfortable touching each other and you, then you will probably feel less awkward when you want to communicate affection by holding and touching. It's like watching a movie character that you really enjoy. By watching her in the movie, you can copy some of the actions and mannerisms you admire. If your parents are reserved or awkward about physical contact, it will probably take you longer to feel good about it yourself.

Talking to Parents About Sex

I have taught a course on human sexuality to about three hundred students per quarter for years now. Since I can comfortably talk about sex in front of that many people, it would seem that it would be easy for me to talk intimately about sex to anyone. This comfort holds true except with my own parents. I know that my parents care for me and are interested in my life and happiness. Yet, discussing sex with them still feels strange. This discomfort is certainly not universal among children and parents, but I would guess that many families do experience it. Often parents awkwardly await the first question about sex from their child, looking forward to the closeness such intimate discussions bring. Yet, if the question does not come, there may be a sense of relief that they did not have to face the discomfort of openly discussing sexuality.

Even in situations where teenagers do try to discuss sex, the results are not always encouraging. In a survey of teens, Aaron Hass asked, "Have you ever tried to talk openly with either of your parents about sex? If you have tried, how did they respond?" Hass reports, "Forty percent of the boys and 54 percent of the girls reported attempts to talk openly with a parent. The common parental responses reported by teenagers were teasing, denial, and punishment. . . . Frequently, a teenager felt lectured instead of listened to."[1]

Let me pose two questions to you:

1. Would you like to be able to talk more openly to your parents about sex?
2. What have you done to approach your parents about this?

If the answer to the first question indicates that you are interested in learning from your parents, then the answer to the second one is critical. Many teenagers assume that it is their parents' responsibility to initiate a talk about sex and, therefore, do nothing themselves. If you wish to discuss your questions and concerns about sex, then *you* may have to take the lead. Bringing up the topic of sex can be just as uncomfortable and confusing for parents as it is for their children.

Understanding Your Parents

If you have tried unsuccessfully in the past to speak to your parents about sex, you and they deserve a second chance. If they tease you or make jokes, try to understand that they too may be uncomfortable. Let them know that you are serious. If they present you with a lecture about what is right and wrong, accept this as their values. It will only be frustrating to you if you try to convince them that their values are wrong or old-fashioned. You probably will have a somewhat different set of values from those of your parents. That does not mean that either you or your parents are necessarily wrong. Listen to what they believe and try to understand why they feel the way they do. Once you understand their values, you can try to evaluate the following:

1. In what areas are my values similar to my parents?
2. In what areas do my values differ from my parents?
3. What are the advantages and disadvantages of each of our points of view?

If your parents happen to be too uncomfortable to talk about sex, you might want to remember that they grew up under different circumstances from you. They were much more likely to have been taught that sex was not to be talked about. It is not that they want you to become sexually maladjusted, never to enjoy sex, or to feel confused. They may just need someone they can talk to themselves before they can talk to you. One mother of teenage girls explained why she had enrolled in the course I teach:

Even though I have tried to answer the girls' questions with honesty, I now know just how little I knew. I grew up in the fifties and sixties when parents refused to even discuss the basics. Even today my mother is unable to talk about anything related to sexuality with me. I have tried to give my girls the opportunity to talk to me about anything and know that if I don't know the answer, I'll try to find it.

Because some parents feel conflicts about sexuality, they may send confusing messages to their children about sexual feelings and behavior. Often, parents or other adults tell you that you should engage in no sexual behavior, other than kissing and holding hands, until you are married. Yet you probably suspect, and rightly so, that many of them did not wait until after marriage to be sexually active, and that married people are certainly not the only ones being sexual.

So how come they want you to be less sexually active than the society around you? Parents and other adults worry about their kids, especially about teenage girls, getting hurt by sexual activity or becoming pregnant. Many girls are exploited and wounded emotionally, and far too many have to face an unwanted **pregnancy** or a **sexually transmitted disease**. Unfortunately, in their attempts to protect you from such painful experiences, adults sometimes make sex sound very negative. Again, an excerpt from *Fast Times at Ridgemont High* illustrates this point.

Stacy herself had learned about sex from her mother, in a supermarket, in the feminine-hygiene section. "There is a certain thing that adults do after they are married," Mrs. H. told her. "The purpose is to have children." She went on to explain the sexual process in such cold clinical terms that Stacy's first question was, "Does a doctor perform the operation?"

"No," said Mrs. H., "your father and I did it ourselves."

In the years that followed, Mrs. Hamilton never mentioned the subject again. Not even a word. Stacy's mother seemed to consider sex an unmentionable obligation performed in unspeakable situations. Sometimes she'd say something like, "You watch out for boys with beer breath; you know what they want."[2]

It is important for you to have someone to help you understand what your body and mind are going through. If you've tried, but really don't feel comfortable sharing all or any of your questions, concerns, and feelings with your parents, then try a brother or sister, a friend, or another adult.

Talking with Brothers and Sisters

As with friends, older brothers and sisters can be a valuable source of sexual information. They may have gone through experiences similar to yours. However, the same cautions that were mentioned about friends apply to brothers and sisters. Realize that both their own comfort or lack of comfort with sex and the circumstances under which you speak to them may affect their honesty and directness in discussing sex with you.

Talking with Other Adults

You probably know at least one adult besides your parents whom you respect and trust. Talking to one or more of them about your questions, feelings, and concerns can be helpful if you are afraid of approaching your parents or if you simply would like to hear some additional views. Try to think of teachers, school counselors, physicians, members of the clergy, relatives, neighbors, or even a friend's parent who you feel will listen and speak honestly with you.

If you cannot think of anyone you already know personally, don't give up. Almost every town has teen centers, counseling centers, telephone hot lines, health clinics, and similar organizations that have counselors especially for that purpose. You don't need to have a major problem to go to one of these places. When I worked in a counseling center, students stopped in all the time just to get some information or to talk about something they were feeling or thinking.

Communicating About Sex: The First Steps

When you speak to someone, much more is communicated than just your words. The tone of your voice, your facial expression, a gesture, a touch, or even the position of your body can change the meaning of what you say. With a subject as emotionally charged as sex, these extra cues from someone's body and face can actually speak louder than any spoken words. For instance, when a teacher looks very uneasy when talking to you about "reproduction," the message that may be communicated is that "sex is dirty." When your friends giggle or whisper about sex, you may pick up the message "I feel very uptight about sex and am trying to cover up my anxiety with jokes." In both cases, what was communicated is very different from what has been said.

Even not saying anything can communicate a message. For instance, when parents are silent about sex, what probably is communicated is "I am embarrassed and would rather not talk about this." Similarly, when you say nothing to your parents, they may interpret your silence as "She's not interested in sex" or "She already knows all she wants to."

Because you do communicate with your family and friends about sex in one way or another, you might as well do a good job. The following questions may be useful in evaluating how well you communicate about sex:

Do I make it difficult for people, such as my parents, to talk with me about sex?
Do my actions make it look as if I want to be left alone or am not interested?
Do I change the subject, make jokes, or act disgusted when sex is brought up?

You can use similar questions to help you figure out who you can get more information from:

Who do I know who doesn't always avoid the topic of sex?
Who do I know who doesn't look overwhelmingly uncomfortable when talking about sex?

Those people may be willing to talk to you more openly. After you've thought of some people you might talk to, the following list of suggestions may be helpful to you in opening up some doors to communication.

Opening Doors to Communication

1. Make a list of the areas of sexuality that are most confusing to you, writing down your major concerns or the questions that occur to you.

2. For each item on your list, write down who you would like to talk to about that concern. Pick someone who you think would have information on the topic, who would be willing to exchange ideas with you, and whom you would feel comfortable enough to approach with your question.

3. Pick a time and place where the two of you can have a discussion without being interrupted or feeling rushed. Make a clear statement to that person about what you want to know or share.

4. The chances are that you will get the information you wish. However, be aware that the person you choose may not have the information you want or may have values that are very different from yours. Even if you don't agree, hear her or him out, without trying to prove them right or wrong. For example, if you approach your parents with a question about **masturbation** and they respond with a lecture about the evils of touching yourself, accept this as their point of view, without feeling obligated to either disprove them or to accept their values.

Helping Communication Along: Asking Questions, Listening, and Clarifying

There are some things to keep in mind while you are discussing sex with others that will help you get the most out of the conversation and help keep the communication going. For one thing, *how* you ask questions can influence how much the person tells you. There are two types of questions. One is "close-ended" questions and the other is "open-ended" questions. Close-ended questions are questions that can be answered with a single word and tend not to encourage any further discussion. Open-ended questions require more than just a single-word answer and they tend to start with *how, why,* and *what.* People tend to respond to open-ended questions by providing a greater amount of information, by talking more openly, and by explaining why they think the way they do. Therefore, you can usually make a conversation flow more easily by using mostly open-ended questions.

As a practice exercise, take the questions that you listed earlier about sex and make them into either close-ended or open-ended questions. Some typical open-ended questions girls ask are:

1. What happens in the body during puberty?
2. How does a woman get pregnant?
3. What helps relationships get better?
4. What happens during an orgasm?

Some of their close-ended questions are:

1. Can a girl get pregnant without having intercourse?
2. Can the pill cause cancer?
3. Do women have orgasms?
4. Is there a safe period when a girl absolutely cannot get pregnant?

Besides the type of questions you ask, the manner in which you *show* someone that you are listening will greatly affect how well the two of you communicate. Stop and think about how you can tell when a friend is really listening to you and is interested in what you are saying. She looks at you, she may lean forward, and she might even nod now and then. If, however, she is bored, disinterested, or too busy, she may look away from you, check her watch a lot, pick at her nails, fidget nervously, or yawn. When someone *looks* interested in what we are saying, we tend to talk more and to enjoy it more. It's not much fun to talk to someone who looks bored or disapproving. In this way you can help the person who is giving you information simply by *showing* that you are listening.

Clarifying what the person has said is an additional tool in good communication. Clarifying can help you to make certain that you understand what the person is trying to say. It is also another way to show that you have actually listened to what has been said. A good method for clarifying is to briefly *summarize* what the person has said *in your own words*. Let's say that you want to clarify what I've said so far about helping communication along. You might say to me, "Let me see if I understand. You are telling me that I can make my conversations about sex better by the way I ask questions, by showing that I'm listening, and by clarifying what the person has said." I'd respond, "Exactly!" and we'd know that we understand each other. If I thought that you had misunderstood me or missed an important point, I might say, "Not exactly," and go on to reexplain so that we could clear up the confusion.

Sometimes you may not understand what someone is saying to you. In those cases, be sure to let the person know that you are getting lost. It is especially helpful if you can tell her what it is that you do not understand. A word might have been used that you don't know the meaning of, or the person may be talking too fast. By letting her know what's wrong, you give her the chance to explain what the word means or to slow down.

3

UNDERSTANDING
YOUR BODY

The Seasons of Your Life

In a sense, life goes through stages, like the year goes through seasons. Each season is separate and distinct from the others, yet all are a part of a continuous process. Likewise, each of the "seasons" of your life is very different from the others. You have already gone through the infancy stage and most or all of your childhood. Thus, you are about to enter, or have already entered, a stage called **puberty** (*pyoo*-ber-tee). This, like springtime, is the season of your life when your body and mind go through an explosion of growth. Understanding what to expect during this period of your life can make it a very exciting time. Not understanding the tremendous change can result in a great deal of unnecessary fear and confusion. The experiences of the following two girls are not atypical.

I was never told what it would feel like when my breasts started to grow and was convinced I had cancer.

When my cousin started her period, she thought she'd been raped in her sleep, because she thought the only way to start your period was after the first time you have sex.

Puberty and Your Sexual Body

Puberty is a stage in your development when many dramatic physical changes occur. Your body begins a period of rapid growth. On the outside it begins to look more like that of a woman than that of a little girl, while on the inside it matures in a way that makes pregnancy and childbirth possible. It is during puberty that a girl is first capable of becoming pregnant. Puberty will probably begin for you sometime between the ages of nine and twelve and will last until you are sixteen or seventeen. However, since every girl develops at a different rate, some girls may start changing physically before the age of nine while others may begin after age twelve. This variation is normal.

Boys usually enter puberty about two years later than girls. This fact can be somewhat upsetting for both sexes. It means that for a couple of years girls tend to look much more mature than their male classmates and friends. Again, this is normal and the boys will catch up in a few years.

You might be wondering what causes puberty and whether there is anything you can do to speed it up or slow it down. As I passed through puberty, I wished that some changes could have occurred immediately and others not at all. I would have been really pleased to grow breasts right away, but never to have gotten acne.

Puberty happens automatically when your body begins to produce more of certain chemicals called **hormones**. These hormones, like messengers, travel throughout your bloodstream and alert the different parts of your body that it is time to change. The timing of the beginning of this increased production of hormones is controlled by the brain and is pretty much fixed by your heredity. If other women in your family had early puberties, you are also likely to start at a younger age. Although it is unlikely that anything you do will speed up the start of puberty, certain life-styles and medical conditions may slow its onset. For example, girls with eating disorders that cause them to be underweight or malnourished, such as anorexia, may undergo some of the changes of puberty at a delayed rate. Similarly, delays are not uncommon in girls who are very active and athletic, such as long-distance runners.

The Growth Spurt

I mentioned three types of changes that occur during puberty. The first is a **growth spurt**. As you enter puberty, you will grow taller at a faster rate than you had been before. Strangely enough, as your whole body is lengthening, your arms, legs, hands, and feet may grow even faster than the rest of you. This takes a bit of getting used to and may lead to you feeling a little clumsy for a while.

Slowly, the growth spurt will begin to taper off and you will stop getting taller. Many girls reach their final height by about age sixteen. Most boys, on the other hand, don't reach their maximum height until about age eighteen.

Changes on the Outside of Your Body During Puberty

The second type of *pubertal* change I mentioned was the external changes in your body that make you look like a woman. These are the ones that are the most obvious to you—and to others. The first change you will notice is that your breasts will begin to grow and start to protrude.

Almost all girls (I actually think it is *all* girls) worry about their breasts. Some girls worry that their breasts are growing too slowly. Other girls worry that they are maturing earlier than their friends and classmates. Some girls fret about them being "too small" and others feel self-conscious about them being "too large." You'll notice that girls are concerned about opposite "problems" and that it seems that everyone is complaining or worrying. That's pretty normal. The two quotes below are from two girls who were self-conscious about their changing bodies, one because she felt hers was developing too slowly and the other because she wasn't ready for her rapid growth.

> In seventh grade I went to a camp for girls. When it came time to take a shower, I saw that the girls in my cabin had already started to develop breasts and pubic hair, and well, I was a "late-bloomer!" I felt very inadequate and embarrassed. Apparently so did my friend Cindy from my school, who was also in seventh grade and a "late-bloomer" also. We had these big lockers in our room that you could fit into easily. We both changed our clothes in these lockers and also avoided taking showers with the rest of the girls. All I could think of was, Thank God the camp only lasts five days! I only showered twice. It's pretty hilarious now, but at the time it sure wasn't.

> In going through puberty, the hard part was not actually having my body change but how attitudes towards me changed. I didn't used to worry about what I would wear or if I was showing "too much." But as my breasts developed and my hips flared, men looked at me differently. They would stare at me or whistle. I was not used to this and hadn't expected it. I became more withdrawn from the guys and became very conservative in what I would wear. I no longer would wear shorts or sun dresses because I felt extremely uncomfortable being stared at.

Despite anything I might say, you will probably still be concerned about how fast you are developing and about the size of your breasts. However, breasts and bodies come in all sizes and shapes, but neither the size nor the shape has anything to do with how feminine a girl or woman is.

A common myth among teenagers is that a girl's breasts are filled with milk. However, the glands in the breast do not begin producing milk until after a woman delivers a baby, and unless she is **nursing** the baby (feeding it her breast milk), the breasts will stop producing milk.

Breasts are made up mostly of fatty tissue. Besides the fatty tissue, the breasts contain the **mammary glands**, which produce milk when necessary, and **ducts** (passageways), along which the milk travels until it reaches the tip of the breast, or **nipple**. This is the area that a baby sucks to get milk from a mother who is breast-feeding. Like breasts, nipples also come in all sizes and shapes. Some may stick straight out and others may turn inward. They tend to get more erect when a woman is cold or when she is sexually stimulated. Surrounding the nipple is a round, darker area called the **areola** (ah-*ree*-uh-lu). The areola may vary in size from small to large, and in color from very dark to pink. Sometimes it has tiny bumps.

After your breasts begin developing, you will notice that your hips will start to widen. This happens, in part, because the pelvic bone itself gets wider and also because some pads of fatty tissue develop. Extra hair sprouts on parts of your body. Hair on your **pubic** (*pyoo*-bik) **area** (a fatty triangle on the part of your body between your legs) starts out fine and may be light in color, then gets thicker, curlier, and darker. Underarm hair and leg hair will also become noticeable. Many girls in our culture choose to shave off the hair under their arms and on their legs. In many other cultures this is not so common a practice.

Acne (*ak*-nee), a skin disorder marked by pimples and blackheads, is a part of adolescence that no one likes. Some hormones cause your skin to get oilier and your pores to enlarge—so some acne is almost always inevitable. You can do some things to make it better, such as washing often and not picking at your pimples. If your acne is very bad, visit a physician. He or she can help you to keep it under control.

One change that many girls don't notice is the maturing of their sex organs. These are the parts of your body that make you a girl as opposed to a boy; the parts that are different in women and men. These are the organs of the body that are

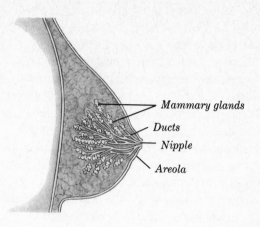

Figure 1   Cross section of a female breast

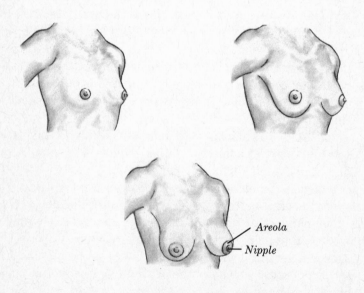

Figure 2   Three various shapes of breasts

involved in sexual activity and in pregnancy.

Although all of us are curious about what we look like "down there," you may have some feelings of being bad for wanting to look at and explore your sex organs. Unfortunately, the slang terms used to refer to female sex organs often sound very negative and may bring about feelings that these areas are shameful or dirty. Be assured that these organs are natural, normal, healthy parts of all females. They are as natural and good as our arms, eyes, legs, and ears. There is nothing shameful or dirty about your sexual organs.

Girls on the Outside

The following diagram shows the female **genitals** (*jen*-uh-tuhlz), or external sex organs. Let's talk about each part and what it does. **Vulva** is a term that refers to all of the female genitals. So when you would like to refer to the whole area pictured in Figure 3, you can simply say "my vulva." Not all vulvas look exactly alike. Like faces, each one is different, but all have the same basic parts. The vulva includes the **mons pubis**, the **outer lips**, or **labia majora**, the **inner lips**, or **labia minora**, the **clitoris** and its **clitoral hood**, and the **vestibule**, which contains both the opening of the **urethra** and the opening to the **vagina**. (I always have my college students define the word *vulva* as one of the questions on their exams. A few people still confuse it with a car made in Sweden, the Volvo.)

The mons pubis (mahns *pyoo*-bis) is the area lying over a bone called the **pubic bone**. Mons pubis means "pubic mound." Pads of fatty tissue protect that area. It is also the area that becomes noticeably covered with springy and curly **pubic hair** during puberty. The mons and the rest of the vulva contain many nerve endings. All these nerve endings make the whole area very sensitive to the touch. Because of all the nerve endings, touching or stimulation is very pleasurable and exciting. However, harsh or rough treatment can be painful.

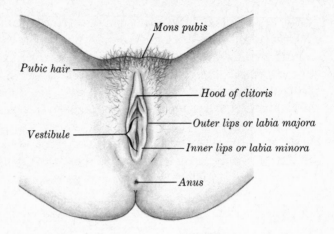

(A) Vulva in normal state and

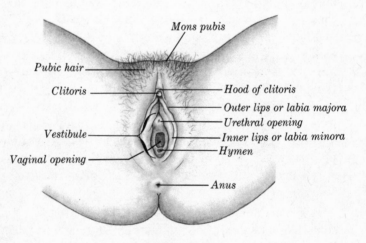

(B) when stretched apart

Figure 3

The outer lips are the two folds of skin that enclose the indentation of the vulva. The outside of these lips is also covered with pubic hair, but the inside is not. The outer lips are fatty and so they protect the inner parts of your vulva. They also contain glands to keep this area moist. Girls sometimes worry about this wetness or moisture, but it is completely normal. The outer lips are also called the labia majora (*lay*-bee-uh ma-*jor*-ruh), which is the term your physician might use. *Labia* simply means "lips" and *majora* means "major."

The inner lips, on the other hand, can be called labia minora (*lay*-bee-uh mih-*nor*-ruh) or "minor lips." These are two folds of skin located within the outer lips. They are *not* covered with pubic hair and are not as fatty as the outer lips. The inner lips are a pinkish or darkish color, depending on your race. They also have glands that keep them moist and have even more nerve endings than some other parts of the vulva. This makes them very sensitive to the touch.

The two inner lips fuse together at the top in a way that forms a hood over another structure—the clitoris (*klit*-or-iss). The clitoris is an amazing part of your body. Although it is small, it has a great concentration of nerve endings and only one purpose that we know of: to produce pleasurable and exciting feelings that may lead to sexual arousal.

The vestibule (*ves*-tuh-byool) is the cleft region enclosed by the inner lips. Within this area are two separate openings. One opening is that of the urethra (yoo-*ree*-thruh), from which urine is eliminated from the body. The other opening is that of the vagina.

In girls, the opening to the vagina is often partially closed by a piece of tissue called the **hymen** (*hi*-muhn), also called the **maidenhead** or "**cherry**." People used to think that the presence of a hymen proved that a girl was a **virgin** (had not engaged in sexual intercourse). Actually the presence or absence of a hymen doesn't mean much of anything. A few girls have very elastic hymens that remain even after they have had intercourse many times, while other girls have their hymens stretched or opened by many things other than sexual activity. Riding a horse and using a tampon are two examples. (See chapter 4 for an explanation of tampons.) Occasionally girls have hymens that completely cover the opening to the vagina. When this happens, menstrual fluid cannot flow out of the body. Therefore, a physician carefully and easily snips the hymen to create an opening.

Changes Inside Your Body During Puberty

The changes that occur inside your body during puberty are at first less obvious, but they have some dramatic results. I already mentioned the first change. Your body starts producing more hormones. These are the chemical substances that cause all the other changes that are occurring in your body. In girls two hormones cause most of the female changes— **estrogen** (*es*-truh-jen) and **progesterone** (pro-*jes*-ter-ohn). You may have heard of them because they are the chemicals put into **birth control pills**.

A second change is that your internal sex organs start to enlarge and begin to function. Internal female sex organs include the **uterus, ovaries, fallopian tubes**, and vagina. Below is a drawing of the internal female sex organs.

Girls on the Inside

All of the organs in Figure 4 are involved in reproduction or having babies, but each has a specialized role in that process. The ovaries (*oh*-vuh-reez) are two almond-sized bodies with two main functions. First, they produce the female sex hormones we just talked about (estrogen and progesterone). For this reason, they are sometimes called **sex glands**. The second thing the ovaries do is to produce small cells called **eggs**.

From the day a girl is born, each ovary contains thousands of tiny eggs. Once she enters puberty, the eggs are released at a rate of approximately one per month until a period called

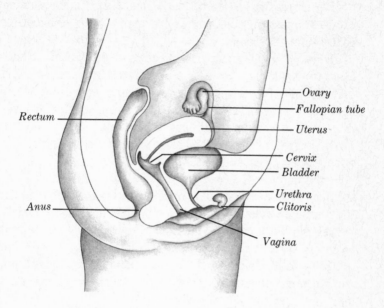

Figure 4   Female internal reproductive organs

menopause, which usually occurs near age fifty. During menopause, the eggs are released less regularly and less frequently until a woman can no longer become pregnant. No eggs are released when a woman is pregnant. For most women, only three to five hundred of these eggs are released during their lifetime. These eggs, also called **ova** (*oh*-vah), can potentially divide and grow into a baby, but only if united with male cells called **sperm**. (See chapter 8.)

Newly released eggs are carried from the ovaries to the uterus through two very small tunnels, called fallopian (fuh-*loh*-pee-an) tubes. These tubes, each about four inches long, are also the place where the union of the female egg and the male sperm occurs. The union or combining of these two different cells into one cell is called **fertilization**. In case you are wondering where the tubes got the name *fallopian*, it is from a sixteenth-century scientist, Fallopius. He mistakenly thought the tubes were ventilators for the uterus, kind of like an air-conditioning system.

The tubes open into a pear-shaped organ known as the uterus (*yoot*-uh-rus). The uterus is a very interesting organ, whose main job is to house and nurture a developing baby. The walls of the uterus are thick and made of muscles running in several directions. Although the uterus is very small, only about three inches long in a woman who has never had children, it expands during pregnancy and becomes as large as it needs to be to hold the baby as it grows in size from a small ball of cells to a full-sized infant. The lining inside the uterus is different from the muscular walls. It is spongy and moist and has lots of blood vessels so that it can provide nourishment for a fertilized egg.

The area right at the bottom of the uterus is shaped like a bottle neck and is called the **cervix** (*ser*-viks). A small tunnel runs through the cervix, providing a passageway between the uterus and vagina.

The vagina is a muscular, tube-shaped organ, about four inches long. It is not a hollow space as you might expect, but rather has walls that touch each other. Its lining is made of soft, moist tissue, very much like the inside of your mouth. The vagina becomes even more moist when you are sexually aroused. During **sexual intercourse**, a man puts his **penis** into the woman's vagina, and sperm is released from the penis. The vagina has also been called the "birth canal," because a baby moves through it on its trip to the outside of its mother's body during the birth process.

Although the beginning changes in your internal sex organs are hidden from you, they are certain to become more apparent when you reach the point in your development called **menarche** (*men*-ar-kee). This is the time of your very first menstrual flow.

4

THE MENSTRUAL CYCLE

One of the most dramatic changes that will occur during your adolescence is the beginning of **menstruation** (men-struh-*way*-shun), or "starting your period." Sometime during puberty, for the first time in your life, your uterus will shed its lining. Since this lining is very rich in blood, it will leave your body as a reddish fluid, seeping slowly out through your vagina. You will probably first notice this event by spots of blood on your underpants. This blood is not the result of injury or sickness, but, rather, it is a normal, healthy occurrence: a signal that your body is maturing and that you are physically growing toward womanhood. It is a process that will repeat itself periodically for about the next thirty or more years of your life.

Although the average age for girls to experience this first period (menarche) is sometime before their thirteenth birthday, the actual age when it may occur for you or your friends may vary widely. Just as there are natural variations between people in height and in hair and skin color, for instance, there are individual differences as to what age girls begin to menstruate. If you have not had any periods by age sixteen, it is a good idea to consult a physician to determine if you have a medical condition that is delaying the onset of your puberty.

Emotional Reactions to Menstruation

A girl usually remembers the day of her first period throughout her life. The emotional impact of this event for you will no doubt be greatly affected by the preparation you receive and the attitudes of those around you. If you have been prepared to expect menstruation and anticipate it as an exciting part of growing up, the memories of this first period will most likely be positive. Understandably, however, girls who are not prepared and have no idea what is happening to them react with fear. Contrast the experiences of these young women. The first related her experience in this way:

> I started my period the summer I was to become twelve years old and also a junior high school student! When I saw that I had drenched my underpants with blood, I literally fainted with worry that I was sick. I ran to Mom, and she gave me a diaper to wear. I mean literally a cloth baby diaper. She told me that for the rest of the week, I was not to shower, run, wear heels, or think bad thoughts. She didn't explain the reason for the bleeding. For the next whole year, one week out of a month I lived with frustration, curiosity, and dirtiness. I hated whatever it was I was going through.
>
> I hated Mom for not telling me about it. But I was afraid to ask.

The second painted a quite different picture:

> At first I got scared when I saw the blood, but then I realized what was happening. My mother had let me know what to expect ever since I was nine. When I told her what was happening to me, she gave me a big hug. Later she and my dad came into my room and gave me a rose that they had picked. It was really a beautiful day.

For the third, getting her period was an important step in feeling like a woman:

My mother was out of town when I started my period. When I told her after she returned, she put her arms around me and hugged me and told me how happy she was for me. From that time on she treated me more like an equal.

Not only will the attitudes of those around you play an important role in your adjustment to this first period, but, in addition, they may influence your attitudes about menstruation for years to come. Many distortions have become associated with the process of menstruation. Some people refer to it as a "curse," or say that it makes you unclean, evil, or weak. One girl told me, "I can remember when I started menstruating when I was about eleven. My mother told me that all my meanness was coming out." The truth is that **periods** are simply a biological fact of life. They are neither magical nor dirty. They are a regular indication that your body is doing what it is supposed to do by shedding the lining of its uterus.

Many myths also exist about what girls cannot do during their periods. Common myths are that you can't exercise, take baths, make decisions, swim, or have sex during your period. In reality, there is no harm in any of these activities. You can do what you normally do, if you feel like it. In fact, daily washing (showers or baths) is important for feeling comfortable, being clean, and for not developing a strong unpleasant odor from the menstrual flow. Also, exercise can be important in reducing menstrual cramps or discomfort.

How the Menstrual Cycle Works

Although menstruation is the part of your menstrual cycle that will make itself most known to you, many other changes will constantly be taking place in your body leading up to your monthly period. These changes make it possible for a pregnancy to occur in a woman. After each menstrual flow the same internal changes repeat themselves again and in the same order and lead to another menstrual period, and then another, and so on. Thus, we get the name **menstrual cycle**.

These internal changes of the menstrual cycle are regulated by hormones, which are the chemical substances that act as messengers from one part of your body to another. Some of the hormones that affect this cycle are produced in the brain, while others, referred to as sex hormones, are manufactured by your ovaries.

The following steps explain the progression of the menstrual cycle. These steps are pictured in Figure 5. If you are having difficulty remembering the parts of the female body as they are mentioned in this chapter, it may be helpful to refer back to chapter 3.

1. Hormones from your brain travel through your bloodstream and tell your ovaries that it is time to start the maturation of one of their many eggs (ova). Usually only one egg (or **ovum**) develops each cycle.

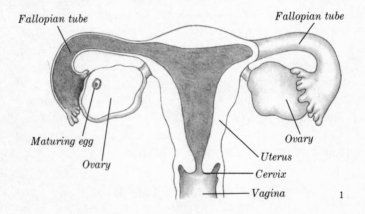

Figure 5   Process of menstruation

2. As the egg is maturing, the ovary starts to produce its own hormones, estrogen and progesterone. Both of these hormones travel through your blood to your uterus and cause its lining to thicken. The lining of the uterus becomes more spongy and rich in blood, so that it can nurture a developing baby.

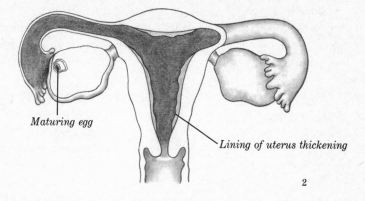

Maturing egg

Lining of uterus thickening

2

3. During one of the days about midway between your periods, the egg becomes mature enough and bursts out of the ovary into one of the fallopian tubes. This process is known as **ovulation** (ahv-yuh-*lay*-shun).

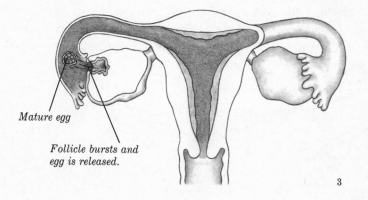

Mature egg

Follicle bursts and egg is released.

3

4. As the egg is traveling through the fallopian tube, the ovaries continue to produce hormones and the lining of the uterus gets even thicker and richer in blood as it prepares to receive the ovum.

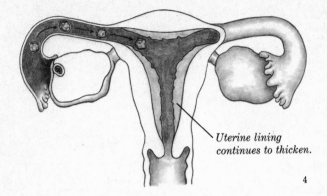

Uterine lining
continues to thicken.

4

5. If the egg does not join with a male's sperm within twenty-four to forty-eight hours after being released into the fallopian tube, it dies. This is the case in most cycles, either because sexual intercourse has not occurred or, if it has, because no living sperm are able to reach the egg in time. The ovaries also stop producing hormones several days after ovulation.

6. Without the hormones from the ovaries, the lining of the uterus breaks down and starts flowing out of the uterus into the vagina and out of your body. This is menstruation.

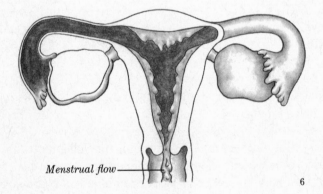

Menstrual flow

6

7. Now the whole process starts over again and repeats steps 1 through 6. Usually an egg from the opposite ovary develops the next time.

Steps 1 through 7 are an outline of what typically occurs during menstrual cycles. However, this pattern can be altered greatly at step 5. If sperm from the male does unite with the egg at this time, fertilization occurs and pregnancy has begun. The menstrual cycle then discontinues until sometime after the pregnancy is completed or terminated, and the hormones resume their regular pattern.

Timing and Predicting Menstrual Cycles

Once you have had your first period, you may want to be able to estimate when you are going to have the next one and how long each will last. Unfortunately, however, menstrual cycles are pretty unpredictable during the early teenage years. At first, periods occur irregularly and their length can vary from a day to a week or more. The bottom line of this "irregularity" is that you can't safely plan activities around your period. It can show up unexpectedly one day, last a few days, then disappear for months. When your cycles are irregular, it is impossible to accurately predict when your period is due. Consequently, it is also impossible to accurately predict when you will ovulate and be **fertile** (that is, capable of getting pregnant). Many teenagers try to guess when they are not fertile in order to pick "safe" times to have sexual intercourse. However, your cycles are far too unreliable during these years for this to be an effective method of birth control. As your body matures during the teenage years your menstrual cycles will tend to become more regular until, eventually, your periods will appear approximately once a month.

Once your periods have started showing up on a regular basis, they will be easier to predict and time. A model used by many textbooks to explain the timing and phases of the menstrual cycle is sketched below.

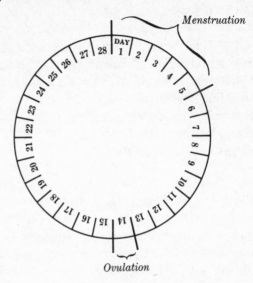

Figure 6   Phases of the menstrual cycle

A "typical" cycle lasts a total of about twenty-eight days. The first day of menstrual bleeding is called Day 1 of the cycle. Menstruation lasts about five days. On about Day 14 of the cycle, ovulation occurs. Fourteen days after ovulation, the cycle is completed and a new cycle begins with the first day of menstruation.

This perfect model of cycles occurs more often in textbooks than it does in real women. Every woman has her own somewhat distinctive cycle. One woman may have a twenty-one-day cycle and another woman's might be forty days. The same is true of how long menstrual bleeding lasts: Three days might be normal for one woman, while six days is typical of another.

Women also vary in how "regular" their cycles are. Some women's periods are very predictable, appearing on the expected date, just like clockwork. On the other hand, some women's periods are so irregular that they may never know exactly what day their period will start. They may wait twenty-eight days between periods one time, then thirty days the next, then twenty-two days, then thirty-six days, and so on.

To make the whole matter even more complicated, the menstrual cycle can be affected by many things. Stress, illness, anxiety, severe changes in body weight, and changes in the environment can throw off the body's typical cycle. Sometimes fear of being pregnant can cause a late period. Consequently, even in a woman who is usually very regular, periods are sometimes delayed or arrive early.

Despite the fact that periods can be unreliable and hard to predict, it is still a *very* good idea to keep track of when your periods do occur on a calendar. Charting which date each period starts and how long it lasts helps you to get to know your body. You'll be able to notice a more regular pattern as your body develops. You may also be able to pick out when your body is not acting in a way that is normal for you. This awareness can help you to recognize physical problems or a pregnancy.

Changes in You During Your Menstrual Cycle

You can bet that with all the changes occurring inside your body during your menstrual cycle, you will also experience some changes in how you look and feel. The different experiences in your body are directly caused by the changes we talked about in the last two sections: different levels of hormones, ovulation, and changes in your uterus.

Quite a few women and girls feel a little different from usual just before and during their periods. You may notice some fullness or heaviness in the pelvic region around your uterus. Your breasts may swell somewhat and become tender. Some other common complaints before or during menstruation are menstrual cramps, backaches, headaches, and slight nausea. Some girls even say that they are more likely to feel down or grouchy at this time. In some women these physical and emotional discomforts become severe. This condition has been called **premenstrual syndrome**, or **PMS**, and can require consultation with a physician.

One reason that these discomforts occur is that your hormones are at a low level during your period, which may lead to some emotional changes. Another reason is that your uterus is cramping in order to expel the menstrual flow. These uterine contractions can be painful. Your body also retains more water at this time, which causes a slight weight gain and the feeling of heaviness.

Besides the physical reasons, another very important fact that can lead to some girls not feeling good during their periods is that they are taught that they should feel bad at that time and come to expect that their periods will be very negative. They are led to believe that menstruation is a bigger deal than it actually is. For instance, although most people associate the loss of blood during periods with physical weakness, the actual amount of blood expelled in the menstrual fluid is quite small—only a few tablespoons. Unfortunately, our culture has portrayed menstruation as a time of instability, which leads many girls to believe that it must be true. When girls have been taught that their bodies and menstruation are dirty and bad, they are likely to feel physically and emotionally upset. Remember, periods are natural and healthy. You are *not* dirty when you have them nor are you unstable or untrustworthy.

There are some things you can do to ease physical discomforts during your periods. Exercise, warm baths, and the use of a heating pad or hot-water bottle all seem to relieve cramps. Aspirin has been used by women for a long time to treat mild cramps and headaches. There are also several other over-the-counter medications on the market that are effective in reducing menstrual discomfort. If you have severe cramps or other menstrual discomfort, consult a doctor.

There are a few other changes you might notice at different times throughout your cycle. One is that some girls have signs that they are ovulating. They feel a cramping or slight pain in one of their ovaries as the egg breaks loose and the ovary bleeds a little. This occurrence has been labeled **Mittelschmerz** (*mit*-tel-shmertz), which means "middle pain" in German. Slight spotting of the underpants with blood may also result at this time.

Also, you will become aware of changes in the wetness and discharge around your sex organs. The cervix, the narrow neck part of your uterus, produces a sort of thickish liquid called **mucus** (*myoo*-kus). You can notice this by feeling in your vagina or you may see some on your underpants. The presence of mucus on your underpants simply means you are functioning as you should. At various times during your cycle the mucus looks and feels different. Just after your period, you may not produce much mucus at all. A few days later mucus is produced and ranges in color from whitish to clear. As ovulation approaches, the mucus becomes more abundant and again its appearance changes. Around the time of ovulation, it feels like egg whites—slippery and stretchy. After ovulation it gets stickier. All of these are normal changes. It is only when the discharge is different from usual (strangely colored or foul smelling) that it might indicate a physical problem.

Practical Matters:
Napkins, Tampons, and Sponges

Several products are available for you to use during your period to absorb the menstrual fluid.

1. **Sanitary napkins** or "feminine pads" are strips of absorbent material that vary in thickness. They are held in place by adhesive strips, elastic napkin belts, or are pinned inside your underpants. When in place, they rest just outside of your vulva and absorb the menstrual flow as it leaves your vagina.

2. **Tampons** are made of absorbent cottonlike material and are inserted into your vagina, where they remain to

catch the flow before it leaves your body. Many brands of tampons are packaged with their own cardboard or plastic inserters. All have a string attached for easy removal.

3. **Menstrual sponges** are available at some health-care centers. They are inserted into your vagina like tampons. These sponges have not yet been approved by the government because their safety has not been sufficiently proven.

To make a choice between these options, you might want to ask your mother, sisters, and friends which they like and why. You can even try different ones to see which you prefer. It is important that you feel comfortable and that your chosen method seems fairly convenient to *you*.

Not only do you need to choose between napkins and tampons, but there are many brands of each kind from which to select. They also come in different sizes. You can read the boxes, which describe what each is like, pick out those that sound right for you, and then just try them out to see what you like. Pamphlets inside the boxes indicate exactly how to use the product and how often to replace it. With all of these products, it is a good idea to change fairly frequently (at least every four to six hours). Frequent replacement helps to prevent odor and the chance of blood seeping through to stain your clothes. On days when your period is very heavy you may even find that you have to change more often than every four hours.

Concerns About Tampons

Many girls worry about how they will be able to urinate if they use tampons during their menstrual periods. The worry is needless. Tampons are inserted into the vaginal opening and so will not in any way block urination. Urine comes out through the urinary opening (urethra), which is located next to the vaginal opening.

Some girls worry that using tampons will destroy their virginity. Tampons do not make you a nonvirgin, although they may stretch your hymen. Whether to use them depends on whether you can *comfortably* insert them and take them out again. If your hymen blocks comfortable insertion, then you should probably try another method.

Another recent concern about the use of tampons is the condition known as **toxic shock syndrome (TSS)**. TSS is a rare but very dangerous disease, and seems to occur most frequently in young women during their menstrual periods. This disease has been associated with the use of tampons and perhaps with menstrual sponges. Because of the danger of TSS, some women have stopped using tampons. The U.S. Public Health Service suggests that if women use tampons, they should alternate tampon use with that of pads within each day of their period. Frequent changing is also advisable.[1]

It is important that you are familiar with the symptoms of TSS so that you can get immediate treatment if any of them develop. You might also be able to recognize them and help out a friend. The symptoms of TSS are similar to those of the flu: a high fever (usually over 102 degrees), vomiting or diarrhea, and dizziness. Some women also have muscle aches, bloodshot eyes, and a sore throat. A rather strange symptom in some women is the development of a sunburnlike rash, which may lead to peeling (especially of the hands and feet). These symptoms are also printed on the side of tampon boxes, in case you forget them. I know of one girl whose life was saved by this information. While the girl was feeling sick, her mother happened to see the symptoms printed on the tampon box. The mother exclaimed, "That's what you have," and rushed her to the emergency room. She was right, and she took the right action—immediate medical attention.

5

BEING COMFORTABLE
WITH YOUR BODY

No doubt you know your face as well as you know anything in this world. You gaze in the mirror every day, sometimes closely examining every detail, or sometimes taking just a quick glance. Maybe you smile at yourself, frown, or simply check to see that everything looks okay. You know every feature and all of the contours and textures of your face. You're familiar with the color of your eyes, the slope of your nose, the shape of your lips. You wash your face, going in and out of all the creases, your hands gliding over the smooth spots and stopping to feel any blemishes. If you put on makeup, you look closely at your face, evaluating which points need high-lighting and which don't.

In fact, you get to know your face so well that you trust it to tell you how you are feeling. You feel your head to see if it is warm, check your eyes to see if they're bloodshot or watery, and check the color of your skin to see if it's pale or flushed.

One purpose of this chapter is to help you to understand that exploring and getting to know the rest of your body is as natural and important as being familiar with your own face. Becoming familiar with your body is essential to keeping it healthy, as well as learning to feel comfortable with your sexuality. Girls and women who know their bodies, their sex organs, and their menstrual cycles can more quickly discover problems, enabling them to get the treatment they need.

Becoming Familiar with Your Body

Infants naturally explore everything they can reach, including their own bodies. It is quite normal for a child to touch her fingers, toes, genitals, or any other part of her body that has a great deal of sensation. Of course, when you did this as an infant, you did not identify this as sexual or say "Hey, I'm feeling turned on," but it no doubt registered in your mind as a pleasurable experience. People tend to repeat experiences that are pleasing to them and to eliminate behavior that causes them discomfort. If there is some pleasure and also some pain, the brain weighs these two feelings and decides whether or not the experience is worth repeating.

It is in this way that this period of self-discovery during infancy and early childhood formed the basis for many of your present feelings about touching your own body. If your parents and other adults around you accepted these early explorations with a positive attitude and allowed them to continue through childhood, then there is a greater chance that self-touching is still pleasurable to you. If, on the other hand, touching your body ended with your hand being slapped or some indication from adults that what you were doing was wrong, then this very natural act of exploration may result in guilt, shame, bodily tension, or some other form of discomfort and may suppress your inclination to touch yourself.

At this point, before going on, stop and think about your own emotional reactions to the idea of getting to know your body. Do you feel neutral, guilty, uncomfortable, scared, eager, proud? You may even feel each of these reactions to different degrees. Whatever your reaction, try to think how these feelings developed. This can be an important step in understanding your own reactions and may help to reduce any discomfort.

If you'd like to learn more about your own body and begin to feel more comfortable with it, you can try the following self-discovery exercises. However, if the exercises make you too uncomfortable, don't feel you need to force yourself to do them. Probably the easiest way to begin to become familiar with your body is to look at yourself in a full-length mirror without your clothes on. Often when women and girls look in the mirror they approach it in a very critical way. They look for flaws and compare themselves to gorgeous models and movie stars. The purpose of this exercise is *not* for you to be critical, but to help you become familiar with your body *as it is*. First, get a general idea of your shape and coloring. Notice some of the signs of your maturation, like breast development, widening of your hips, and the growth of underarm and pubic hair. Next, you can touch different parts to notice textures, contours, and sensations. Every part has a distinctive feeling to your fingers.

Now, take a look at your genitals. A good way to explore them is to sit in a comfortable position and part your legs. The aid of a hand-held mirror will reveal them for your viewing. You might find it helpful to refer back to chapter 3 as you are learning about yourself. Hold the book open to page 30 to compare yourself with the diagram. Just as faces are different, so are sex organs. Consequently, when you compare yourself with the diagram, each of the important parts will be there, but the exact shapes, sizes, and shading will be different.

Notice the entire vulva and the pubic hair around it. Next find the outer lips. If you part them, you'll locate the inner lips. These inner lips come together at the top to make a hood over your clitoris. The clitoris looks like a small bump and you might identify it more by the intense sensations that touching it produces. Within the inner lips you can find the small opening of the urethra on top and the vagina below. Your vagina may be partly covered by the tissues of the hymen. Some women say that female sex organs look like lovely flowers.

As you are exploring your genitals, begin to become familiar with shapes, colors, sizes, textures, and even their wetness and smell. Try to develop an awareness of what is normal for you. Once you know what is normal for your body during each phase of your menstrual cycle, you will be able to recognize any abnormalities that develop.

Self-Pleasuring and Masturbation

Touching your body in order to bring pleasure to yourself may sound weird, but if you think about it, most likely it is something you do every day without ever giving it a second thought. You may stroke your face softly, feeling the smoothness of your skin, or enjoy the sensation of rubbing powder or suntan lotion onto parts of your body. You may enjoy the feelings of gently pulling a brush through your hair or massaging your scalp while shampooing it. Self-touching that becomes more focused on the genitals and breasts and has the goal of causing sexual excitement is referred to as **masturbation** (mas-ter-*bay*-shun).

An incredible number of negative myths about masturbation have been passed down over the centuries. If you are having trouble trying to separate the myths from the realities, you are not alone. Even many of us who now have a pretty good knowledge about sex believed some of the ridiculous myths about masturbation when we were going through the strains of adolescence.

Masturbation has been blamed for blindness, insanity, acne, sterility, and epilepsy. All of these are myths. One of my all-time favorite myths is that it can make hair grow on the palms of your hands. We used to tell this one in junior high and then watch to see who would anxiously check out their palms. There is absolutely no evidence to indicate that masturbation is in any way physically unhealthy. Nor are there any set number of times per week or month in which masturbation is normal, or a cutoff point beyond where it becomes abnormal. Today, research clearly indicates that there are no harmful side effects caused by masturbation itself.

Actually the only problems that seem to regularly be associated with masturbation have to do with the unfortunate and unnecessary guilt instilled by people who are uncomfortable with or disapproving of masturbation. Usually, however, these negative messages that masturbation is harmful or immoral do not eliminate it, they just cause people to do it in secrecy and with guilt. It is easy to assume that you are the only one. One woman told me,

> By the time I "confessed" to "my sin" I was in my late twenties, had three children, and my marriage was breaking up. The first person I told my secret to was a marriage counselor. Her reaction was, "What's the big deal?" to which I asked her whether she had ever done such a thing. When she answered, "Of course," I think my jaw dropped to the floor.

It seems unfortunate that so many women feel it necessary to keep masturbation their personal secret. Certainly the desire for privacy during sex play is understandable, but privacy and secrecy are not the same thing. Privacy is simply the need to experience an event without the pressure of others to interfere with the experience. The need for secrecy, in contrast, stems from a desire to hide what you are doing—often from a sense that it is evil or shameful. Sadly, although masturbation is a normal and natural event, it often still remains an embarrassing secret. Even college women who I found to be very open in discussing their sexual experiences with boyfriends clammed up and blushed when the subject of masturbation was mentioned.

Some girls say that they did not hear any negative myths about masturbation—that no one told them anything about it at all. As one girl said,

When I was just thirteen, I discovered by accident how good it felt when running water flowed on my clitoris. I must add that at that time I did not know about clitorises, masturbation, orgasms, or the like. Consequently, I felt I had discovered something that no one else knew about and that it must be very bad. For one thing nobody talked about it, and I had never heard of anybody doing what I did.

Other girls expressed their belief that only boys masturbate and that it wouldn't be proper for a girl to do so.

I also did not know that girls masturbated. I know this may be hard to believe but I never even considered touching myself.

The fact is that most people do masturbate. However, differences exist as to when people start and how frequently they do so at various times throughout their life span. More teenage boys report masturbating than do teenage girls. According to a survey by Aaron Hass, in the age group from fifteen to sixteen, 75 percent of boys and 52 percent of girls said they masturbated; whereas in those seventeen to eighteen years of age, the figures increase to 80 percent of the boys and 55 percent of the girls.[1] There are many possible explanations as to why there is a difference between the number of boys and girls who say they masturbate. For one thing, boys might fall into this practice more easily as a result of handling their penises during urination. Also, the messages boys receive about their sexuality tend not to be as harsh as those received by girls. The idea that "good" girls aren't sexual may inhibit some girls from masturbating and others from admitting that they do. It also appears that boys are more likely to teach other boys about masturbation than girls are to teach other girls. In fact, many women report that they started masturbating only after they had first been involved in sexual activity with a partner. One woman told me,

I was eighteen years old before I was able to really touch myself. Even at that, I would have never done it without help. My fiancé and I had been together for almost three years at the time, and we had established an excellent communication system. We could talk about anything and everything, so discussing masturbation was no problem for us. However, for me, doing it was. He had always told me I should get to know my body in order to relax and be more comfortable with it, know what made me feel good so I could tell him, and just plain enjoy it. I knew he was right, but I could not bring myself to do it. I don't know if I was scared of it or what. I didn't feel comfortable about it. Anyway, I thought, What's the use? I could never really make myself feel good even if I did try it. He helped me to see that I was wrong.

The number of women who regularly masturbate increases during the adult years. And, despite the myths that masturbation is "immature" and only used to relieve oneself in the absence of a partner, most adults, men and women, married and single, continue to masturbate. A majority of women in a survey by Shere Hite indicated that masturbation was an important part of their adult sex lives.[2]

Of the many reasons that people masturbate, the central one is, of course, that it is enjoyable. Self-pleasuring simply can feel very good. In addition, it is a safe way of releasing sexual tensions. Either when you do not have a partner, or when you simply want to enjoy your body without the complications of being involved in a sexual encounter with another person, masturbation can be a satisfactory release. Furthermore, you cannot get pregnant from self-pleasuring.

Masturbation gives you an opportunity to explore not only your genital area, but also the sensations of your entire body. It can be a chance for you to find out where and in what ways you enjoy being touched. In this way you can find that your needs and sensitivities change from day to day, and even second to second. You can become familiar with different ways of touching your body and new areas of sensitivity.

Consequently, in a sense, masturbation becomes a rehearsal for later sexual encounters with a partner; a rehearsal where you can feel safe in the knowledge that you can experiment as you wish without feeling pressured by another person's presence. Later, it will be considerably easier to share your needs and wants with a partner, thus removing from him the burden of trying to guess how you enjoy being touched. In my role as a sex therapist I see many women who find it impossible to describe how they like to have their bodies touched, simply because they really do not know. For this reason, masturbation often becomes an important part of sex therapy.

No one can instruct you on the best way to touch yourself or even on whether you should or should not masturbate. As I said at the beginning of this book, you are an individual, different from all others. Not everyone likes to be touched in the same ways or the same places. Nor does everyone feel comfortable with self-pleasuring. You are the expert on your body, your feelings, and your values. This book can only share information on how other people stimulate themselves and help you to find out more about your own feelings.

Girls and women have many ways of masturbating, but probably the most common is to use their fingers to stroke their vulval areas, particularly the areas around the clitoris. Many say that the clitoris itself is too sensitive to directly stimulate for any length of time and, instead, they touch the area beside it. Some girls prefer to rub their vulvas back and forth against the bed or pillows. One girl explained how she discovered this technique:

I heard from other girls in the fourth grade that if you lay on your stomach and spread your legs, you would get pregnant. So I tried. I didn't get pregnant, but I discovered a pleasurable feeling.

Other girls simply tighten the muscles around their vaginas as a way of creating sexual pleasure. Another fairly common method is to use a warm stream of running water from the faucet in a bathtub or a shower massage. Electric vibrators have also become popular with many women. In addition, women often use sexual fantasies while masturbating as a way to intensify their experience.

Some women prefer different forms of lubrication, such as creams and lotions, to make the vulva more slippery, thus changing the type of sensation and also reducing irritation of the skin. To be on the safe side in minimizing the risk of having an allergic reaction to the creams, it is best to use a nonperfumed, **hypoallergenic** lotion or cream. Two good lubricants are K-Y jelly and Abolene. These can be purchased in a local pharmacy. However, it is best *not* to use petroleum jelly (Vaseline), which we will discuss in the following chapter.

Masturbation Is Not for Everyone

Despite the fact that masturbation is normal, and is a healthy part of sexuality for many women, masturbation is not for everyone. Because of certain religious prohibitions, parental restrictions, or other personal pressures, the conflict associated with touching yourself for the purpose of producing pleasure may lead to a great deal of guilt. Consequently, sometimes masturbation may cause more problems than enjoyment. If this is the case for you, now may not be a comfortable time to experiment with masturbation. Rather it might be wise to postpone this until a time when it feels right for you, if that time develops. You don't need to make up a reason to yourself or anyone else for not masturbating. When and if you are ready you can begin. It may be that you will never reach a point of feeling comfortable with masturbation as a form of sexual satisfaction for yourself. This, too, is fine. I know that I said that masturbation is a way of becoming familiar with your body's sensations, but this can also be accomplished by a patient, trial-and-error learning process in a later relationship with a partner.

Whether or not to masturbate or where and when to masturbate are two important considerations you will have to face as you mature physically and emotionally. These are not decisions you *must* make now, nor are these decisions unchangeable. They are decisions that you will be continually evaluating during your entire life.

If you decide that masturbation is something you wish to explore, it should be an enjoyable and rewarding process for you. If it becomes work or a constant struggle, then the circumstances of your self-touching need to be reevaluated.

6

KEEPING YOUR BODY HEALTHY

When you become comfortable enough with your body to examine yourself regularly and are familiar with what is normal for you, you've come a long way toward taking good care of yourself. Developing this ease should allow you to maintain your body in a healthy manner and alert you to potential problems, so that you can seek early treatment. This chapter will cover some of the aspects important in helping you keep yourself healthy. It will discuss **hygiene** (*hi*-jeen), preventive health tips, how to recognize problems, vaginal infections, physical exams from a physician, and breast self-exams.[1]

Hygiene

Just as the rest of your body needs washing on a regular basis, so do your genitals. If your vulva is not cleansed, secretions from its **glands** will build up, creating a smelly cheeselike substance called **smegma**. In addition, keeping this area clean also reduces the chances of developing an infection. Gentle washing with a mild soap and water is sufficient. Make certain that you wash the folds between the lips and around the clitoral hood since it is easy for substances to hide there. It is unnecessary and may even be harmful to scrub this area roughly or to use harsh or perfumed soaps. Sometimes girls find that the soaps they are using are irritating to the tender vulval tissue. If this turns out to be a problem for you, switch to a milder soap.

The advertising media have caused some women to go overboard with hygiene, particularly in the marketing of perfumed vaginal douches and so-called feminine deodorants that are sprayed on the genitals. The deodorants are unnecessary and, in fact, have been harmful at times, due to the harsh chemicals in them. Regular washing is sufficient to prevent the development of a strong odor from the vulva, unless an infection or a foreign body is present (such as a tampon or diaphragm left in the vagina too long). In either of these cases, you don't want a deodorant to cover up the odor, which is your signal that something is amiss. Frequent douching, similarly, can have harmful side effects. It causes an imbalance in the chemical makeup of the vaginal walls, which ordinarily do a very good job of taking care of themselves.

Many **health care practitioners** advise against applying petroleum jelly (such as Vaseline) to the genitals for any reason. Because petroleum jelly is not water soluble, it can both block the urethral opening and harbor the growth of bacteria in the vagina.

Preventing Vaginal Infections

Certain conditions may make you more susceptible to vaginal infections. These conditions include not getting enough sleep, living under stress, eating poorly, having diabetes, using birth control pills, and taking antibiotic medications. In contrast, there are a number of suggestions that health care practitioners make about how to prevent vaginal infections. The following list of tips is adapted from a health book for women called *Our Bodies, Ourselves*.[2]

1. Keep your genitals clean by regularly washing your vulva and anus. It is not a good idea to use other people's towels and washcloths because diseases can be transmitted to you from them.

2. As was mentioned earlier, it is best to avoid "feminine deodorants" and harsh soaps because they can be irritating to your genitals.

3. Clean underpants and pantyhose with cotton crotches are preferable to those with nylon crotches. Nylon tends to keep the vulva warmer and damper, which may help harmful bacteria grow.

4. Although they may be fashionable, it is better not to wear pants that are tight in the crotch because they can irritate your vulva.

5. In order not to move bacteria from your anus to your vagina and urethra, always be sure to wipe yourself from front to back after a bowel movement.

6. And if you are sexually active:

a. It is important that you and your sexual partner maintain clean hygiene. For instance, a boy should wash his penis daily, particularly before having sex.

b. **Condoms** can reduce the likelihood of passing on some sexually transmitted diseases. (See chapters 12 and 13.)

c. Don't continue to have intercourse if you are experiencing significant pain. Painful intercourse can be both physically and psychologically harmful to you.

d. The best lubricant for intercourse is that produced by the vagina itself when you are sufficiently aroused (see chapter 10). If you decide to use extra lubrication, be sure to buy a sterile, water-soluble product. K-Y Jelly is a good example. Birth control jellies and foams can also be good lubricants. Besides helping to reduce your chances of becoming pregnant, they may also help protect you from some diseases because the chemicals in them slow the growth of some bacteria. (See chapters 12 and 13.)

Recognizing Problems

Often when your body is having a problem of some sort, it lets you know this in one way or another. Consequently, it is important for you to become familiar with these signs and to take appropriate measures when they occur. Many times these signals are in the form of discomfort or pain. Infections, for instance, are often accompanied by burning, irritation, itching, and even a fever. On the other hand, you may not experience pain, but you may notice that your body feels, looks, or even smells different from the way it usually does. Important changes to note are any lumps, swelling, redness, sores, tenderness, heavier or lighter than normal periods, blood in your urine, and/or a strangely colored or foul-smelling discharge from your vagina. As an infection spreads deeper into your pelvis, severe pain may result.

It is always a good idea to consult a health care practitioner if you develop any of these symptoms. The sooner you get treatment, the easier it will be to cure an infection or disease and the less likely it is to cause any serious complications. Untreated infections can cause dangerous long-term and even permanent problems, including sterility, possibly cancer, and on rare occasions even death. In chapter 13 symptoms of specific sexually transmitted diseases (STDs) will be discussed. However, you do not have to be sexually active to have a vaginal or bladder infection.

Unfortunately, some diseases do not warn you with early symptoms. For instance, as you'll learn more about in the chapter on STDs, many women have no early symptoms of **gonorrhea** and may not know that they have it until it has caused permanent damage. For this reason, regular checkups are very important in maintaining your health, particularly if you are sexually active.

Vaginal Infections

Vaginitis is a term used to describe any infection or irritation of the vagina. You can probably expect to have one or more bouts with vaginitis during your life. One of the most frequent kinds is **candidiasis** (kan-duh-*di*-uh-sis), which is usually referred to as a **yeast infection**. It is quite common in women and often is *not* transmitted sexually. A yeast infection is caused by an overgrowth of a fungus normally found in the vagina (also in the intestines and even the mouth). A number of different conditions can cause the overgrowth of the fungus: use of birth control pills, pregnancy, use of antibiotics, and diabetes. The typical symptoms of a yeast infection are a white, cottage cheese–like discharge and redness, soreness, and itching of the genitals. Yeast infections are treated with the use of prescribed creams or suppositories.

Other causes of vaginitis, such as gonorrhea, **trichomoniasis**, and **chlamydia**, will be discussed in chapter 13 on sexually transmitted diseases. It is important to have all vaginal infections treated, because persistent infections may make you more at risk for developing cancer of the cervix.

Having a Pelvic Exam

Sometime during either your adolescence or young adulthood you'll have your first **pelvic exam**. You may have already had one. A health care professional conducts this examination in order to make sure that both your internal and external sex organs are problem-free. There is no single rule as to when you need to get your first pelvic, but there are some guidelines that might be helpful. The following is a list of situations that indicate that a pelvic exam is necessary:

1. Symptoms of bladder or vaginal infection, pelvic pain, or severe cramps.
2. Trouble with your periods, especially heavy bleeding or bleeding for more than ten days.
3. Trauma to the genital region, such as from a fall or from being sexually assaulted.
4. No sign of puberty by age fourteen or no sign of periods by age sixteen.
5. If you wish to obtain certain contraceptives, such as the pill, IUD, or diaphragm.
6. If you become sexually active. Once you become sexually active, you should have a pelvic exam on a regular basis. The recommended time can range from every six months to every two years, depending on your medical history and sexual life-style.
7. If your mother ever used the medication **DES** prior to your birth.

I remember being pretty nervous the first time my mother told me that I was going to have a pelvic exam. My periods were all messed up, lasting a couple of weeks at a time, and the physician felt it was necessary to check on my internal sex organs. I had heard rumors that pelvics were horrible, painful experiences. This turned out *not* to be the case. Two things helped me a lot. First, my mother calmed me down and told me that the exam was important and that it would probably be somewhat uncomfortable, but not nearly as bad as I was anticipating. Second, the physician was very gentle and understanding about my fears. Many girls have said that knowing exactly what to expect reduced their anxieties greatly.

There are two points that are important prior to your initial pelvic exam. First, let the doctor's staff know that this will be your first examination. This will enable them to schedule sufficient time to ask their questions and to answer yours.

Second, prior to going in for the visit, prepare a list of any questions you have about your health, body, or about birth control. This will ensure that you don't forget to ask the questions you need answered. Don't be afraid to include all the questions you have. There is no such thing as a silly or unimportant question. If it concerns you, it is important enough to ask.

What follows is a description of the typical procedures that are used. Exact methods vary somewhat from clinic to clinic and from physician to physician. Also, although the pelvic exam here is described as being performed by a physician, in many agencies they are also performed by other health care professionals, such as nurse practitioners. These health care workers receive special training and can competently conduct these procedures.

Probably the first thing that you will do is to fill out a medical-history questionnaire. Then, a nurse or medical assistant will escort you to an examining room and ask you a few questions about such things as how regular your periods are and whether you are experiencing any physical problems. Two questions that will be asked during almost any checkup are the date your last period started and how long it lasted. Consequently, it is a very good idea to keep track of that information. The physician will talk to you next, asking more questions and explaining what the exam will be like. The doctor will then leave the room for a few minutes so that you can undress privately and put on a hospital gown (a white cotton or paper robe that ties in the back).

In most cases a female nurse or helper assists during the exam if the physician is male, handing the doctor the necessary tools. Having another female present puts many girls and women more at ease. The assistant will help you onto the examining table, which looks similar to the examining table in any other doctor's office except for the addition of foot supports (stirrups) at one end of the table. These stirrups help you to keep your legs steady during the exam.

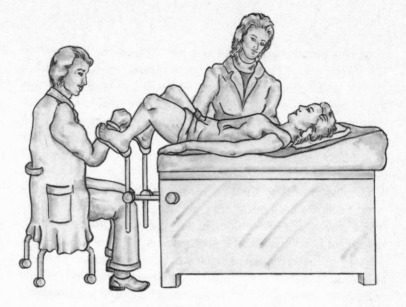

Figure 7 The pelvic exam

The total exam may consist of a breast exam, an abdominal exam, a pelvic exam, and a pelvic-rectal exam, although all four are not necessarily performed each time. During each phase of the examination, the physician looks at and feels each area, checking for lumps, abnormalities, enlargement, sores, irritation, tenderness, and discharge. I really don't know anyone who didn't experience some embarrassment during her initial examination. However, sometimes it helps to keep in mind that this is a very routine exam for the doctor. Chances are that she or he has done this hundreds, if not thousands, of times.

The breast exam is usually done first, while you lie down on the table. It will be similar to the breast self-exams described in the next section of this chapter. The doctor will feel your breasts, nipples, and underarm areas, pressing gently in a circular motion. Next the doctor will tap and feel around the abdomen, especially if you came in complaining of pain in that area.

At this point the assistant will help you to put your feet in the stirrups and then to slide your hips down to the end of the table. In this position your legs will be spread and your knees bent toward the ceiling, so that the doctor can easily examine your genitals and pelvis. A white sheet may be draped over your bent knees, creating a little tent and privacy for you. Many physicians will explain each step to you as they go along, so that you won't be startled.

The doctor will now put on rubber gloves, turn on an extra lamp to light the genital area, and then visually inspect the whole vulva. The speculum exam of the vagina follows. A **speculum** is a duck-billed instrument with handles that cause the two rounded blades to separate. Some are made of plastic and some of metal. After lubricating the speculum, the doctor will slowly insert it into your vagina in its closed position with the two duck-bill blades together. Once it is inside the vagina, the handles are used to spread the duck-bills and open the vagina. Since the walls of the vagina are expandable, this should not be painful, but it can be somewhat uncomfortable. With the speculum in place the physician is able to see your cervix, as well as the walls of your vagina.

Figure 8 Speculum

The physician can also obtain cultures from your vagina and cervix for lab tests. If there is concern about the possibility of an infection, a long cotton swab is used to take a sample of mucus from the opening of the cervix. A second cotton swab is used to take a sample from deep in the vagina, especially if an area with discharge or a sore is spotted. Finally, a **Pap smear** is obtained by scraping a few cells from the cervix, using another cotton swab or a narrow wooden spatula similar to a long Popsicle stick. These cells will be examined in a laboratory under a microscope. The Pap smear has detected abnormalities and cancer of the cervix early enough to save the lives of many women. At the end of this phase of the exam, the speculum is slowly closed and then gently withdrawn from the vagina.

Next, the doctor inserts two lubricated fingers into the vagina and puts pressure down on the bottom part of the vaginal wall to feel the cervix. The other hand is then placed on your abdomen. This is called a bimanual examination, and is used to check your uterus, fallopian tubes, and ovaries. First, your uterus is felt between the physician's two hands to make sure that it is normal in size, shape, and placement and to check for any tenderness. Then your doctor will feel your fallopian tubes and ovaries in a similar manner. To do this adequately, the doctor must use a fair amount of pressure, making this one of the most uncomfortable, yet important, parts of the exam.

The final step is a pelvic-rectal exam. Two fingers are used for the exam: The index finger is inserted into the vagina and the middle finger into the rectum. The physician is now able to feel the bottom side of your uterus and to examine the rectum. When the pelvic-rectal exam is over, the physical examination is complete. The assistant will help you slide back up the table, away from the edge and out of the stirrups. You can get dressed and discuss the doctor's findings.

The time that follows the actual physical exam is an extremely important part of your visit, a part that should not be overlooked. It is your opportunity to ask any of the questions that were not answered for you during the examination. If the doctor gives you an answer that you do not understand, speak up so that it can be answered in a way that makes sense to you. This is the time to voice any fears or questions you have about your physical condition. If you feel very intimidated by your doctor or if your doctor is unwilling to take the time to answer your questions, give consideration to trying another physician for your next examination. You might ask your friends if they have a doctor with whom they feel more comfortable.

Examining Your Breasts

Along with noticing the changes in your body and going for physical exams on a regular basis, it is important that you begin a process of breast self-examination. You might think that it is incredibly early for you to learn to do a breast self-exam, since breast cancer and other breast diseases are very rare at your age. However, there are some very good reasons for including information on breast exams in this book.

First, while rare, breast diseases, including cancer, *have* occurred in teenage girls. Second, getting familiar with your breasts and examining them regularly are wonderful habits to develop early in life rather than waiting until you are older. Breasts are normally rather lumpy and vary in how they feel to the touch during different phases of the menstrual cycle. It is very difficult to recognize an abnormality in them unless you know how they usually feel. Therefore, health care practitioners recommend that you begin doing regular breast self-exams as soon as "you have a breast to examine, in your teens, or as soon as your menstrual cycle is at all regular."[3]

A third reason for you to know the essentials of breast exams is so that you can share the information with your mother, older sisters, grandmothers, and aunts. The risk of breast cancer increases in women over thirty-five and is highest for women over fifty. Breast cancer runs in families, so that if anyone in your family has had breast cancer, all of you should be especially conscientious about doing self-exams.

Breast cancer is one of the leading causes of death in women. Approximately one out of eleven women get breast cancer at some point in their lives. Until very recently, it was the most prevalent cause of female cancer-related deaths. (A large increase in the number of women who smoke has resulted in a corresponding increase in the number who die of lung cancer. Hence, lung cancer has become the number-one cancer-killer in women, while breast cancer has become number two.)

Early detection and prompt treatment are the keys to eliminating the cancer and saving women's lives. Usually, that early detection is made by the women themselves. In fact, the American Cancer Society estimates that breast cancer is self-discovered about 95 percent of the time. Waiting for a physician to detect a lump or abnormality during an annual physical is not good enough, because it can be too late. Still, most lumps turn out *not* to be cancerous, so you don't need to panic each time you notice something different in the consistency of your breasts. Breasts are somewhat lumpy naturally and many women regularly get cysts and other benign lumps in their breasts. Cancerous lumps tend to be hard and painless.

The best time to conduct a breast self-exam is about a week after your period. Breasts tend not to be as tender and swollen at this time. You should examine your breasts *every* month at about the same time in your cycle. It is important to go to your doctor as soon as possible if you should discover a lump, a dimple, an enlarged breast, or a discharge from your nipple during your self-exams. Again, it would be unlikely that you have cancer, but it needs to be checked out.

Below are the instructions on how to do breast self-exams published by the American Cancer Society.[4] They suggest a three-step procedure. It is necessary to complete all three steps, and it is suggested that they be done in this order:

1.

In the shower: Examine your breasts during bath or shower; hands glide easier over wet skin. Fingers flat, move gently over every part of each breast. Use right hand to examine left breast, left hand for right breast. Check for any lump, hard knot, or thickening.

2.

Before a mirror: Inspect your breasts with arms at your sides. Next, raise your arms high overhead. Look for any changes in contour of each breast, a swelling, dimpling of skin, or changes in the nipple.

Then, rest palms on hips and press down firmly to flex your chest muscles. Left and right breast will not exactly match—few women's breasts do.

Regular inspection shows what is normal for you and will give you confidence in your examination.

3.

Lying down: To examine your right breast, put a pillow or folded towel under your right shoulder. Place right hand behind your head—this distributes breast tissue more evenly on the chest. With left hand, fingers flat, press gently in small circular motions around an imaginary clock face. Begin at outermost top of your right breast for 12 o'clock, then move to 1 o'clock, and so on around the circle back to 12. A ridge of firm tissue in the lower curve of each breast is normal. Then move in an inch, toward the nipple, and keep circling to examine *every part of your breast,* including nipple. This requires at least three more circles. Now slowly repeat procedure on your left breast with a pillow under your left shoulder and left hand behind head. Notice how your breast structure feels.

Finally, squeeze the nipple of each breast gently between

thumb and index finger. Any discharge, clear or bloody, should be reported to your doctor immediately.

The message from this whole chapter is that it is up to you to learn about and take care of your body. You are in the best position to become an expert about what is normal for your body and to recognize when something is wrong. The more aware you are of your body's phases and functioning, the more easily you will be able to detect changes that could indicate problems.

7

THE MALE BODY

I remember thinking I was pretty cool at about age eight when my sister, who was four years younger, asked, "How do you tell boy babies from girl babies? Do they cry different or something?" We were driving home from a movie and I laughed and rolled all over the backseat because I couldn't believe how "dumb" her question was. After all, thinking myself to be a sophisticated eight-year-old, I thought I knew it all: Boys have penises and girls have vaginas.

On the outside, that's the way it looks. To a young girl noticing the physical differences between herself and a young boy, that is all there is to it; he has a penis and she has a vagina. However, as I later found out, the differences go far beyond that. On the inside, men's and women's bodies are really quite different, not only because each has a unique set of internal organs, but also because their bodies contain different balances of internal chemicals. These differences begin to become especially magnified during puberty, the time when boys and girls begin their sexual development.

Boys and Puberty

Like girls, during puberty boys go through a series of changes that transform their appearance and make sexual reproductive functioning possible. Just as in girls, it is the hormones, the body's unique chemical messenger system, that alert the body to begin and to continue these changes. Although both males and females have the same hormones in their bodies, females have larger concentrations of estrogen and progesterone. In males, the abundance of **testosterone** (tes-*tos*-ter-ohn) is the key to unlocking the dramatic changes of the maturation process. As mentioned in chapter 3, boys typically begin puberty about two years after girls do, but continue physically maturing a few years longer.

One of the most dramatic changes in boys, as it is in girls, is the growth spurt. In addition to growing taller, boys' bodies broaden and they get stronger as their muscles grow at a fast pace. Like girls, boys grow pubic hair and underarm hair and, in addition, they may begin to grow hair on their chests and stomachs. Eventually, facial hair shows up and boys start to think about shaving. The amount of hair on any part of the body is hereditary, just as it is in girls.

Boys' bodies undergo a couple of modifications that girls' bodies don't. Vocal cords stretch as the rest of the body is growing. Their voices begin to deepen and for a period of time their voices often "crack" or squeak. Most of them feel pretty self-conscious when their voices "change," and a little understanding from you during this trying time may help ease their anxiety.

Another conditon that is sometimes embarrassing to teenage boys is a temporary enlarging of their breasts, called **gynecomastia** (ji-nuh-koh-*mas*-tee-uh). This occurs in about 80 percent of boys going through puberty and is a result of normal hormonal variations. Furthermore, testosterone, the predominant male hormone, tends to increase the production of skin oils more than do the female hormones. Consequently, boys tend to have even more trouble with acne than girls do.

Again, just as in a girl, a boy's internal and external anatomy matures during puberty in a way that makes sexual functioning and reproduction possible. Whereas for girls the most dramatic signal that puberty has begun is the day of their first menstruation, for a boy it is the day when a thick whitish liquid called **semen** (*see*-men) spurts from his penis. Often this first **ejaculation** (e-jak-yuh-*lay*-shun) occurs in a young man up to a year or two after his body has already experienced the first changes of puberty. Ejaculation usually comes about as the result of sexual excitement. It may happen in what is referred to as a **nocturnal emission**, or **wet dream**, while a boy is sleeping.

Boys on the Outside

Boys tend to know more about their outside sexual body parts than girls do about their own. This is because these parts are more visible and are handled regularly during urination. Basically, there are two body parts to remember: the penis and the **scrotum** (*skroh*-tum). The external sexual anatomy of boys is pictured in Figures 9 and 10.

The penis is a cylindrical organ that is involved in two bodily functions. It is important for sexual functioning and is also used in urination. Like the clitoris in your body, a boy's penis contains lots of nerve endings that make it very sensitive to touch. Consequently, touching the penis is sexually arousing to males, just as touching the clitoris (and the rest of the vulva) is to females. There are even more nerve endings on the **glans** (glanz), or head, of the penis than there are on its **shaft**. The glans is the cap-shaped portion at the end, and the shaft is the longer, tube-shaped part.

Penises come in somewhat different shapes and sizes. Each one has its own characteristic features. They may be wide or narrow, long or short, or even more or less shriveled. Even the tips (glans) can look different.

As you'll note in the illustrations above, one large difference in the way penises appear is that some are circumcised and some are uncircumcised. **Circumcision** is a procedure in which the **foreskin** of the penis is removed. The foreskin is a loose

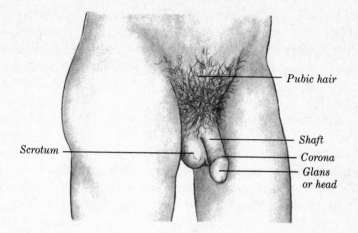

Figure 9   Circumcised penis

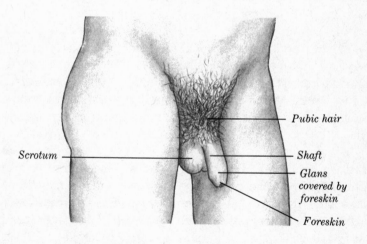

Figure 10   Uncircumcised penis

piece of skin that surrounds the glans of the penis when a boy is born. This skin is cut off surgically, as a way of promoting cleanliness and reducing the risk of infection. Circumcision is usually performed during the first week of a boy's life. It is a very common procedure in the United States, but is much less common in most other cultures.

An interesting aspect of the penis is that at times it becomes longer, thicker, and more rigid, in what is called an **erection**. Slang terms for an erection are "**boner**" or "**hard-on**." Often erections occur because a boy is feeling sexually excited ("turned-on") either as a result of sexual stimulation or just from sexual thoughts. However, other stimulation, motion (such as riding in a car), or even a hot bath can also cause them.

Even though it may sometimes seem like there are bones in the penis, there are none. The inside of the penis is basically made up of three areas of spongy material with nerve endings and blood vessels going to them. Erections take place when, on signal from the brain, spinal cord, and nerve endings, the spongy material fills with blood. Like a long balloon being filled with air, the penis becomes longer, wider, and more rigid, and the skin stretches tight. Boys often complain that erections pop up at the most embarrassing times, such as when sitting among a group of girls or getting out of a swimming pool.

Although the length of the penis is not important for sexual satisfaction or any other reason, boys and men often seem to use the size of the penis as a yardstick of how mature or masculine they are. In locker rooms, guys are constantly checking each other out through the corner of their eyes. Boys worry about penis size the same way girls worry about breast size. They let it affect their self-esteem and confidence, even though there is much more to being a man than having a long penis.

Just beneath the penis is the second important part of the external male sexual anatomy. The scrotum is a loose sack of skin that houses two organs known as **testes** (*tes*-teez). The singular of testes is *testis*. Although the testes appear to be two solid lumps and in slang are often called "balls," they are actually two egg-shaped organs that contain tiny spaghettilike tubes. If stretched out, these tubes would be longer than a few football fields. The testes, or **testicles** (*tes*-tih-kuhls), as they are sometimes referred to, are the male equivalent of ovaries. They produce male hormones (particularly testosterone) and sperm (male sex cells).

Boys on the Inside

The internal sex organs of males are pretty much made up of a sperm factory and a sperm delivery system. Actually, to be more accurate, it is really a semen factory and semen delivery system. The parts are shown in Figure 11.

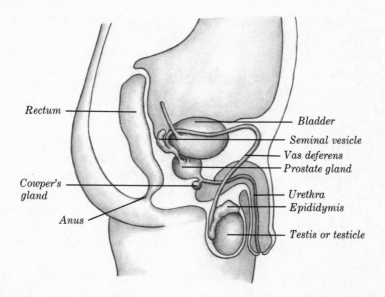

Figure 11 Male internal reproductive organs

Although boys often refer to the sticky, white liquid that spurts from the penis during ejaculation as sperm, this is not entirely correct. Actually, sperm account for only a tiny portion (about one percent) of this fluid called semen. However, it is the microscopic sperm and their ability to create new life that make semen so important.

During sexual intercourse about 400 million sperm are ejaculated into the woman's vagina. This may seem like a tremendous number, but actually the sperm are so tiny that about 120 million of them can fit into one drop of fluid. These sperm look like tiny tadpoles when viewed under a microscope. Like tadpoles, they use their powerful tails to swim inside the woman's body. If just *one* of them reaches a mature egg in the woman's body and joins with it, the woman becomes pregnant. The sperm that do not penetrate an egg eventually die.

The way in which a male's body produces sperm is intriguing. To do this, the body acts almost like a small factory. The sperm are produced by the testes at the rate of about 50,000 each minute (72 million each day) from puberty until old age. The sperm factory is so complete that it even has a way of regulating its own temperature. Since the temperature inside the body is too warm for sperm production, the body's way of adjusting for this is to place the factory in an external sack. In that way, the scrotum maintains an environment that is just right for producing sperm. Muscles in the scrotum can even further regulate the temperature of the testicles by moving them closer to or farther away from the body. When the temperature is warm, the muscles in the scrotum let the testicles hang loosely to be cooled by the surrounding air. When it is cool, these muscles pull the testes close, to be warmed by the body.

After being produced, the sperm move through a series of ducts or tubes inside a male's body. From their creation in a testicle, the sperm move to a large tube called the **epididymis** (ep-ih-*did*-ih-mis). The epididymis is actually compactly wound up and feels like a bump on the side of each testicle. The sperm stay in the epididymis and mature for up to six weeks. During this time the weaker sperm die and are absorbed into the body.

The remaining stronger sperm are moved by microscopic hairs from the epididymis up the eighteen-inch sperm duct, the **vas deferens** (vas *def*-er-enz), and travel up into the pelvis until they reach one of the **seminal vesicles** (*sem*-ih-nuhl *ves*-ih-kuhlz). These seminal vesicles are sacklike structures that secrete a substance that seems to start the tails of the sperm whipping.

The vas deferens and seminal vesicle from each side of a man's body join together inside another important male gland, the **prostate** (*prahs*-tate) **gland**. Here the sperm mixes with the rest of the sticky fluid that makes up the semen. These secretions help to nurture and protect the sperm. When the semen is ejaculated, it moves through the urethra, which is the tube that starts deep in the body at the prostate, runs through the penis, and out at its tip. Since the urethra is the same tube used for both ejaculation and urination, during ejaculation a tiny valve closes the urethra off from the bladder to ensure that the semen does not mix with urine.

One more set of tiny but potentially very important glands are the pea-sized **Cowper's glands**, which are located under the prostate gland and open into the urethra. When a male first becomes sexually excited, these glands emit a small amount of fluid, which can contain stray sperm. This occurs *before* he ejaculates. Because of this, *pregnancy is possible during intercourse even if the male withdraws his penis before he ejaculates.* Actually, if the penis even touches the vagina, even if the male never enters or ejaculates, pregnancy is a possibility. We'll talk about this more when we cover conception in chapter 8 and contraception in chapter 12.

8

PREGNANCY
AND CHILDBIRTH

Conception

Whether you are interested in avoiding an unwanted pregnancy or simply gathering information for the day when you decide to have a child, understanding the process of **conception** is important. This process normally begins with sexual intercourse. The male places his erect penis into the vagina of the female, and moves in and out until he ejaculates, releasing millions of sperm in the whitish liquid called semen. Even if the male withdraws *prior* to ejaculating, however, enough sperm may have been deposited to result in a pregnancy. In fact, it is essential to understand that any method by which sperm are carried to the opening of the vagina, whether by the penis or by somebody's hand, whether by accident or on purpose, could begin the process of conception.

As we saw in chapter 4, you have the ability to become pregnant once your ovaries begin releasing eggs. Usually a girl doesn't begin ovulating until sometime after she has had her first period. However, it has been found that some girls ovulate *before* their first menstrual flow. Therefore, if you are sexually active you must use contraception to avoid an unwanted pregnancy—whether you have experienced your first period or not.

Once deposited inside the female's vagina, the microscopic sperm propel themselves with their tails, swimming their way up through the opening in the cervix into the uterus, and finally, all the way into the fallopian tubes. If it is around the time of ovulation in the woman's menstrual cycle, one of the millions of sperm may eventually burrow into the ovum (egg), resulting in fertilization. The two cells, the ovum and the sperm, unite into one cell. This union is conception, the first moment of pregnancy. All that is required for conception is one egg and one sperm.

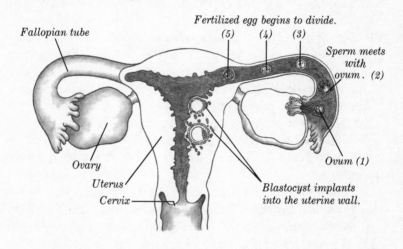

Figure 12 Uterus and the process of fertilization

After conception has occurred, the fertilized egg begins to divide, first into two cells, then four, eight, sixteen, and so on. At the same time, the egg slowly moves down the fallopian tube toward the uterus. Once at its destination inside the uterus, the mass of cells first attaches itself and later becomes buried within the uterine walls. Slowly, over a period of months, the mass of cells begins to differentiate into the layers of the unborn child's body. The developing baby is called an **embryo** for the first eight weeks of its development and a **fetus** afterward, until birth.

Twins can be formed when there are some variations in this typical process. There are two different kinds of twins: fraternal (or nonidentical) and identical. Fraternal twins are the most common, coming about when two separate sperm from the father fertilize two separate eggs (ova) from the mother. Although usually only one egg matures and is released during each menstrual cycle, on some occasions two or more eggs burst from the ovaries at the time of ovulation. If sperm find each of the eggs, more than one baby can be started. Identical twins are formed when a single egg is fertilized by a single sperm, but then goes on to divide into two separate structures rather than remaining one.[1]

Similarly, triplets, quadruplets, and so on, can occur when more than one egg is fertilized or when a single fertilized egg divides into three or four babies. In fact, both ways of conceiving multiple babies can work together at the same time. For instance, triplets can be formed in three different ways: by three separate eggs and sperm; by one fertilized egg that divides into three structures; or even by two eggs, if one of the eggs divides into identical twins while the other develops singly.

You might wonder what the chances are that you'll have twins someday. Your chances of having identical twins are about the same as those of any other female. Identical twins are born in about 1 out of 250 pregnancies. Your chances of having fraternal twins, however, depend on a number of personal characteristics, such as your race, heredity, age, and the number of times you've been pregnant in the past. Records show that black women have more fraternal twins than white women, who, in turn, have more than Japanese women. Fraternal twins tend to "run in families," so that you are more likely to have them if other women in your family have a history of giving birth to fraternal twins. The chances of having twins also increase as the age of the mother and the number of previous pregnancies increase. It has also been discovered that women who have been taking medications to help them get pregnant (fertility drugs) have more multiple births than women who don't take these drugs, because these medications can cause more than one egg to be released during ovulation.

As a final note on conception, you might be interested to know that medical science has now developed some ways to help out people who are having difficulty getting pregnant. You may have noticed that at the beginning of this chapter I said conception "normally" begins with sexual intercourse. Conception still requires the union of an egg and a sperm, but some creative ways to get them together have been devised. One method that has been used for many years is **artificial insemination**. This is a procedure in which a physician mechanically places healthy sperm into a woman's vagina or cervix. From that point, the process of conception can take place as it would under normal conditions. In another achievement of modern medicine, the first "test-tube baby" was born in 1978 as the result of fertilization that occurred outside the mother's body, in a laboratory. An ovum was surgically removed from the mother and fertilized in a dish by sperm from the father. Once conception had taken place, the fertilized egg was reinserted into the mother. These and other new methods are continually being researched as a means of helping couples who wish to have a child but for medical reasons find it difficult to conceive.

Signs of Pregnancy

The first thing that makes most women wonder whether they are pregnant is a late period. This is because menstruation ceases during pregnancy. Women can miss this key sign for a few different reasons, however. For one thing, instead of having no menstrual bleeding at all, some women have much lighter periods during early pregnancy and are fooled into thinking they are not pregnant. Some women's menstrual cycles are so irregular that it is difficult for them to determine when a period is indeed late. Other women don't keep careful enough track of their cycles to even notice that a period was due at a certain time. As you learned in chapter 4 on the menstrual cycle, periods can be thrown off by many things other than pregnancy. Therefore, having a late period does not prove that a woman is pregnant, but it is certainly an indication that she might be.

There are some other common symptoms or signs many women notice early in their pregnancies. Breasts can become very tender and tingly. Also, nausea and vomiting are fairly typical. Because this nausea is most common in the morning hours, it is called **morning sickness**. Often pregnant women feel more tired than usual and find that they need to urinate frequently.

It is very important for any woman who believes that she is pregnant to have a pregnancy test. She can then make the exciting plans for promoting a healthy pregnancy or have sufficient time to face the difficult decisions involved in an unwanted pregnancy (see chapter 16, "Dealing with an Unplanned Pregnancy").

Pregnancy tests work by measuring the level of a certain hormone, called **HCG**, in the woman's body. The fertilized egg begins producing this hormone soon after conception, and the hormone continues to be produced as the pregnancy progresses. The most common type of pregnancy test measures the level of this hormone in the woman's urine, but with the usual urine test for pregnancy, a period typically has to be about two weeks late before this type of test can detect the hormone. Newer blood and urine tests are more sensitive and can diagnose a pregnancy much earlier. Home pregnancy tests are now also available (see chapter 16).

When a woman has a positive pregnancy test, the next step is to have a pelvic exam (see chapter 6). A physician can estimate how far along the pregnancy is by the size of the uterus. The uterus and cervix get softer when a woman is pregnant, and the physician can feel this during the exam. Sometimes potential problems with the pregnancy can also be picked up at this time.

As a pregnancy develops, a woman's body undergoes many

visible changes. The most obvious is that her abdomen enlarges and protrudes as the baby grows in size. Her breasts and nipples enlarge and veins may become visible in them. Eventually the baby's heartbeat and movements can be noticed. Special techniques now even exist that can safely take pictures of the baby inside the uterus.

Stages of Pregnancy

From conception to birth an average pregnancy lasts just under 9 months—about 266 days. Sometimes a pregnancy is measured from the first day of the last menstrual period rather than from the day of conception. In that case the average number of days is 280.

The stages of pregnancy are divided into three consecutive three-month periods called **trimesters**. The first trimester starts with conception. The fertilized egg, or **zygote**, begins rapidly dividing into more cells and rolling from the outer portion of the fallopian tube toward the uterus. About one week after conception the ball of cells (now called a **blastocyst**) has implanted itself in the lining of the uterus. At the time of implantation, this blastocyst is only 4/100 of an inch in diameter. Some of these cells evolve into the embryo itself and some evolve into structures that protect and support the embryo.

As development continues, the embryo is suspended in a fluid-filled sac called the **amnion**, which is in turn surrounded by another protective sac, the **chorion**. These sacs protect the embryo and fetus from injury by cushioning shocks and blows, giving it room to grow without pressure, and providing an even temperature. Within its sacs inside the mother's uterus, the fetus receives nourishment and oxygen from the mother by way of a special structure called the **placenta**. Waste products from the fetus are also passed through the placenta to be eliminated by the mother's bloodstream. The fetus is attached to the placenta by its **umbilical cord**.

In the first trimester the embryo (or fetus) begins to form

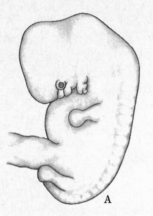

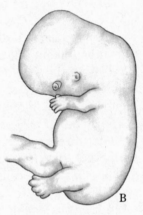

Figure 13 Fetal development

(A) Embryo at five weeks (B) Embryo at six weeks (C) Fetus at ten weeks (D) Fetus at twenty weeks (E) Fetus at twenty-six weeks

D

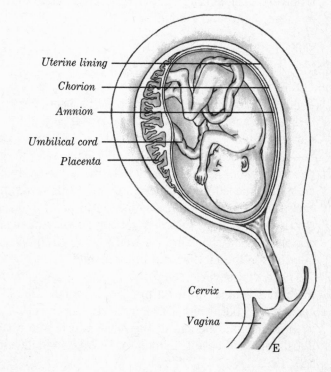

Uterine lining

Chorion

Amnion

Umbilical cord

Placenta

Cervix

Vagina

E

arms, legs, eyes, fingers, and toes. Internal organs also initiate their development during the first three months: the heart, brain, spinal cord, nervous system, digestive system, and bones. By the end of the first trimester, twelve weeks after conception, the fetus is about 3½ inches long. Its major organs have been formed, but they are not complete.

The fetus continues to grow and mature during the second trimester. The external genitals develop, so that the sex of the fetus can be seen by the end of four months. Lips, eyebrows, and eyelashes become visible. The mother can begin feeling movements of the fetus during this time. At the close of the second trimester, the fetus is about 12 inches long and weighs from 1.3 to 1.5 pounds.

The fetus grows larger and stronger during the third trimester. The brain and nervous system complete their maturation. The fetus is referred to as "full-term" at the end of the third trimester. The average full-term fetus is about 20 inches long and weighs around 7 pounds.

Prenatal Care

Prenatal care means taking the steps necessary to have a pregnancy that is most likely to result in a healthy baby and mother. Ideally, prenatal care is an extension of an already healthy life-style, so that the mother begins her pregnancy in good condition. As has already been mentioned, having a pregnancy diagnosed early gives the mother time to initiate this care during the critical first few months of fetal development. Good prenatal care includes getting regular medical advice, education, and checkups, as well as living a life-style that is healthy for the mother and unborn child.

There are several purposes of the initial comprehensive medical examination for a pregnant woman. One is to make certain that both the mother and fetus are healthy. A second is to determine the age of the fetus in order to estimate the due date and to be able to monitor the expected developmental milestones of the pregnancy. The third is to help the woman prepare for the next steps in her pregnancy. Any special risks can be identified; education about pregnancy, prenatal care, and childbirth can be provided; and schedules for regular checkups and prenatal classes can be discussed.

An important aspect of this initial education is to become aware of major warning signs that a complication is developing:

1. Any vaginal bleeding;
2. Swelling of face or fingers;
3. Severe or continuous headaches;
4. Dimness or blurring of vision;
5. Abdominal pain;
6. Persistent vomiting;
7. Chills or fever;
8. Painful urination;
9. Escape of fluid from the vagina.

Any of the above symptoms should immediately be reported to the woman's health care practitioner. In addition, it is helpful for the mother and, if possible, the father to be educated as to what to expect for the remainder of the pregnancy and delivery. Unprepared parents can easily become unduly alarmed about the many physical changes that occur normally during the pregnancy. Classes on child development and parenting skills can further help new parents take on this important and challenging role.

Traditionally, monthly medical checkups have been recommended for the first seven months of a pregnancy, increasing to every other week during the eighth month, and to once a week in the last month. This schedule is modified to meet the needs of the individual woman, however. During these visits the doctor can monitor the normal fetal development, as well as do special tests to detect birth defects and abnormalities of the fetus.

It is important that a woman consult her physician *before*

taking any medication during pregnancy. This is true for both prescription and over-the-counter drugs. Medications can have an effect on the fetus. Some tragic deformities have been caused by medications. In most cases the results are more subtle, but even aspirin has been found to have the potential for negative effects on the fetus.

Of special concern is the mother's consumption of certain common toxic substances. These include street drugs, tobacco, and any alcohol—even beer and wine. Street drugs, such as heroin, opiates, "uppers" (amphetamines), and "downers" (barbiturates), can have devastating effects on the fetus, including death. Tobacco and alcohol also have been found to have negative effects. The children of mothers who smoked cigarettes during pregnancy have been found to have lower birth weights, higher rates of prematurity and hyperactivity, and to have decreased IQs, school achievement, and motor skills. Women who smoke also have more spontaneous abortions. Heavy alcohol intake during pregnancy has been related to decreased growth of the fetus, damage to the brain and nervous system, facial abnormalities, mental retardation, and hyperactivity. More current research even indicates that light to moderate drinking may have adverse consequences for the child. We also now know that the active chemicals in marijuana cross the placenta into the blood system of the fetus. The possibility of damage to the fetus and of miscarriage are now suspected risks of marijuana use in pregnant women.

While pregnant, the woman herself is in charge of maintaining a life-style that promotes health: good nutrition, adequate rest, proper hygiene, and moderate exercise. A nutritionist can suggest the type of diet best for the mother and her child. In general, she will need a diet high in protein, minerals, and vitamins to assure adequate weight gain for the mother and growth for the fetus. Poor nutrition has been related to such things as slower fetal growth, premature birth, low birth weight, and mental retardation of the child.

Moderate exercise is usually positive. The idea is to use common sense by avoiding dangerous activities that risk bodily harm and by not exercising to the point of heavy fatigue. There are some high-risk pregnancies when even light exercise is not wise, but the doctor can advise the woman in these cases. Likewise, there is no indication that engaging in sexual activity during the first seven months is harmful during most pregnancies. Opinions on the effects of sexual intercourse during late pregnancy vary. Again the physician can advise the woman whether there are any reasons for her to restrict sexual activities during any stage of her pregnancy.

Childbirth

The process of childbirth is called **labor** and is divided into three stages. Although how long a woman is in labor varies with individual women, the first stage is the longest. The length of this stage also varies depending upon whether or not it is the woman's first child. The first stage commonly lasts between ten to sixteen hours for first children, but usually shortens to four to eight hours in subsequent pregnancies. Sometimes a woman can tell she is about to go into labor when a plug of bloody mucus is expelled from the cervix. You may have heard this occurrence referred to as the *bloody show*.

Labor actually begins with strong, regular, involuntary contractions of the uterus. The cervix dilates (opens up) gradually. The amniotic sac may break open and release the fluid inside it. Many women call this "breaking the bag of waters." In some cases, the waters break before labor begins, and is another sign that labor is not far off. Contractions become more intense throughout this first phase of labor. This stage ends when the cervix is fully dilated and ready for the baby to pass through it.

During the second stage the infant descends into and through the vagina (or birth canal). This stage commonly lasts from about one-half to two hours. It is completed when the baby is born.

Within about a half-hour after the baby has been delivered,

the placenta detaches from the wall of the uterus and is also expelled through the vagina. This process makes up the third stage of labor and is often called **afterbirth**.

Complications in Labor

Many girls and women are very frightened by the idea of giving birth. They regard it as horribly dangerous and painful. In fact, 80 percent of births are uncomplicated, and because of medical advances rarely is there a life threat to the vast majority of the remaining 20 percent.

Special instruments, equipment, and procedures are available for use during any of these difficult deliveries. For instance, **forceps** are a surgical instrument like tongs that can help pull the baby out of the vagina. In a special delivery procedure called a **cesarean section**, or **C-section**, the fetus is removed through incisions cut in the mother's abdomen and uterus. Labor can also be introduced artificially through the administration of certain drugs if there is some concern about letting the fetus remain in the uterus. An *episiotomy* is a procedure in which an incision is made in the skin and muscle surrounding the opening of the vagina, reducing the chances that these tissues will tear during childbirth.

Alternative Types of Childbirth

Many women and health care practitioners are now questioning whether some medical "advances" have gone too far. Although advanced technology is certainly necessary in complicated births, some people feel that they are overused and unnecessary in routine births. Some of these procedures introduce their own risks: painkillers given to reduce the pain of contractions can slow down labor, make it difficult for a woman to push during delivery, and even affect the baby's heartbeat; injuries to the child have occurred with forceps; and cesarean sections (C-sections) have higher rates of post-pregnancy complications. Others complain that traditional hospital deliveries have made childbirth too mechanical and less personally meaningful for the parents. Hence, a number of alternative approaches have been developed in answer to these criticisms.

Natural childbirth was first popularized by Grantly Dick-Read, a British physician. He believed that the pain and anxiety women experienced during birth could be greatly reduced if they were more prepared. Such preparation may make anesthesia less necessary for many women. Classes that teach women more about birth and give instruction in relaxation techniques have evolved from his philosophy. The Lamaze Method, named after a French physician, teaches specific breathing and relaxation exercises to ease the process of labor and delivery. These methods also get the woman's partner involved in the baby's birth. The partner attends classes with the pregnant woman and serves as a coach during her labor.

The LeBoyer Method, developed by another French physician, focuses on the birth experience from the infant's point of view by trying to make the child's entry into the world as nonalarming and gentle as possible. Dimmed lights, soothing water baths, a quiet atmosphere, and immediate contact with the mother's belly are techniques that are used.

Many medical centers have responded to requests for less impersonal deliveries by creating birthing clinics, which are designed to be more homey than typical hospital rooms. Some of these are located within hospitals and some are separate centers. Home births have also become somewhat more popular again. Medical professionals stress, however, that there is always the danger that a birth can become more complicated than anticipated and backup emergency care should always be available.

9

MAKING DECISIONS ABOUT SEX

No one ever has to make a decision about sex in the movies or on TV. Things just seem to happen. A man and woman melt into each other's arms, and the decision is made for them. It appears that having sex is an almost routine process; but in reality sex is anything but simple. This chapter is designed to help you understand the complexity of factors that influence sexual decision making and to assist you in making constructive decisions more easily.

In reaching the best sexual decisions for yourself, there are three critically important steps: (1) understanding the facts; (2) establishing your own values; and (3) listening to your own emotional reactions. Ignoring any of these three steps could result in serious difficulties. Not paying attention to the facts could mean having sex unsafely and suffering serious consequences, such as an unwanted pregnancy or a sexually transmitted disease. Ignoring your values can leave you with deep feelings of guilt or a lack of self-esteem. Finally, ignoring your feelings can leave you deeply scarred by hurt, anger, or other unpleasant feelings.

Without a doubt, it is difficult to consider each of these steps when you are about to make an important decision, but accepting adult responsibilities takes work. Certainly, if you were about to buy an expensive stereo or a car, you would take the time to make a careful evaluation of the alternatives. The decisions that go with making you a healthy sexual person deserve at least the same amount of consideration.

Looking at the Facts

Sex doesn't just involve excitement and romance. It also involves some concrete realities. Since having sex exposes you to a number of risks, including pregnancy, diseases, and emotional distress, it is important that you understand how these risks can be minimized and how the pleasurable aspects of sex can be enhanced. To do that you need to know the facts.

Below are a series of questions whose answers you should know *before* engaging in sex. If you are even slightly unsure of any of the answers, make certain to read the chapters from which the questions originated, rather than finding out the answers the hard way.

1. How does a girl get pregnant? How can this happen without her having intercourse? Why is there no "safe" time of the month during which a teenage girl can be certain not to become pregnant? (Answers in chapters 4 and 8.)

2. What contraceptive techniques are available? Why is withdrawal an ineffective method of birth control? Why is there no method of birth control that is 100 percent effective? What are the side effects, health risks, and benefits of the method you presently use or may be thinking about using? (Answers in chapter 12.)

3. How can a young woman tell if she is pregnant? Where can she go to get a pregnancy test? Where can she get counseling if she is pregnant? What are the options open to a young woman facing an unwanted pregnancy? Why is it essential to have a pregnancy accurately diagnosed as early as possible? (Answers in chapters 4, 8, 12, and 16.)

4. What are some of the symptoms of sexually transmit-

ted diseases? Why are sexually transmitted diseases even more dangerous if a woman does not have any symptoms? How can STDs be prevented? Where can you go to get examined or to receive treatment for an STD? What are the possible consequences of not getting treatment? What is PID? (Answers in chapters 6 and 13.)

These are not the only facts that are important in preventing some of the possible serious consequences of sex, but they are the ones that are most vital when you choose to be sexually active. This book is full of information that is essential to making completely informed sexual decisions. Know your facts before you leap into a possibly dangerous situation.

Sexual Make-Believe

One factor that complicates our attempts to use factual knowledge when making sexual decisions is that much of what we learn about sex is make-believe. Without a doubt, some of your ideas about sex are already unrealistic. All of us have some exaggerated expectations about sex and sexuality. You live in a world of exaggerations. On TV and in the movies men are superstrong and women are supersexy. It is impossible to get away from the exaggerations. Almost every woman you see in an advertisement is beautiful, large-breasted, and seductive. Movies make intercourse seem like a natural part of every male-female relationship. Sex sometimes seems like a two-person sport, as casual as tennis or bowling. As you watch a movie or the television screen, you are no doubt aware that what you are watching is not real and is only a fictional story. However, sometimes it is difficult to realize that the way sex is portrayed is likewise a world of make-believe.

The reason for these distortions is simple. People pay attention to sex. Sexy men or women in advertisements sell products. Sex sells books and magazines. The more exaggerated the sex appears to be, the more people seem to pay attention. Along with capturing your attention, however, these distortions will most likely give you false expectations. And, every false expectation has the potential to influence you to make an unwise sexual decision.

Understanding and Developing Your Own Values

Not all of the influences upon your sexuality will be as obvious as those caused by the exaggerations of the media. Many of your sexual attitudes, opinions, and actions will be shaped by much more subtle influences, such as the words people use (or misuse) in talking about sex.

Many people will confuse facts with opinions when talking about sex. If someone says that a girl may become pregnant if she engages in intercourse, that is a fact. If that person says that it is good or bad for her to engage in intercourse, that is their opinion. Opinions and facts are not the same.

By learning to recognize other people's opinions and how to distinguish them from facts, it will be easier for you to develop a set of sexual values.

As a teenage girl, you are faced with developing a set of values that will work for you. In talking with other teenage girls, certain value questions come up all the time. One major concern is to define under what circumstances it is all right or even good to have sex: Should it only be when a couple is married or going steady? How committed should the couple be? Is casual sex okay, or do the people need to be in love? Is it immoral to have sex with more than one person? Is heavy petting acceptable if intercourse isn't?

A second critical value concerns abortion. Since pregnancy is a realistic risk of sexual behavior, sexually active girls (and boys) need to figure out how they will handle an unplanned pregnancy and whether abortion is an acceptable option for them. Certainly other value questions come up and are debated, but these two appear to be central.

Whether you realize it or not, you already have developed some sexual values of your own. And, like everything else about your sexuality, your values are uniquely yours. They may be similar to those of your friends, or they may be similar to those of your parents, but when you really get down to it, no one has values exactly like yours. Put simply, values are what you believe is right or wrong. They are standards that you feel are appropriate for yourself and others. You may even have one set of values for yourself and a different set for others. For instance, you might believe that it is all right for a friend to have premarital intercourse, but not for you.

Everyone around you has sexual values, and either openly or subtly, they are constantly sharing their values with you. Everyone believes that his or her values are the right ones. If they didn't believe that, they would change their values to something else. Therefore, don't be insulted if people challenge your values. All they are doing is giving their opinions. You don't have to agree with them.

Other people's opinions can often be a very powerful influence in determining what sexual decisions a teenager makes. Our values about sexual behavior develop from a number of different influences: our culture; religious teachings; watching the behavior of those around us; TV, books, and movies; the laws governing sexual behavior; what our parents have taught us; what our friends say; and even the results of our own experiments with sexuality. However, it is important to recognize that whatever final decisions you make are your responsibility. If you choose to follow someone else's advice, that is up to *you*. If you choose to go it alone and not listen to anyone else, that too is up to you. Ultimately, you are the one who chooses your sexual direction. And, you are the one who faces the consequences of your decisions.

Before making important decisions concerning your own sexuality, it is essential that you first understand your own values. Below is a simple exercise designed to help you clarify your values involving a few major issues that often confront young women. Read through this list of questions, thinking about the opinions you have heard in support of each of the various sides. If these concerns are not relevant to you and others are, change the questions so that the exercise will be more meaningful for you. Write out your own opinion about each issue and what information you have to support it. Make a statement like "I believe it is (good/not good/wrong/right/ etc.) for me to (engage in heavy petting/have intercourse before I get married/etc.)

1. Under what circumstances is heavy petting okay?
2. When is it all right to have intercourse?
3. Is masturbation okay?
4. Is being sexual more acceptable for boys than it is for girls?
5. Should a girl initiate sex?
6. Should a girl ever consider an abortion?

Remember, the point of this exercise is to help you understand what your present values are. Even if you have chosen a certain value now, this doesn't mean that you are stuck with it. As you gather more information it is likely that a good many of your sexual values will be altered. Even when you become an adult, it is likely that you will have different values for your children than you presently have for yourself.

On some questions you might not feel ready to reach a conclusion. Instead you might want to collect additional information by reading or by watching and listening to people who have differing values. Then, after putting all of your information together, you can arrive at your own set of values to help you make decisions.

Looking at Feelings

Just as facts and values are critical in making sexual decisions, so are feelings. The best sexual decisions are made only when all three of these factors are taken into account. If you were to purchase a new dress, you wouldn't just buy something because it was the right size and the right color. You would buy it because it made you *feel* attractive or because it made you just *feel* good. Likewise, in making a decision about yourself as a sexual person, your feelings are crucial. Even if you understand the facts about sex perfectly and if your values permit you to engage in intercourse, doing so even if it feels bad can cause considerable regret and emotional distress. On the other hand, making a decision solely based on emotions can be equally unwise. To decide to make love with a guy just because you feel that you love him can be disastrous if you overlook such crucial facts as the risk of pregnancy or sexually transmitted diseases (STDs), or if you fail to consider your values.

Emotions probably developed originally as a guide for our survival, to warn us when something was dangerous and to encourage us to continue actions that were healthy for us. As such, emotions can continue to function as signals to you that something can hurt you or can make you grow. This is not to say that emotions are always 100 percent accurate in predicting whether something will be positive or negative. Many times we are afraid of things that are not really dangerous, such as speaking in front of a room full of people. Other times we get excited and want something that turns out to be harmful, such as eating too much chocolate or drinking too much wine. Consequently, important decisions should not be made on the basis of feelings alone, but after considering what you want, what you value, and what the realistic consequences or facts of the situation are.

How can you use your emotions then? They are wonderful cues. You can ask yourself, *How do I really feel about this action?* such as having intercourse with this person. Then pay attention to your own emotional reactions. What feelings become prominent? Excitement, tenderness, joy, or anxiety and fear? There is often a mix of these feelings, to different degrees. If the idea of sex with this person makes you uncomfortable, you can stop to analyze why this is so. Perhaps you don't trust the relationship; perhaps you don't hold the value that sex is good in this situation; or perhaps you know that you haven't adequately protected yourself against pregnancy.

Just for practice, try the following: Find a quiet place, and get your body into a very relaxed position. Now, close your eyes and visualize each of the situations listed below. As soon as you get a clear mental image of each scene, pay attention to any messages your body might be sending. Do you feel tension anywhere? Is there a sense of excitement, joy, or tenderness? Do you feel any fear? Does your body feel generally comfortable or uncomfortable? Notice which feelings stand out.

1. Making out with a boy for the first time.
2. Making the decision to have intercourse.
3. Having your doctor tell you that you are pregnant.

Your body will send you messages. Sometimes the messages may be much clearer than at other times, but if you pay careful attention, your feelings will become apparent.

Whenever your feelings about any sexual activity are highly negative, it is not a good idea to force yourself into it. Engaging in sex when you don't want to or are scared can create many problems. Certainly it is not likely to be enjoyable. Furthermore, sex therapists have found that people who continue to engage in unpleasurable sexual activities often develop sexual problems. When used together with your chosen values and a knowledge of the facts, feelings can be a powerful tool in helping you make healthy sexual decisions.

Love

One emotion that deserves special attention when discussing sex is love. Often we see love portrayed in ways that make it seem almost magical. In songs, TV shows, films, poems, books, and even in real life, there seems to be a belief that if you are in love, everything will work out well in the end. We even have expressions like, "Love conquers all," "Love is beautiful," "Love is bliss," and "Love makes the world go round," all feeding that same unrealistic expectation that being in love will lead to only good things.

Without a doubt, love is wonderful and can create a terrific feeling of well-being, but the other side of that reality is that love also can be painful and that, by itself, love is not sufficient to make a relationship work. All good relationships take a great deal of effort, communication, respect, sharing, and trust.

Making decisions about sex is often complicated by confusing emotions. It becomes difficult to separate sensations of physical attraction from emotions like being in love. Just because you like a boy, enjoy being with him, and are sexually attracted to him, this doesn't mean that you love him. Similarly, having sex with someone does not ensure you of either an exciting romance or of close emotional intimacy. All three can go together, but they don't always. Having sex can certainly be romantic and intimate, but usually only if the feelings of romance and intimacy already exist. Often girls are disappointed when they have sex with someone, hoping that it will bring emotional closeness or deepen the relationship. Sometimes couples who already share a special relationship find that sex does deepen their intimacy, but many times it works the other way. If there isn't much emotional closeness in a relationship, sex is probably not the missing ingredient. Trust, communication, and caring are more likely what is needed. Many people find that sex too early in a relationship can actually dampen the romance and get in the way of developing intimacy.

Although it is difficult to be objective about romantic relationships, being able to evaluate the quality of your relationships would certainly help you to make better decisions about sex. In reality, the vast majority of teenage romances don't last. Even couples who feel that they are really "in love" and who believe that they will be together "forever and ever" usually break up. Even though you probably cannot count on a relationship being permanent, you can still try to be honest with yourself about how good the relationship is and how likely you are to get hurt. You might want to ask yourself the following questions about your relationship when deciding whether or not to have sex:

How healthy is this relationship? How long have we known each other?

How much do I know about the other person? What is the level of commitment in the relationship? Does this person have other sexual partners?

What do we plan to do if I get pregnant? Is there a chance that this person has a sexually transmitted disease?

Can I trust this person to be honest with me and to care about my feelings and welfare?

Some people need to be in love to enjoy sex. Others can enjoy sex if they simply care about the other person. Still others find that sex can be enjoyed simply as a physical act, without any emotional ties with the other person. You will have to set up your own guidelines as to what importance love will play in your sexual relationships. The key is to *be honest with yourself* about what you need. Don't fool yourself by confusing physical attraction, love, intimacy, and sex. Don't pretend that casual sex is cool with you if it's really not.

Two cautions deserve mention here. First, sex should never be used as a proof of your love. If at any time a boy says to you "if you love me, you'll have sex with me" as a way of pressuring you into doing something you are uncomfortable with, *don't do it*. If he really cares about you, he will accept you in the relationship without making you prove it. Likewise, don't do the same thing to your partner. Second, sex should never be used as a cement to hold a relationship together. Becoming sexual with a boy, simply because you are afraid that the relationship is slipping away, will not, in the long run, keep things together.

Putting It All Together to Make a Decision

Again, before you make any major decisions about engaging in sexual activity, it is essential that you assure yourself of three points:

1. Know that the activity you are considering is right for you—that it conforms to your values.
2. Have enough factual information to feel confident that you can handle any possible consequences.
3. Check your feelings to make sure that this is something you truly desire and feel comfortable about doing, not just something you are doing to make someone else happy or to prove yourself.

After you have done all that, the next step would be to discuss your feelings, values, and practical concerns with your partner and to find out his views as well. Many of the hurts and feelings of betrayal that occur in relationships happen because people don't talk openly about what they want from each other. They find out later that they had different expectations. For example, if you believe that sex means a commitment while your partner sees it as only a "good time," resentment is inevitable.

If you and your partner can discuss your views openly, then any potential problems can be minimized. The more serious you are about a relationship, the more important it becomes to discuss your needs and your views as to how you wish to relate to each other. Following are a few topics that are especially important in this regard:

- Who will take primary responsibility for birth control?
- What is the best way to deal with a pregnancy?

- What are each of your expectations in regard to the other one dating or having other sexual partners?

Sometimes decisions seem very easy, and sometimes they seem impossible. Whatever decisions you make, be sure they are decisions that you are making freely for yourself.

One girl who waited until she was ready wrote,

All through high school I was a virgin. During most of this time I was embarrassed by this fact. When people at parties would talk about sex or joke about those who were virgins, I would feel very out of place. I felt that I would be rejected if anyone knew I was a virgin. I never said I had had intercourse, but I never denied it. Sometimes, I would think that I could never go out with the popular boys because they would want to have sex. I was afraid that they would not like me as much as other girls because I was a virgin. I often imagined going to bed with one of them, though, and being the best lover they ever had. In a way, I felt that sex was the ticket to "catching" a really cute guy.

Even though at times I felt sex was the way to be popular, I knew that I was not ready to be sexually active with anyone. . . .

Today I'm happy that I did not lose my virginity in the back seat of a car, that I waited till I was ready. I have a lot of self-respect because I was positive that making love to my boyfriend was the right decision.

One final aspect of decision making is essential. In addition to never letting yourself get forced into doing something because you think it will save a relationship, *never* get into a position where drugs or alcohol are making a decision for you. Many times girls allow themselves to be manipulated or in other ways forced into doing something sexually that they later regret. Stand up for your own values and be clear on what your limits are in a relationship.

Being Assertive

For a lot of people, talking about sex is harder than having sex. Even important conversations with a sexual partner are often avoided because of the awkwardness of initiating them. I'm not just talking about what goes on between teenagers, but between adults as well, even married adults. This section should help you in communicating your values and limits to your partner.

The key to learning to communicate effectively with a partner about sex is *assertion*. Being assertive means expressing yourself directly and honestly in a way that shows you respect both yourself and the person you are talking to. Not being assertive means that you are treating yourself as if your own feelings and opinions are not important.

There are many different forms of assertive statements: expressing your positive feelings about someone, giving compliments, expressing your opinions, telling someone that you don't like something they are doing, and standing up for yourself by saying no to something that you don't want to do.

For many girls, some ways of being assertive are very difficult. They tend to disregard their own opinions and often avoid saying that they don't like what someone is doing. Standing up for themselves and saying no are also forms of assertion that many women do less firmly than men. Some people confuse assertion with aggression, but these two types of communication are very different. Aggressive behavior may be direct and honest, but it doesn't involve treating the other person with respect.

In learning to communicate assertively, it is important to pay attention both to what you say and how you say it. What you say, your verbal message, should be clear and straightforward. The manner in which you say it, the nonverbal message, should support what you are trying to communicate. For example, some clear assertive verbal messages would be:

"I care about you."

"I feel angry."

"I do not want to have sex."

"No, I don't want any wine."

"I like it when you call and say that you have been thinking about me."

Although each of these statements is very different, each is direct, honest, and clear.

The intent of any of the above messages could be spoiled, however, by the nonverbal delivery. If, for instance, you say "I feel angry" and laugh because you are nervous about saying it, the person is liable to think, Well, she couldn't be too angry with me. Or, if you say, "No, I don't want to have sex," but you sound very unsure of yourself, your partner is liable to think, She really doesn't mean it. She is just playing hard to get. Such things as eye contact, voice tone, loudness, fidgeting, and giggling can all make a difference as to whether you look like you mean what you say. You are more likely to be taken seriously if you look directly at someone, speak clearly without mumbling or whispering, and if you don't move around nervously or laugh at your own opinions.

Being able to tell another person assertively what your values and feelings are really increases your chances of getting heard and being respected. If you don't feel that the other person is responding to you with understanding, you might first think about whether you have stated what you wanted to say clearly. If necessary, either repeat what you said or restate it in different words. If you feel that the other person isn't listening or is putting pressure on you to accept his views or desires over your own, bring the conflict into the open. Tell him that you don't feel he is listening or that you are feeling pressured. Remember, it is up to you to stick up for yourself. Don't give in to something you really don't want to do.

Being assertive is not always easy, especially with the opposite sex. If you find asserting yourself to be difficult, an excellent book to read would be *Self-Assertion for Women*,

108 | *A YOUNG WOMAN'S GUIDE TO SEX*

by Pamela Butler.[1] Also, courses on assertiveness training are frequently offered by many schools and community agencies.

What Do You Do If You Make a Mistake?

Actually, there is *no* chance that you will get through your teenage years (or your life, for that matter) without making mistakes. All adults look back at this time and say "If only I hadn't done such and such," or "If only I *had* done such and such." Consequently, it's not really a matter of what you should do *if* you make a mistake, it's a matter of what you should do *when* you make a mistake. The answer is simple: Learn from your errors. There is no sense in punishing yourself for "blowing it." Just think about how you might handle the situation differently the next time, and how you can make the best of the situation at hand.

Sadly, many girls condemn themselves for making a mistake, rather than using the mistake as a painful learning experience. Often they call themselves names, or put themselves down in other ways. This doesn't help the situation, and, in fact, can further damage their self-esteem and sometimes lead to depression. If you find yourself falling into this pattern, try treating yourself as you would a friend who had made the same mistake. Probably you would be supportive and understanding, and encourage her to be wiser in her choices the next time. If you can be supportive to a friend, do the same for yourself.

In the event that you continue to be overcritical of yourself or get quite depressed, talk to someone about it. If possible, choose a friend who has been through a similar situation, or an understanding adult. Professional counselors can also be helpful if you continue to feel down or don't have anyone you feel comfortable in talking to. If you find yourself repeatedly making self-destructive decisions, this is also a sign that professional counseling might be in order.

10

SEX: WHAT IT'S ALL ABOUT

Many adolescents, and even many adults, seem to equate sex with intercourse. Yet, in reality that is *not* all there is to sex. Actually, any behavior that leads to the excited feelings of being "turned on" (sexually aroused) can be considered sexual.

Certainly, intercourse is the sexual behavior that the most fuss is made about. There always seems to be talk among adolescents about who "went all the way" and who didn't. Virginity still seems to be the yardstick that most teenagers use to measure how sexually experienced a girl is. Yet, the truth is that intercourse is only one way of experiencing your sexuality, and for many young women it is not even the most enjoyable of sexual activities. In an interesting survey, thousands of questionnaires were distributed to women of all ages. A majority of these women described other forms of touching as more consistently pleasurable and satisfying than intercourse.[1]

This does not mean that sexual intercourse cannot be a very pleasurable experience. It simply means that other forms of sexual activity can be important sources of sexual pleasure. Kissing, rubbing, holding, touching, and even dreaming and thinking can each be important parts of the experience we refer to as "sex."

Feelings and Fantasies

One of the most enjoyable parts of adolescence, and often one of the most confusing, is having sexual fantasies (daydreams). You can enjoy the satisfaction of gazing at a boy from across the classroom and experience a romantic encounter without the threat of being rejected, or fantasize about being loved by your favorite rock star without the slightest possibility of anything happening that might spoil the romance. Like a magical adventure, you can have all of the fun without any of the risks.

On the other hand, some of these imagined adventures may seem very threatening. Sometimes girls worry that they are perverted or oversexed merely because they experience these very normal sexual feelings and fantasies, or because some of these feelings and thoughts extend to members of their own family. This, too, is quite normal. You might catch a glimpse of your brother while he is changing clothes or wrestle with him and feel a tinge of sexual excitement. Yet because our society frowns upon sexual relationships between close relatives, these reactions tend to create unnecessary feelings of guilt and self-doubt. Also, because of the taboo associated with such feelings, it is doubtful that your friends will talk about similar experiences. Each of you will be left with these secret fantasies, feeling uncomfortable and strange, only to find out much later in your life that these are normal thoughts for your age.

Allowing yourself to enjoy sexual feelings and thoughts does not mean that you will translate these fantasies into actions. If they are appreciated and it is understood that these adventures into your mind are a normal part of your growth, they can become an enjoyable aspect of both your adolescent and adult sexuality. If, on the other hand, these feelings and thoughts become associated with feelings of fear, guilt, or anxiety, they can slow your sexual development. As your adolescence progresses, it is likely that your sexual feelings and fantasies will continue to intensify and occur more frequently.

Starting to Touch

Ease or discomfort in touching others appears to be rooted in early childhood. Physical contact between you and your parents during infancy and childhood form the earliest notions of what it is like to touch and be touched by others. Also, the example that your parents set by their physical contact with each other influences your later comfort in touching. If your parents touched you comfortably and appeared relaxed in touching each other, then touch is more likely to be a relaxed and natural experience for you.

As childhood continues, touching other children becomes a natural part of playing and fighting, and sometimes may even result in the children examining each other's bodies. This mutual exploration is often referred to as "playing doctor" or "show and tell." Since girls usually play with girls, and boys tend to stick with boys throughout most of childhood, many girls have their earliest experiences of bodily exploration with other girls. Even somewhat more extensive touching and physical exploration between girls during childhood or early adolescence is not unusual.

Touching others is not necessarily a way of being sexual. In many circumstances touching is merely a way of communicating feelings. It may be an expression of caring, affection, playfulness, or even hostility. In general, girls appear to be much more relaxed about touching each other than boys are. Often, girls will hold hands while walking along and seem more able to show their affection through physical contact. This can be a very reassuring and rewarding source of support throughout life.

Certainly, as you mature, the meaning of touch may take on more sexual implications. Touching may begin to feel like a need fueled by some mysterious inner drive. The playfulness that once existed between you and boys may become mixed with a sense of excitement and adventure. This "sexualization" of anything that involves touching may be even more true for teenage boys. For an adolescent boy, touching can often be interpreted as a sexual act, even when a girl means it simply as an expression of caring.

It is unfortunate that many teenagers and adults rush through the pleasures and joy of touching to get to the genital aspects of sexuality. Unfortunately, this rushing can cause them to miss out on the closeness that holding, hugging, caressing, and kissing can bring to a relationship. By pushing themselves to be more "grown-up" and sexually experienced, the romance and sensuality in the relationship actually diminish.

Kissing

Not all kisses are sexual. There is an obvious difference between kissing your grandmother good-bye, affectionately kissing a boy good-night, and kissing someone with sexual passion. Sexuality is really a feeling that lives inside you. When you are ready to express it, your body will let you know, and kissing will take on a different meaning.

Like most girls, before I ever kissed a boy, one of my greatest concerns was whether or not I would be good at kissing. I practiced studiously in front of the mirror and with my pillow. One friend gave the rest of us tips on how to position our heads slightly to the side and to part our lips a bit. I also worried about how to avoid damaging the guy for life with my braces.

One girl talked about her first reactions to being introduced into the world of kissing:

I can't remember my first "peck on the cheek," but I do remember my first "passionate kiss." . . . After the dance we went to another party. When we got into the car after the party, we started talking and laughing. We did have a good night. Then he asked me to sit next to him—close. All my little-girl fantasies vanished and I started getting scared. Here I was, only fifteen, and I was in this car with an eighteen-and-a-half-year-old-hunk. He put his arm around me. He was quite smooth; obviously an old pro. Next thing I knew he was kissing me gently on the cheek. He didn't waste any time—he went straight for the mouth. And I was experiencing my first French kiss. Since I was a new beginner, I just kind of followed. It was nothing like I had imagined. The thoughts that were going through my head! "So this is what it's like!" "Is this what everybody is so excited about?" "This is gross!" Well, the night ended quickly. I was quiet on the way home. When I did get home, the first thing I did was brush my teeth. I thought that kiss was the most disgusting thing I had ever experienced. I vowed I'd never do it again. Obviously I was wrong. Practice makes perfect!

As this girl discovered, kissing and other early sexual encounters aren't always as romantic and wonderful as in the movies. Just as in learning to dance, for some girls comfort develops only after considerable practice and experience.

Making Out and Petting

Usually the term "making out" describes kissing, touching, and hugging, while **petting** is used to describe the same activities when they include touching of the breasts, vulva, and penis. However, often these terms are used interchangeably, so that neither has an exact meaning.

When teenage girls begin to get involved in making out, a number of concerns tend to emerge. One concern you may have is what limits you want to set for petting to ensure that you don't go "too far." Since teenage boys may try to push you beyond your level of comfort, it is usually best if you decide beforehand what your sexual limit is. Don't let yourself get pushed into something you will later feel bad about. This is a very important decision for you and one that only you can make. Since many of your teenage friends may exaggerate their own sexual adventures to impress you, and since you are the person who must live with the consequences of your actions, set your sexual limits according to your values and your own level of comfort, not those of your friends. You may find chapter 9 helpful to you as far as sorting out your values and communicating them to a boy in a way that he will take seriously.

At the same time that girls are trying to develop a set of values about sexual behavior, they are often trying to figure out how to attract boys and how to be "sexy" partners. They may borrow tips from friends or from movies and TV as to ways to dress, perfumes to wear, and various techniques to turn guys on. Yet, despite the fact that hundreds of books have been written about how to attract men and how to be a good lover, there really is no one method that is guaranteed to work. Every person is different. What one boy perceives as exciting and attractive won't necessarily be a turn-on to another. Your best bet is to dress and act in ways that are acceptable to you. If you do get involved with someone, the best way to obtain information about what is or is not pleasurable for each of you is by sharing your preferences and feelings.

Another serious concern among teenagers who are beginning to experience the new emotional and physical sensations of making out is the fear that what they are experiencing is not normal. Some worry that what they are feeling is abnormally intense, making them oversexed. Others experience less excitement than they expected, and label themselves as undersexed. Again, it is important to remember that every girl is different, and what you are experiencing is normal for you. A survey of teenage sexuality by Aaron Hass provides us with some interesting confirmation of just how much teenage girls vary as to their individual reactions. In response to the question: "If your breasts have ever been touched by a teenage boy, how enjoyable was it?" only 42 percent of the fifteen- and sixteen-year-old girls who responded said that it was very enjoyable. Another 53 percent indicated that it was moderately enjoyable, and 5 percent responded that it was not enjoyable at all.[2] The point is that every girl is different.

What Is Intercourse Like?

Some girls may think that because this book contains sections on intercourse, I am implying that you *should* be "going all the way." That's not the case. The information is here for you for whenever you need it—now, two years from now, or after you're married. Even though my personal bias is that most girls are not emotionally ready for intercourse in their early teenage years, the reality is that large numbers are sexually involved. My hope is that this information can help prepare you for making your own decision about sexual intercourse.

Before engaging in intercourse, it is important for the couple to spend time touching each other so that each becomes aroused. During intercourse, the male's erect penis is placed inside the female's vagina. That sounds easy enough, but typically it's not that simple the first few times. For one thing, it can be awkward for an inexperienced male to find the opening of the vagina, especially in the dark. Second, if the woman's hymen has not been broken or stretched previously, it may take a fair amount of pressure from the penis to push through it. Some bleeding and pain can result when it does break. Third, because of nervousness, or the fact that the couple didn't engage in **foreplay** long enough, sometimes women do not produce enough lubrication to help the penis slide in easily. Again, proceeding slowly, gently, and at one's own pace is very helpful.

As the penis is inserted into the vagina, the vaginal walls gently surround the penis and adjust to its size. It is because of this accommodation that the size of the penis has nothing to do with the sexual pleasure of either the male or female. The vagina will adjust to surround any size penis.

The two partners usually then proceed to move their bodies in a rhythmic manner, with the penis moving back and forth inside the vagina. The movement may vary from gentle to fairly vigorous, usually until one or both partners reach orgasm. During initial experiences of intercourse, boys tend to **"come"** fairly quickly, while their female partners seldom experience **orgasm**. Later, as the partners become more sexually experienced, orgasm becomes easier for the female to achieve, although teenage males are usually more consistent at reaching orgasm. After intercourse is completed, many couples use the time to communicate feelings and to experience closeness and tenderness.

Sexual Positions and Variations

There are probably as many different ways of enjoying sex as there are people who enjoy it. Every person has her or his own sexual preferences. Some people find pleasure in a relatively set sexual routine, enjoying sex in a single position with little or no variation. Others enjoy sex in a much more spontaneous way, varying many aspects of their sexual positions.

As a teenager, you will be exposed to many words and expressions that refer to various positions. Some of these will sound kind of bizarre and may bring on a sense of curiosity, while others may bring on feelings of excitement, disgust, or various other feelings. Whatever your personal reaction, remember that when you are in a sexual relationship, you and your partner will be making your own decisions. There is no rule that you must try all of the variations you hear about, nor for that matter is it necessary that you even try any of them.

However, since it is likely that you will hear many of these terms, and in some cases may not know exactly what they mean, below are the definitions of various words and common slang expressions associated with different sexual positions. These are not the only sexual positions that exist. The number and variety of sexual positions you may someday enjoy is limited only by the creativity of your imagination and your personal preferences.

Male-superior position (missionary position)—a position of intercourse where the male lies in a face-to-face position on top of the female.

Female-superior position—a position of intercourse where the female is in a face-to-face position on top of the male.

Lateral position—a position of intercourse in which the couple lies in a side-by-side position, facing each other.

Oral sex (oral-genital sex)—a general term for any sexual stimulation in which the mouth is used to stimulate either the male or female genitals.

Cunnilingus (kuhn-ih-*ling*-gus)—the type of oral sex in which the mouth is used to stimulate the female genitals.

Fellatio (fuh-*lay*-she-oh)—the type of oral sex in which the mouth is used to stimulate the male genitals.

69—a combination of cunnilingus and fellatio at the same time. This position is referred to as *69* because the positions of the bodies form a figure that looks similar to the number *69*.

Anal sex (anal intercourse)—a type of sexual contact where the penis is inserted into the partner's rectum.

What Happens in Your Body During Sexual Response

One sexuality expert, Helen Singer Kaplan, explains that sexual response has three phases: desire, arousal, and orgasm.[3] Whether male or female, **heterosexual** or **homosexual**, young or old, these stages of sexual response still apply.

The desire phase has to do with a person's general level of feeling sexual. It is a sort of readiness to feel turned on or excited. It is during this phase that our sexual thoughts and fantasies become stimulated. One experience common to most adolescents, male and female, is that during the teen years there is usually a dramatic rise in the level of sexual desire. This is due largely to the same increase in sex hormones that is also responsible for the body's maturation.

The second state of sexual response, arousal, is what people are referring to when they say they feel turned on. Arousal can result from having sexual thoughts, viewing pictures, touching someone, touching yourself, or from any intense sexual behavior. You might even have dreams that cause you to become sexually aroused. Feelings of arousal can vary greatly, ranging from feeling mildly tingly to being very excited.

Trying to understand the pleasure and the physical sensations that often accompany intense sexual arousal is like listening to someone describe their experience with a rich, whipped cream–topped ice cream sundae without ever having tasted one. You can imagine the experience in your mind, but the excitement and pleasure of actually devouring the sundae can't be described with words. In the same way, the following paragraphs describe the reactions of the body during sexual arousal and orgasm, but not the intense emotional experience that can accompany these events.

One of the first changes that occurs as a woman begins to respond sexually is a moistness in the vagina and area of the vulva. As arousal intensifies, the heart quickens its beat and pumps the blood more quickly to different parts of the body. The increased blood flow causes tingly and flushed sensations that may even result in a rashlike redness on a woman's chest. In males the increased blood flow causes the penis to become hard, while in females the result is that the clitoris stiffens.

With increased arousal, breathing becomes faster and a fine layer of perspiration forms on the body. During this stage, muscles become more tense and twitchy, and often the nipples of the breast become erect. Many people report that they feel intense longing and excitement.

The excitement and physical sensations of arousal may continue to heighten until they sometimes reach a point of extreme intensity. Then, the muscles surrounding the vagina and uterus begin to spasm, followed by a feeling of intense relaxation. This is orgasm, the third phase of sexual response. Typically, orgasm is a very pleasurable and intense experience, both physically and emotionally. Usually it results from a great deal of sexual arousal, including some stimulation of the genital area. Although orgasms are similar in both sexes, there are some significant differences. When a male reaches the point of orgasm, he will almost always ejaculate, and semen—a thick, whitish liquid—will squirt from his penis. Rarely do women expel a liquid in any large quantity. A few women do report that they expel a small amount of mucus-type liquid during orgasm, some even referring to it as an ejaculation, but this does not seem to be the common experience of most females. Another difference is that males tend to experience a single orgasm lasting a few seconds, followed by a **refractory period**, during which they feel totally sexually unresponsive. The experience in women can be quite different in that this dramatic decrease in sexual drive is much less likely. In fact, many women can sustain the orgasm for long periods of time or experience additional orgasms immediately or soon after the initial one.

It is not necessary to have intercourse in order to reach orgasm. Both males and females can reach orgasm through masturbation, manual (hand) or oral stimulation by a partner, sexual dreams, intercourse, or virtually any other form of intense sexual stimulation.

It is important that you realize that enjoying one phase of sexual response does not commit you to journey to the next step. Enjoying your sexual thoughts and desires in no way obligates you to act out your fantasies, nor does becoming sexually aroused mean that you must become further involved in sex play. All the physical reactions of sexual arousal are temporary and will fade whether or not you or your partner have an orgasm. It is true that maintaining prolonged and intense arousal can be somewhat frustrating, emotionally and physically. Women experience this as a congested and tense feeling in their pelvis, while males feel this as a pelvic ache that is commonly referred to as "blue balls." However, neither condition is harmful, and both will shortly pass.

Responsibilities and Sex

The excitement of sex can be so overwhelming that it is easy to overlook some important responsibilities that go with the sexual experience. One important responsibility is to be honest with yourself and your partner about what sex means to you and how far you really want to proceed. No matter how aroused either you or your partner becomes, neither of you is obligated to go further sexually than you want. *Do not let yourself be pushed into actions that you don't feel comfortable with or that you will later regret.* If you are forced into sex as a proof of your love or as a test of whether or not you are a woman, you will no doubt regret it later. Both of you not only have the right to say no and to set your own limits, but each of you actually has a responsibility to set those boundaries. To force yourself or your partner into sexual acts in which either of you is not freely willing to participate will result in both of you being uncomfortable. Your self-esteem will suffer and most likely your relationship will, too. Sex cannot hold a relationship together for long.

People often assume that any pressure to engage in sex is applied by boys upon girls, but boys also can be pushed into having sex when they don't feel like it. Sometimes they are teased that they are not "men" unless they are sexually experienced. This pressure may come from girls or from their male friends. In any case, an honest discussion about sex can sometimes eliminate needless pressures and prevent either person from being hurt. Chapter 9 is designed to help you make decisions about your sexual behavior and to assist you in communicating your standards to another person.

It is also crucial when engaging in sex play for you to understand how to avoid such hazards as sexually transmitted diseases (see chapter 13) and unwanted pregnancies. *Even during petting, it is possible for a girl to become pregnant without ever having intercourse.* This can occur if the boy ejaculates and any semen is accidentally carried to the vaginal opening. If you and your partner engage in touching each other's genitals, be very cautious once he ejaculates to avoid accidentally rubbing your genitals together, or accidentally carrying semen to the vagina with your hands or clothing. All it takes is one drop of semen to become pregnant. Also, as you've already read in chapter 7, the fluid secreted from a boy's Cowper's glands during the arousal phase of sexual response may contain sperm and, likewise, should not be allowed to come into contact with the vaginal area. It is extremely important that you read chapter 12, about how to prevent a pregnancy, before engaging in any serious sex play.

11

FIRST SEXUAL EXPERIENCES AND CONTINUING SEXUAL RELATIONSHIPS

Sexual Intercourse: First Experiences

Girls tend to remember their first experience with sexual intercourse throughout their lives. Years later, if you ask a woman what her first time was like, she can usually tell you who the boy or man was, where it happened, what it felt like, and how she felt afterward. One woman related her memories of her first experience:

> After about eight months, we decided to make love. The first time we tried, it hurt so much that we had to stop. We tried again in a couple of days. I felt it was worth the pain to put our feelings into motion. It was beautiful. I remember us both crying in each other's arms afterwards just because we loved each other so much.

Another commented about hers:

> I must point out that the night I "lost" my virginity (it really wasn't giving) I was in a daze. I felt no emotion, no passion,

and no pleasure or love. I was a robot. We didn't have much foreplay and when he entered me I asked, "Is this all? This is what all the love songs and stories are talking about?"

A third woman told me,

> When it was over he was exhausted and I ached all over. . . . I still loved him but I think I loved myself a little less afterward. I was wrapped in guilt because I wanted to be a virgin when I got married.

As the stories above show, the quality of the first experience is different for every woman. Some find their initial lovemaking to be warm, intimate, and pleasurable, while others are disappointed and think the whole business has been overrated. Many young women experience such feelings as pain, guilt, and fear. In fact, several studies indicate that for most young women the first experience with intercourse is somewhat negative.[1] In a survey of 1,067 teenagers, Robert Coles and Geoffrey Stokes found that although only 11 percent of the girls surveyed said they were "sorry they had the experience," only 23 percent reported they were "glad." Sixty-one percent of the girls indicated that they had mixed feelings, and 4 percent said they had no feelings at all.[2]

There appear to be a number of different influences that take the shine off the first lovemaking experience for teenage girls: feeling pressured into intercourse before being emotionally and physically ready; fearing pregnancy and diseases; having unrealistic expectations; not being sufficiently aroused; and feeling tense or physically uncomfortable. One young woman offered to share her feelings about early sexual encounters and her insights into why they were unsatisfying for her.

> I was extremely young by most of my friends' standards, but at the time I felt I was much too old to still be a virgin. Looking back I can't figure out why at fourteen I felt I was destined to be a spinster and forever a virgin, but I did. It

might be because a good friend of mine when I was twelve told me about how many times she had had intercourse. It also might be because I had started being pressured by boys I knew and dated at age twelve to "go all the way." I felt as though I was a tease to kiss a boy without wanting to have intercourse. Well, whatever the reason, I did have guilt feelings for not allowing the boys I dated to make love to me. The boy I did finally "give in" to was seventeen. We began dating when I was about fourteen and our relationship was strictly physical. I found it very hard to talk about anything of importance to him. Every time we would get to this point we would go through the same discussion as to why I wouldn't have sex with him. I knew too little about being assertive to offer any kind of a rebuttal, except a weak "I don't want to." Eventually I gave in, for fear of losing him, and because I felt it was inevitable anyway. Because I was not very stimulated, this process was extremely painful and took what seemed forever.

Below are some considerations that can help you avoid some of the potential pitfalls that many young women experience when making love for the first time and may increase your chances of having this event be a pleasant memory.

1. *Go at your own pace.* Don't let yourself be pushed into intercourse before you are ready. Wait for circumstances that are right for you. Virginity is not something that you need to be embarrassed about. A girl who had been embarrassed about being inexperienced throughout her high school years wrote,

After I came to college I found out that many girls were virgins, and discovered that many of my friends had never dated before. The inexperience I had been so embarrassed about was no big deal. I want to let all the confused, desperate girls out there know they can be proud to be themselves, whether a virgin or a nonvirgin. Don't push yourselves until you're ready.

Girls who end up feeling guilty or exploited often have had sex at least partially in response to pressures from partners, friends, or even as a result of their own unrealistic expectations. Since you only get to have your first sexual experience once, reread chapter 9 on sexual decision making before you make this momentous decision.

2. *Wait and choose a partner whom you can trust to share your first time with.* When women were asked in a survey to look back at the quality of their first act of intercourse, the ones who had gentle, considerate, and loving partners were much more likely to have had a positive experience. Those who described their partners' behavior as rough or inconsiderate tended to have negative memories, even if that partner was someone with whom they were engaged to be married or had a committed relationship.[3] A girl contrasted two of her very different experiences with sex:

We went to his room. The minute we were in behind his closed door he became very aggressive and I was scared. I told him I just wanted to sleep with him—to me that sounded very romantic. His next words were, "You aren't a virgin are you?" I reeled. I was, but the way he said it was as if it were a terrible thing. I quickly stammered "Oh no" because I thought that was what he wanted to hear. It happened so fast. I was tense, I wasn't lubricated, and I was scared. He pushed into me and it hurt badly. I gritted my teeth and it was all over soon.

I'm glad to say, though, that the second time I had intercourse, I was truly made love to. It was warm and tender and I was caressed and hugged and ready through and through. Ronald made me feel wanted and I can remember that occasion with many smiles.

3. *Before you do anything that even approaches intercourse, make sure that one or both of you is using a safe form of birth control, and using it properly* (see chapter 12). Don't just assume that your partner is going to take care of it; ask him

before you begin. Even if you know he has a condom, make sure he knows the correct way to use it. Besides, it is best to use contraceptive foam in addition to a condom to even further reduce the chances of getting pregnant. Don't take any chances on leaving things to luck. A young woman said,

> I was eighteen and in love with a boy I thought I would marry when I first had sex. It was a wonderful experience, but the aftereffect was a confused jumble of emotions that lasted for months. I felt guilty, scared that I was pregnant. The fear and anxiety I had over not using any contraception were not worth it.

There is a myth that a girl cannot become pregnant the first time she has intercourse. *This is absolutely untrue.* If the two of you are not using proper birth control methods, your chances of becoming pregnant are as good the first time as they are any other time.

4. *To learn how to reduce the risk of catching or of spreading a sexually transmitted disease, read about how to prevent them in chapter 13.*

5. *Proceed slowly and gently and allow yourself to engage in enough sex play to become aroused.* In this way you can reduce the physical discomfort that many young women experience the first time. If there has been considerable touching and petting (foreplay) prior to intercourse, your vagina will generally create its own lubrication, and your partner's penis will slide in more easily. Also, if you anticipate having intercourse, it is possible to begin stretching the hymen with your fingers slowly over several weeks' time during petting so that it is not as painful when it tears.

6. *Don't expect your first time to run as smoothly or romantically as in movies or in the exaggerated descriptions found in many books and magazines.* There is bound to be some awkwardness and tension. Let your partner know your anxieties. If he is also inexperienced, it will allow the two of

you to talk and joke about your lack of experience and reduce the pressure you both feel. If he is experienced, he can lead the way. As with any other new experience, the tension and awkwardness that often plague initial attempts at intercourse will probably be replaced by relaxation, comfort, and enjoyment only after you become somewhat more experienced.

Intercourse and the Law

As crazy as it may sound, there are laws in your state that govern your sexual behavior. All states have laws about the sexual activities of their residents. In many states there are laws against having intercourse if you are not married, and there are other laws against oral sex, or even masturbation. In fact, in some states, any person who engages in sexual activities that do not include the potential for a child being conceived is committing a crime. Rarely, if ever, are these laws enforced, but they do exist in some state law books.

Probably the one group of laws regarding sexual behavior that are most important to teenagers are those regarding **statutory rape**. As defined by California law (and by most other states as well), it is unlawful for a male to have intercourse with any female under the age of eighteen, *even if she gives her consent*. In some states a person may be charged with child molestation instead of statutory rape. Depending upon which state you live in, the age of consent will vary from fourteen to twenty-one. Interestingly, statutory-rape laws usually apply only to underage girls. If the boy and girl are both younger than the age of consent, it is usually only the boy who is prosecuted for a crime.

There is one additional law that may become important if you get pregnant and have the baby. Your sexual partner is legally the father of that child. A court of law can require him to contribute some amount of money to the support of your child.

As Sexual Relationships Continue

As you become more sexually experienced, the nature of your sexual relationships will change. The changes are not exactly the same for all women, but nevertheless, women begin to feel different about sex. Even though 61 percent of the girls surveyed by Coles and Stokes indicated that they had mixed feelings about their first sexual experience, their attitudes toward sex seemed to improve greatly over time. When asked "How much do you enjoy intercourse?" 70 percent responded either "a large amount" or "a great deal." Only 3 percent responded "not at all" or "a small amount."[4] This increasing comfort seems more likely to happen in the context of a mutually respectful and caring relationship.

For other young women, sex remains a negative experience. Often this occurs when they continue to engage in sex due to pressure or in violation of their own moral values. Ongoing fears of pregnancy can also interfere greatly with sexual enjoyment. Some girls who are at first more enthusiastic come to be disillusioned with their sexual activity over time. Sex sometimes starts to dominate their relationship in a way they don't like, or they feel hurt and used when a relationship breaks up. Combining those who were never very comfortable with intercourse and those who later become uncomfortable, one researcher estimates that as many as 30 percent of nonvirgin teenagers are troubled by their sex lives.[5]

If you find yourself continuing to engage in sex that you don't enjoy or feel bad about, use chapter 9 to reassess your motives for doing so. It is perfectly all right to decide to stop having intercourse or engaging in any other sexual activity, no matter how many times you've done it in the past. Below is a good example of a young woman who eventually came to that conclusion herself after years of poor sexual relationships.

The only sex I have ever experienced has been affairs and one-night stands. I am fortunate, however, in that I am beginning to be able to understand how I am feeling about a situation and if I feel negatively about going to bed with someone, I can express that without feeling incredibly guilty. In other words, I have learned to say "no," a very simple word. It is surprising that it took twenty-one years to add it to my vocabulary.

Sexual Communication Between Partners

One skill that is too often ignored as being an important part of sex is communication. If you try to maintain a long-term relationship, clear communication is essential. Communication is the only way for each partner to learn about the other's likes, dislikes, and feelings. One girl explained how important communication has been in her relationship:

> We were honest with each other in expressing our feelings and desires. Through sex, we were able to open another line of communication that made us closer to each other. I'm glad that we turned to each other with our problems about sex instead of others. Now after two and a half years, we have a healthy and open sex life. We communicate before, during, and after sex—with honest and encouraging words.

In any relationship there is communication, whether it is intended or not. If a boy pays attention to you, smiles at you, and talks to you, you may understand his message to mean "he likes me." If he does nothing, and simply ignores you, you may understand his message to mean "he isn't interested in me." If you take a boy's hand, one message is communicated; if you don't, you communicate another. In each of these situations, messages are being exchanged between the two of you. Every movement of your body, and every expression on your face sends a message. Every word you speak and every gesture and touch of your hand communicates something.

Communicating with Touch

Because of the close physical contact involved, touch becomes an especially important form of communication in a sexual relationship. Every touch, and every avoidance of a touch, communicates a message. As an experiment, examine the following list of actions that might be a part of your relationship with a boy. Read each one and imagine two or three messages he might interpret from each action.

- A gentle hug.
- A lengthy embrace.
- Aggressively taking his hand.
- Not taking his hand.

As you can conclude from your imagined responses, messages communicated through touch have a lot of room for being misinterpreted.

If each of the messages in the example above could have two or three possible interpretations, then a great deal may depend upon other messages you send, or possibly even what kind of mood your partner is in. In the last example above, if the boy is in a good mood, he might interpret your not taking his hand as an indication that you are shy. If he is feeling insecure, he may take it as a rejection. The lengthy embrace in the second example could be interpreted as feelings of closeness and trust, but it could also be seen as an invitation to sexual intercourse. In fact, a series of recent interviews with teenagers revealed that boys are much more likely than girls to interpret a number of actions as invitations for sex.[6] Therefore, it is important to be aware that your touch is an important means of communication, but one that is easily misinterpreted. This will allow you to send clearer messages to your partner and to clarify what message you are trying to send.

Verbal Communication

Although spoken messages, like nonverbal messages, are sometimes misinterpreted, words are probably the best tool we have for communicating clearly. Yet, because many people are not comfortable talking about sex, or because they feel that sex is a thing that should happen between people without any words being spoken, sexual messages often end up unclear.

When people think of the organs of the body that are important in sex, their first thoughts commonly turn to the penis and the vagina. However, as the following section makes clear, in many sexual relationships your ears may play a considerably more important role than either the penis or vagina. Not because your ears feel good during sex, but because of the vital role they play in verbal communication.

In a sense, words and touch are tools that we use to communicate messages. As with any other tool, they are effective when used properly and ineffective when not. If you use a knife to cut meat, it works fine. If you use it as a screwdriver, sometimes it works and sometimes it doesn't. Words and touch are, likewise, effective when they are used properly as tools of sexual communication.

Communicating Effectively

In a sense, good sexual communication can be boiled down to honestly listening and talking to each other. Back in chapter 2 a few basic principles were discussed in regard to communicating with your parents. Some of those same principles apply to communicating with your sexual partner. The sections on how to be a good listener and how to encourage conversations have hints that should work just as well in a romantic relationship as with your parents. When it comes to expressing yourself rather than just listening, one apparently simple rule is essential: Let your partner know clearly what you want and don't want. What seems like a simple rule, however, can be deceiving. Often couples, even those who have been together for many years, run into problems due to one of the following reasons.

One of the most common difficulties that couples experience with sexual communication is that one of them follows the rule (lets the partner know what is wanted), while the other partner doesn't. This tends to make the relationship one-sided, with one partner getting most of what he or she wants, while the other partner ends up unsatisfied. Although it would appear that this would be great for the partner whose needs are getting met, the frustrated partner is likely to feel resentful, sometimes to the point of breaking off the relationship.

A second common difficulty is that one or both partners become comfortable at saying what they *don't* want, but fail to communicate what they *do* want. Rather than constantly criticizing your partner by telling him what he is doing wrong, give him guidance as to what you would like from him. If your partner hears only what you don't like, he must guess in order to figure out what pleases you. In addition, after a while it is likely to become frustrating and depressing for him to hear only about his mistakes. For instance, suppose that you feel he kisses you too roughly. Instead of telling him that he's "an inconsiderate animal" or a "lousy kisser," you can ask him to kiss you more softly and tenderly, and when he does so, tell him how much you enjoy it.

Another critical area of communication for sexual relationships is setting limits. You can use the information in chapter 9 on assertion to help you communicate your limits effectively.

Learning to say no to your partner is extremely important. However, it is helpful to do it in a way that makes it clear that you are rejecting the sexual activity rather than rejecting him. Giving in because you feel obligated is not a good solution. As mentioned previously, try to let him know what you *do* want. Give him an alternative, for example, "Don't kiss me when my friends are around; I'd rather you only do that in private."

12

CONTRACEPTION (OR BIRTH CONTROL)

The last thing that most adolescents want is a child. Yet, every day in the United States nearly three thousand girls become pregnant. Few of these do so intentionally. It has been estimated that of every 10 girls who turn fourteen this year, 4 will become pregnant while still in their teens.[1] The fact is that to engage in intercourse, or any serious sex play, without *correctly* using some effective means of contraception (a birth control method or device) is like playing Russian roulette: You may not become pregnant the first time, or the tenth time, but the odds are that unless you use an adequate method of birth control, you *will* become pregnant. Wishing, hoping, or carrying a lucky rabbit's foot are not adequate forms of birth control.

This chapter may very well be the most important one in the book for a sexually active teenage girl. It will give you in-depth information about the various forms of contraception— the ineffective methods as well as those that can significantly reduce the chances that you might someday face an unwanted pregnancy. It will also present a list of criteria you can use to evaluate which means of birth control might be most effective for you.[2] Refer to chapter 8, "Pregnancy and Childbirth," for information about how babies are conceived. It is essential that you understand conception, whether you want to have a child or want to avoid becoming pregnant.

Deciding to Use Contraception

Since *con*ception is the process of becoming pregnant, *contra*ception (*contra* meaning "against") is the process of avoiding pregnancy. Whenever you engage in intercourse, there is a good possibility that you will become pregnant, unless some form of birth control is used and used properly. **Contraceptives** are devices that *reduce* the chances that a girl will become pregnant, but they do not completely eliminate this possibility.

Since it takes two people engaging in sex to produce a pregnancy, ideally each should take equal responsibility if they wish to avoid conceiving a child. Realistically, however, a male partner may not have the knowledge about birth control necessary to protect you adequately. Furthermore, he might not be as motivated by the fear of pregnancy, since he is not the one who will have to face the most serious consequences if you do become pregnant.

Many young women feel that it is easier to avoid making a decision about contraception or to leave that responsibility up to their sexual partner. Yet, ultimately, you will end up being responsible for the decision about how you can best protect yourself against an unwanted pregnancy. If you are sexually active, or think that you might be in the near future, you must decide either that you *will* protect yourself against the possibility of an unwanted pregnancy or that you *won't* protect yourself. *Not taking any action is a decision not to protect yourself.*

Teenagers give many reasons for failing to use contraception. Some say contraception spoils the romance and spontaneity of sex. However, compared to the harsh realities of facing an unwanted pregnancy, taking a little time for birth control really isn't that much of a hassle. Besides, even birth control can be romantic if you approach it with a creative, positive attitude of sharing.

Other teenagers don't like to admit to themselves that they are going to have sex, and so avoid preparing themselves for it. Still others pretend that somehow they will magically escape pregnancy. As one girl wrote, "At the age of fifteen, I was experiencing the typical 'but I thought it would never happen to me.' Well, it did, and I found out I was pregnant."

I have heard girls say that they were too embarrassed to talk to their partners about birth control. Yet, an open and honest discussion about this can help you get a great deal of information not only about contraception, but also about the boy with whom you are involved and about your relationship with him. It can help you figure out how emotionally mature your partner is and his level of concern for your safety and welfare. A boy who isn't willing to take on the responsibilities that go with sex is not really ready to have intercourse or doesn't care about you.

Some teenagers seem to have been scared by all the negative publicity about various birth control devices. However, it is important to put the risks of using birth control into perspective. All of the methods result in fewer health risks to teenagers than a pregnancy does. They are also less hazardous than motorcycling, smoking, driving, power boating, and rock climbing. This is not to say that there aren't important health factors to take into consideration when choosing and using a contraceptive method. It is just that it is a good idea to educate yourself fully about the risks of not using contraception as well.[3]

Finally, many young women decide that they are interested in using some form of birth control, but are embarrassed to talk to a parent or to go to a professional in order to obtain a contraceptive device. However, there are agencies, such as Planned Parenthood, that will be sympathetic to your needs and that are experienced in dealing with frightened and embarrassed teenagers. You can use appendix A of this book to help locate the appropriate agency nearest you. Remember, the uneasiness you might feel will be a small price to pay in order to avoid the potential traumas that accompany an undesired pregnancy.

Incredibly Ineffective Methods

A number of incredibly ineffective methods have been used by teenagers over the years. You'll probably laugh at some of them and be surprised by others, but the truth is that people have unsuccessfully relied on some very crazy methods. Some people assume that having intercourse in certain positions, like standing up, prevents pregnancy because they believe gravity will pull the sperm away from entering the uterus. This just isn't how it works. Sperm are excellent swimmers in all directions. You can get pregnant no matter what position you use, even if you do it on a trapeze flying through the air.

Some teenagers mistakenly believe that for conception to take place both people must have an orgasm and, therefore, think that a girl cannot get pregnant unless she, too, has had an orgasm. This belief is a myth. You can get pregnant if both of you have orgasms, neither of you has an orgasm, or only one of you has an orgasm.

Teenagers have also used **douching** (*doosh*-ing), or washing out the vagina, as a method of contraception. They have also tried water, lemon juice, vinegar, commercial douches, and even shaken-up Coca-Cola. However, no matter what you douche with or how quickly you do it, it won't help. Even if you are a track star and could jump up and run to an awaiting douche as soon as the boy ejaculated, it would be too late. Sperm enter the uterus within moments after ejaculation. The propelling action of the douche may actually push more sperm up into the uterus and make a pregnancy more likely. Douching also has the potential of leading to vaginal infections.

One of the ineffective methods most frequently used by teenagers is **withdrawal** (known professionally as **coitus interruptus**, or interrupted intercourse), in which the male partner attempts to withdraw his penis from the girl's vagina prior to ejaculation. As mentioned in chapter 7, sperm contained in the clear fluid released from the penis into the vagina *before* ejaculation are quite capable of causing a pregnancy. Furthermore, it is very difficult for males, especially aroused teenage boys, to withdraw in time. For this reason some people call withdrawal the "oops" method. A standing joke among health care practitioners is: "What do you call a boy who uses withdrawal?" "You call him Daddy."

The "Natural Methods" or Fertility Awareness Methods

The **natural methods** are all based on trying to predict when a female is fertile (capable of becoming pregnant), and refraining from intercourse during those times. Since a woman is only fertile around the time of ovulation, it might seem that this is an easy and safe method to use. Unfortunately, however, predicting ovulation is very tricky, especially in teenage girls. Periods tend to be so irregular during these years that these methods just don't work very well. They are more effective with older women, but even then, ovulation (and hence the time of fertility) can be thrown off by many things—even in women with periods that are usually regular. Mood, illness, and stress can all affect when ovulation occurs. Furthermore, women have been known to ovulate more than once per cycle and even during their periods, which should be the safest time. Consequently, this method has sometimes been compared to Russian roulette.

A second problem with natural methods is that occasionally sperm have been found to live in a woman's body for up to five days after intercourse. Consequently, even if you engage in intercourse many days before you ovulate, it is possible for you to become pregnant. Another reason why these methods often fail is that teenagers don't actually abstain from intercourse every time they should. Sometimes in the heat of passion, it may become difficult for a couple to keep from having intercourse, even though they have previously decided that it is not a "safe" time of the month. Even under the best of circumstances, the natural methods can be very risky.

Three different fertility-awareness methods are used to predict when a woman is fertile. One form is known as the **calendar**, or **rhythm, method**. It requires that the woman keep an ongoing chart of her menstrual cycles. The length of each of the eight most recent cycles is used to figure out which days during her *next* cycle she is likely to be fertile. Ovulation typically occurs somewhere between periods—about fourteen days prior to the subsequent menstruation.

The first "unsafe" day of the cycle is determined by subtracting eighteen days from the shortest cycle. The last "unsafe" day is obtained by subtracting eleven days from a woman's longest cycle. For example, suppose that the *shortest* cycle you have had in the last eight months was twenty-one days, while your *longest* cycle lasted twenty-eight days. You are most likely to be fertile from the third to the seventeenth day of your current cycle.

A second natural method, called the **basal body temperature**, or **BBT**, method, requires taking your temperature with a special basal temperature thermometer as soon as you wake up each morning to establish your usual pattern. It so happens that there is often a slight drop in temperature just prior to ovulation and a small consistent rise after ovulation. Consequently, after you have measured the rise in temperature for three consecutive days, it is likely that you are not fertile.

A third method is the **mucus method**, in which one learns to recognize the change in cervical mucus at different stages of a menstrual cycle.

Fertility-awareness methods become more effective if you combine them rather than relying upon only one form. One such combination procedure is called the Sympto-Thermal Method. It is based on recording both mucus and temperature changes, as well as other signs of ovulation such as Mittel-schmerz (see page 45).

If you do choose to use one or more of the natural methods, you must obtain a thorough education on their use from a trained health care practitioner. Once you've learned how to use them, they require extreme conscientiousness on your part. You must chart cycles regularly, take your temperature, check your mucus, and, of course, follow through on not having intercourse during the times of highest fertility.

The benefits of the natural methods include that they are acceptable to members of certain religions who otherwise are prohibited from using artificial birth control, and that they are a good way to learn about your body. However, again, they tend not to be very effective means of preventing pregnancy for young women.

Vaginal Spermicides: Foams, Creams, Jellies, and Suppositories

Contraceptive foams, creams, and jellies all work by creating a chemical barrier that kills sperm, and are therefore called **spermicides**. Foam can be used as a contraceptive method by itself, but it is much more effective if you use both foam and condoms ("rubbers") at the same time. The creams and jellies, however, should only be used with a **diaphragm** because they do not spread out sufficiently in the vagina.

Foam comes in an aerosol can and has a separate plunger-type applicator. Its texture is a lot like shaving cream. In order to use it, you must first shake the can thoroughly (about twenty shakes) and then fill the applicator. Then you insert the applicator, full of foam, deep into your vagina and push the plunger to disperse the foam. Some brands require two applications of foam. Foam should be inserted *prior* to having intercourse in order for it to kill the sperm, but because it loses its power over time, it should be inserted no more than thirty to sixty minutes before intercourse. If a longer time goes by, you must insert more foam. It is also important to use additional foam every time you engage in intercourse. You need enough spermicide to work on all the sperm. Once you've had intercourse, wait eight hours before doing anything (like douching) that would wash out the foam from your vagina. The box that the foam comes in will contain complete instructions.

The major problem with foam is that although it is more effective than the natural methods, it is less effective in actual use than the other means of contraception. These lower rates may be due in large part to inconsistent use. Foam's effectiveness can be maximized if you use it each and every time and place it deep into the vagina so that it covers the cervix. Another problem with foam has been that it is hard to tell

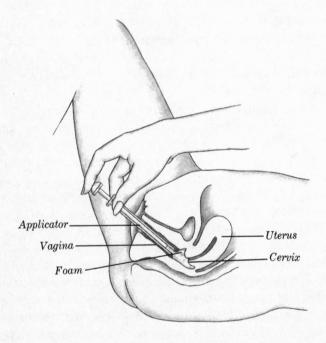

Figure 14 How foam is inserted into the vagina

from looking at the container if you're about to run out. Therefore, always keep an extra container of foam as a spare.

Used in conjunction with condoms, foam actually becomes an excellent method of birth control. Foam also helps protect women from sexually transmitted diseases and PID, and is a good back-up if you mess up another form of birth control. For instance, if you forget to take your pill, or if a condom breaks, you can use foam for added protection. (Although foam should be inserted before intercourse, immediately afterward is better than not at all.) Another advantage of foam is that it is available in drugstores and many grocery stores and does *not* require a prescription to be purchased. Hence, it is easy for you to obtain. There are no reported serious health risks associated with foam use. Allergic reactions to the chemicals have occurred on a rare basis. Despite earlier concerns, foam does *not* seem to lead to an increase in birth defects for infants who are conceived while the mother was using foam as a contraceptive.

Spermicides now also come in suppository form. The suppositories are wrapped in foil or plastic and contain chemicals similar to those in contraceptive foam. The main difference in using them rather than foam is that you have to allow ten to fifteen minutes for the suppository to melt and disperse after placing it deep inside your vagina. On some occasions the suppository fails to dissolve completely, which lowers its effectiveness and can lead to irritation of the penis or vagina. You need to use another suppository each time you have intercourse and should not wash out your vagina for eight hours after intercourse. Some people feel that suppository-type spermicides are a little less messy than foam and easier to conceal in your purse.

There is a vast array of creams, ointments, douches, and other vaginal products on the market that have nothing to do with contraception. They will in no way stop you from getting pregnant. Consequently, make certain that what you buy clearly says "contraceptive" on it. Women have made the mistake of trying to use the wrong vaginal product for birth control.

Vaginal Contraceptive Film (VCF)

Vaginal contraceptive film, or VCF, is a new contraceptive product that received approval from the Food and Drug Administration in early 1986. The product consists of paper-thin, two-inch-square films that contain a spermicide. A square is inserted into the vagina no less than five minutes and no more than two hours before intercourse. The film dissolves on its own and is washed away with the vagina's natural fluids. A new film needs to be inserted for each act of intercourse. As with other spermicides, some women have experienced minor irritation as a side effect.

The Diaphragm

The diaphragm is a small, dome-shaped, flexible rubber cup that is inserted into the vagina so that it covers the opening of the cervix that leads to the uterus. It is always used with contraceptive cream or jelly, which is placed inside the dome and around the rim of the diaphragm. Consequently, it works in two ways: The diaphragm provides a barrier that stops sperm from getting into the uterus and, if any sperm should slip by, the contraceptive jelly or cream kills the sperm with spermicidal chemicals.

Diaphragms are fitted by a health care practitioner. Therefore, you must obtain them from a clinic or physician's office. The fit is important to ensure that the diaphragm stays in place during intercourse. Consequently, do not borrow a friend's diaphragm and expect it to work for you. The health care practitioner can also help you learn to insert it properly. Be certain to practice inserting it and to have the practitioner check the placement while you are still in the clinic. Otherwise, you will always be nervous that you are doing it wrong. And this may indeed be the case.

Diaphragm

Contraceptive jelly or cream

A

(A) Contraceptive jelly or cream is placed inside the dome of the diaphragm and spread around its rim. (B) Diaphragm is squeezed and inserted into the vagina until it covers the cervix. (C) Diaphragm is placed over the cervix and is checked to assure that it is correctly in place.

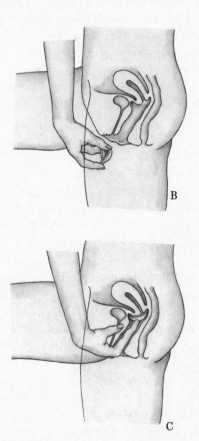

B

C

Figure 15   How a diaphragm is inserted into the vagina

In order to use a diaphragm, first squeeze about a tablespoon of contraceptive cream or jelly into the dome and spread some of it around the rim. The diaphragm must be inserted into the vagina *prior* to intercourse, preferably not more than an hour or two ahead of time (so the chemicals in the spermicide will still be strong enough). However, it is better to insert it many hours before intercourse than not to use it at all. After inserting it, use your fingers to check that your cervix is covered, that the front rim is snugly behind the pubic bone, and that the back rim is behind the cervix. It must remain in place six to eight hours after intercourse. Additional spermicide must be inserted each time you have intercourse during the time that it is in place. However, *do not remove the diaphragm to put in the spermicide*. Spermicides (cream, jelly, and foam) come with an applicator that you can use to put them directly into your vagina. Do not leave your diaphragm in place for more than twenty-four hours. For a diaphragm to be effective, *it must be used each and every time you have intercourse*.

In order to remove the diaphragm, merely insert your finger into your vagina, hook the rim of the diaphragm, and pull it down and out. Wash it with warm soapy water, dry it thoroughly, and always store it in its plastic container. You should never use talcum or perfumed powder on it nor should you use petroleum jelly (Vaseline) as a lubricant for intercourse. All of these products will cause the diaphragm to deteriorate. Inspect it regularly for defects or holes and always take it with you for your annual physical checkup. Also, consult your health care practitioner if you feel discomfort from the diaphragm, have difficulty urinating with it in place, or lose or gain ten pounds or more.

The diaphragm has very few side effects:

1. Women or their partners are occasionally allergic to the chemicals in the spermicides, or to the rubber of the diaphragm itself, and need to try different brands;

2. If fitted incorrectly, it can aggravate bladder and urinary problems, or cause pelvic discomfort, cramps, or pressure on the rectum;

3. Proper fitting appears to be difficult with a few women due to their anatomical structure;

4. Yeast infections can develop more easily if the diaphragm is not well cleaned and dried between each use;

5. If left in place too long (over twenty-four hours), the diaphragm develops a strong, unpleasant odor and can even lead to a heavy discharge.

6. Although the risk is very low, toxic shock syndrome (TSS) may have occurred in association with diaphragm use. This risk can be reduced by:

a. not leaving the diaphragm in place for more than twenty-four hours;

b. Using a condom and/or foam rather than a diaphragm during menstruation;

c. not using a diaphragm for several months after giving birth;

d. not using a diaphragm when you have an abnormal vaginal discharge;

e. not using a diaphragm if you have previously had TSS, or not using a diaphragm at least until it is certain that you have been completely cured of the bacteria causing it.

The major benefit of the diaphragm is the very low occurrence of health risks. In fact, it is helpful in reducing rates of sexually transmitted diseases, PID, and cervical cancer.

Diaphragms can be a very effective method of birth control, but only if used conscientiously and consistently. One study found a 98 percent effectiveness rate.[4] However, it doesn't work if you go out somewhere and leave your diaphragm at home in your drawer. Therefore, before choosing this method, be honest with yourself as to how responsible you are.

The Cervical Cap

The **cervical cap** is similar to the diaphragm in that it fits over the cervix and works as a barrier, preventing sperm from entering the uterus. It is smaller than a diaphragm, however, is thimble-shaped, and fits snugly on the cervix by suction.

Cervical caps are fitted to the size of a woman's cervix by a health care practitioner, who gives the woman careful instructions on insertion and removal. Because many women seem to have trouble inserting and removing the cap at first, it is important to practice this before leaving the practitioner's office. It is now recommended that a spermicide be used with a cervical cap. The cap should be filled about one-third full with contraceptive jelly or cream before being inserted into the vagina. Unlike the diaphragm, no additional jelly is necessary after each act of intercourse. Although when the cap

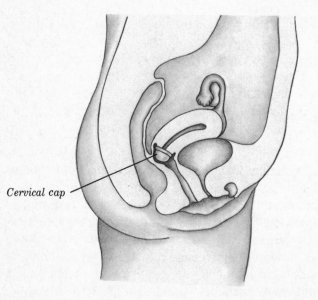

Cervical cap

Figure 16   The cervical cap in place on the cervix

was first introduced, instructions said that it could be left in place for extended periods of time, it is now advised to leave it in place no longer than thirty-six to forty-eight hours.

The cervical cap is still being studied in the United States and has not been approved by the Food and Drug Administration. Therefore, it is not widely distributed. It is available at some women's health centers, clinics, and private physicians' offices. Studies published in England found its effectiveness rates to be similar to those of the diaphragm, but reports in the United States have not been as favorable. Information on potential side effects and health risks is sparse. There is some concern about the risk of TSS, of irritation of the cervix, and of pelvic infections.

The Contraceptive Sponge

The **contraceptive sponge** is a soft, plastic sponge that works similarly to the diaphragm. It is inserted into the vagina and fits over the cervix. However, unlike the diaphragm, the sponge contains its own spermicide and doesn't require the application of creams or jellies. It is disposable, doesn't require a prescription, and is available at drug counters.

To use it, moisten the sponge with water and insert it into your vagina prior to sexual intercourse, making sure that it covers the cervix. Moistening it is essential not only because it makes insertion easier, but more importantly because it activates the spermicide. Once you've inserted the sponge, check to make certain that it is sitting snugly against your cervix, with the strap side pointed out toward the opening of your vagina. Also check that it has remained in place after you have had intercourse. It must be left in place six to eight hours after intercourse and it can safely be left in place for up to twenty-four hours. Repeated intercourse is possible during that time and, unlike the diaphragm, it is not necessary to apply additional spermicide. It has a soft cotton strap de-

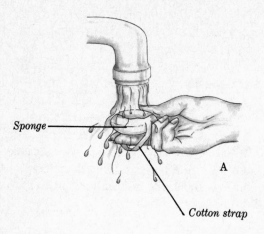

Sponge

Cotton strap

A

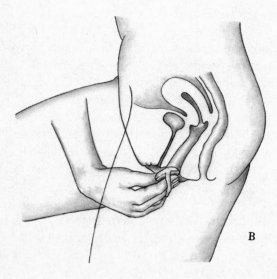

B

Figure 17 How to use a contraceptive sponge

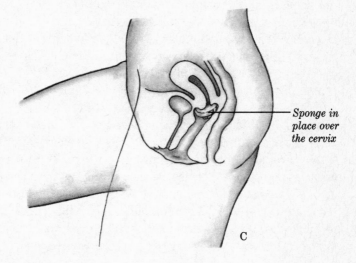

Sponge in
place over
the cervix

(A) Apply clear tap water until the sponge is dripping wet.
Squeeze gently, then fold in half. (B) Squat slightly with legs
apart and slide sponge up into vagina. (C) Check sponge edge
with finger to assure that cervix is covered.

signed for easy removal. Once removed it should be thrown away, because it is not effective a second time.

There have been some concerns about sponges being related to toxic shock syndrome (see chapter 4), similar to the concerns about tampon use. Therefore, it is important to follow instructions for proper use carefully. In particular, the sponge should not remain in your vagina for more than twenty-four hours, nor should it be used during menstruation, for the first few months after giving birth to a child, or when you have an abnormal discharge from your vagina. If you do have intercourse during your period, use an alternate form of contraception. Other side effects include occasional irritation or allergic reactions to the spermicide, and vaginal dryness.

The main advantages of the sponge are its wide availability and easy use. As with other spermicide-plus-barrier methods, it may provide protection against some sexually transmitted diseases and against cervical cancer. Initial research has found its effectiveness comparable to that of the diaphragm for women who have never given birth to a child. Somewhat surprisingly, women who have had previous births appear to have higher failure rates with the sponge than those who haven't.

Condoms (or "Rubbers")

Condoms (or **"rubbers"**) have been around for centuries, and are one of the few ways your male partner can take primary responsibility for protecting the two of you from a pregnancy. Because it is the boy who uses the "rubber," you might think that it is unnecessary for you to learn about it. However, before you relax, the truth is that boys *commonly* make mistakes in using condoms, so you may need to provide a few very important tips.

Condoms are thin sheaths, resembling long balloons, made out of latex or animal membranes that fit over an erect penis. They work by catching the semen when it is ejaculated, thus stopping the sperm from getting into the vagina. They come in different colors, textures, and with or without lubrication. The lubricated ones seem to break less often and some people report that they feel better. Since some condoms are dated, check to make sure that any you buy are not more than a year and a half old. If they are stored in a cool, dry place, however, condoms can last for as long as five years. They deteriorate more quickly if stored in the usual places boys like to keep them: in wallets in their back hip pockets or in hot glove compartments of cars. Some of the more expensive brands from drugstores may be safer than the cheaper ones. Sold in packs of three or more, each condom is usually individually wrapped in a foil or plastic wrapper.

Condoms need to be used *every* time intercourse occurs and they must be put on before intercourse begins. They are more effective when used with contraceptive foam, especially since the foam provides a backup in case the "rubber" breaks. After removing the wrapper, the rolled-up condom should be rolled down onto the boy's erect penis. I have heard of boys trying to be "prepared" for a date by putting them on prior to going out. This strategy doesn't work because they fall off when the penis is limp.

Some condoms come with special tips to hold the semen after ejaculation. If the one you and your partner are using doesn't have this kind of tip (called a reservoir tip), it is important to make a space by leaving about one-half inch of room at the tip of the condom. This space is necessary so that the semen has some place to go when it spurts out under force.

Since males lose part of their erection right after ejaculation, the condom will become loose. Therefore, your partner should withdraw his penis very soon after ejaculation, *holding on to the base of the condom while he withdraws* to ensure that the condom doesn't slip off inside the vagina and spill its contents of semen. The condom should then be thrown away. There will still be some sperm on the tip of his penis, so be careful not to allow his penis to come in contact with your vagina. If you decide to have intercourse again, use a fresh condom.

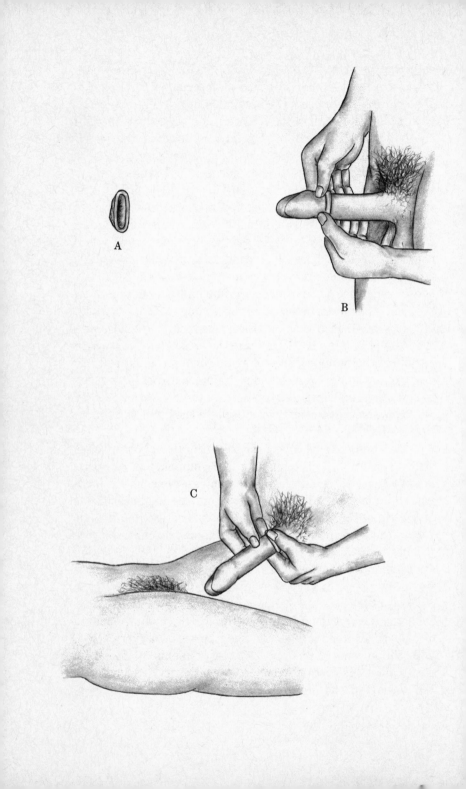

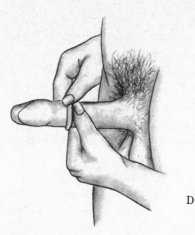

D

Figure 18   How to use a condom

*(A) Take the rolled condom. (B) Unroll
condom onto erect penis, leaving room at
the tip for semen to accumulate. (C) After
intercourse, hold condom while withdraw-
ing penis from the vagina. (D) Remove
condom from penis while away from partner's vagina. (E) Dry penis and discard
used condom before approaching partner.*

E

Petroleum jelly should *never* be used as a lubricant because it can cause deterioration of the latex condom.

If a condom should happen to break during intercourse, use foam immediately. It is, of course, much better if you put in foam before intercourse, but a late application is better than nothing. Also check for tears after use. There is now one brand of condoms, Ramses Extra, that has a spermicide already on the condom itself. This spermicide kills sperm inside the condom very effectively.

Condoms present *no* serious health risks and are highly effective *if used consistently*. The major complaints teenagers have about them are that they cut down on the sensitivity of the penis and that they interrupt the spontaneity of making love. Both of these concerns can be dealt with. Natural-skin and lubricated latex condoms seem to interfere less with the sensations on the penis. You and your partner can also be creative in putting on the condom to make it a fun part of lovemaking rather than an interruption.

Condoms are easily available, inexpensive, and do not require a prescription. One extremely important benefit of condoms is that they are the best product available for guarding against sexually transmitted diseases and, consequently, may reduce your chances of developing some of the dangerous complications of STDs, such as cervical cancer and **sterility**. In fact, it is always a good idea to use a condom in order to reduce the possibility of picking up a sexually transmitted disease when you are with someone who may have had other sexual partners. Some boys like condoms because they help them to delay ejaculation.

Intrauterine Devices—IUDs

Intrauterine devices (IUDs) are small devices that are inserted by a health care practitioner into a woman's uterus. At the time this book is going to press, only one type of IUD is

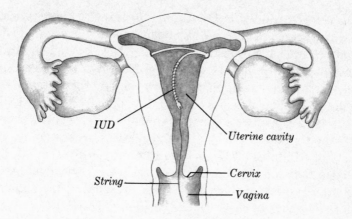

(A) IUD inserted in the uterine cavity

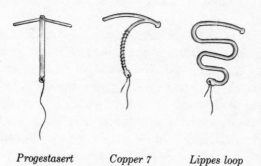

Progestasert   Copper 7   Lippes loop

(B) Three types of IUDs

Figure 19

still being marketed in the United States, the Progestasert. Many women already have other types in place, however, and many clinics have remaining stock of other IUDs. Therefore, this chapter will include some information on them as well. All IUDs are made of plastic. However, in order to improve effectiveness, some IUDs such as the Copper 7 and Copper T also have a copper wire wrapped around portions of the plastic, and the Progestasert contains and releases progesterone. In the United States all IUDs have thin strings attached to the bottom that run through the opening in the cervix and hang out into the top of the vagina. The presence of the strings makes it easier to check on the position of the IUD.

Exactly how the IUD works is not absolutely known, but three theories have been proposed. The most widely accepted theory is that the IUD acts as a foreign body in the uterus, irritating its lining and preventing a fertilized egg from implanting. The other two theories are that if an egg should start to implant, the IUD may knock it loose, or that the IUD may also cause a low-grade infection inside the uterus that kills sperm.

Many clinics and agencies, including most Planned Parenthood branches, will no longer insert IUDs in teenage girls (except in very unusual circumstances). Some, in fact, will only supply them to adult women who already have children. This is due to the risk of sterility from PID and from perforation of the uterus. For any woman, deciding on whether or not to use an IUD should be done only after careful consultation with a health care practitioner. One reason for this is that teenage girls and women who have never been pregnant expel IUDs more often than other women. Second, it is important to have a discussion about your medical history and life-style to make certain that you don't have any contraindications for using the IUD. These contraindications include such things as a history of pelvic infections or ectopic pregnancies, the desire for future pregnancies, or a history of multiple sex partners. You are equally at risk if your partner has sex with others. Third, it is essential that you understand the possible complications that can occur with an IUD and how to recognize them. These include:

1. Pelvic inflammatory disease (PID) (see page 180).
2. Perforation of the uterus or cervix, and embedding itself in the uterus.
3. Pregnancy, with higher risks of infection, spontaneous abortion, or that the pregnancy will be ectopic.
4. Difficulty removing the IUD.
5. Lost IUD strings and other string problems, such as irritation to the partner's penis.
6. Expulsion of the IUD, especially in the first year.
7. Cramping and pain, which may only be bothersome or which may indicate one of the more serious complications.
8. Spotting, bleeding, hemorrhage, and anemia.

The authors of *Contraceptive Technology* have listed dangerous warning signs in a way that is easy to remember. If you look at the first letter of each danger signal you will notice that they spell out *PAINS*.[5]

EARLY IUD DANGER SIGNS

Period late (pregnancy), abnormal spotting or bleeding
Abdominal pain, pain with intercourse
Infection exposure (such as gonorrhea), abnormal discharge
Not feeling well, fever, chills
String missing, shorter, or longer

Once an IUD has been inserted by a professional, you have two main responsibilities. The first is to regularly check the placement of the strings of the IUD. Any change in length could mean that the IUD has moved. Your second responsibility is to watch yourself for any of the side effects mentioned above. If any of these develop, you should go to a physician to have them checked out. Untreated problems with the IUD can be very dangerous. They have resulted in sterility and, on rare occasions, even in death.

Failures with the IUD are most likely to happen during the first three months of use. Consequently, a back-up method of contraception (like foam or condoms) is a good idea during that time. You should have a complete yearly checkup when you use an IUD. Never remove an IUD yourself. If it is causing problems, go to a professional. Some women who don't have problems with their IUDs keep them in indefinitely. The ones with copper or progesterone need to be replaced regularly, as follows: the Copper 7 every three years, the Copper T every four years, and the Progestasert every twelve *months*. If you know anyone who still has a Dalkon Shield, strongly encourage her to have it removed as soon as possible.

The Pill—Oral Contraceptives

No doubt the most publicized and most popular of all birth control methods is the birth control pill (**oral contraceptive**). Currently, the only oral contraceptives available in the United States are for women, although someday there are likely to be pills available that men can use. Birth control pills are actually a preparation of synthetic female hormones; each different brand varies as to the type or amount of hormone contained in it. There are two general varieties of pills available in the United States: the "**combination pill**," which contains both estrogen and **progestin**; and the "**mini-pill**," which contains only progestin. In the combination pill, the estrogen prevents eggs (ova) from maturing and being released from the woman's ovaries. Consequently, there is nothing for the sperm to fertilize and thus no pregnancy can occur. With the mini-pill, on the other hand, women sometimes continue to ovulate. However, the progestin causes a change in the mucus of the cervix, making it difficult for sperm to penetrate into the uterus.

The mini-pill was developed as a way to avoid negative side effects caused by estrogen and is thought to have fewer serious health risks than the combination pill. On the other hand, it is slightly less effective than the combination pill and requires special care in remembering to take every pill and at about the same time every day. In addition, use of the mini-pill can result in very irregular periods, which can make it more difficult to determine whether or not you are pregnant.

Before deciding that the pill is the contraceptive means for you, it is necessary to have a complete physical examination and a thorough discussion with a health care professional about your own and your family's medical history. This is important in order to confirm that you do not have any of the contraindications that make taking the pill dangerous. This also gives you the opportunity to discuss the relative advantages and disadvantages of the combination versus mini-pill in your case. Since the combination pill comes in an array of strengths and with different balances of estrogen and progestin, all of which influence the side effects, the professional will need to decide which is best suited to you.

If you do decide to use the pill, it is important to learn warning signs associated with serious problems. Below is a list of the danger signals, again arranged by the authors of *Contraceptive Technology* in an easy way to remember them. This time the first letters of the symptoms spell out *ACHES*.[6]

EARLY PILL DANGER SIGNS

Abdominal pain (severe)
Chest pain (severe), cough, shortness of breath
Headaches (severe), dizziness, weakness, numbness
Eye problems (vision loss or blurring), speech problems
Severe leg pain (calf or thigh)

See your clinician if you have any of these problems, or if you develop depression, yellow jaundice, or a breast lump.

Your pill packet will supply complete instructions for use, as will your doctor or nurse. Follow their instructions exactly. When starting pill use, it is a very good idea to learn about and obtain a *second* birth control method at the same time, such as condoms or foam. You'll *need* this back-up protection with your first pack of pills, and it can become handy later if you run out of pills, forget to take some, or decide to stop using the pill for any reason. With the mini-pill, it is often suggested that you use a back-up method during the first several months and even during each midcycle. Since birth control pills now contain lower dosages of hormones, it is important to take them consistently, at about the same time each day. If you often forget to take pills, this is not a good method of contraception for you. If you miss more than one or two pills, you will probably need to use a back-up method of birth control for the rest of that cycle. A back-up method should also be used if you are sick for several days with severe vomiting and diarrhea, since the chemicals may not be getting into your bloodstream in sufficient strength to be effective. Consult your clinic about a possible pregnancy test if you miss your period. You will definitely need a pregnancy test if you miss two periods in a row.

While using the pill you should have a yearly physical exam. Whenever you are being seen for other medical conditions, let your doctor know that you are using the pill, especially if you need to go to the hospital because of illness or for surgery. The pill can interact with other medications and affect other symptoms.

Side effects of the pill range from some rare, but life-threatening, conditions (like blood clots and heart attacks), through serious problems (like gall bladder disease and hypertension), to bothersome, but nondangerous effects (like nausea and weight gain). Some women also experience mood changes like depression when using birth control pills. If you are having bothersome side effects from the pill, report them to your doctor. Sometimes switching pill brands can modify or lessen them. You should also be aware that the pill is much more dangerous for women who smoke, especially if they are older than thirty-five years of age. Knowing this may help you to advise your mother. Some of the best advice you can give *anyone* is to stop smoking.

The greatest advantage of the pill is that it is extremely effective. Theoretically, if used correctly it should be 100 percent effective. In addition, shorter, lighter, and less painful periods usually accompany pill use. Another advantage is that if you remember to take your pill on time, you don't have to carry them around with you or fumble with another means of contraception prior to intercourse. Finally, recent findings are that birth control pills may decrease the chances of getting the more severe forms of pelvic inflammatory disease (PID) (see page 180) and perhaps help to protect against cancer of the ovary and of the lining of the uterus.

Post-Intercourse Contraception

A few post-intercourse contraceptive procedures are available if you have had unprotected intercourse. Physicians can prescribe what has been called a **morning-after pill**. These are high doses of hormones that, if taken soon after unprotected intercourse (within twenty-four to seventy-two hours), appear to be fairly effective. They are most effective when taken within twenty-four hours of intercourse. Side effects from these pills can be quite troublesome, however, and they are not considered to be a safe form of ongoing contraception. Morning-after IUD insertion is also used in some cases.

Sterilization

Although **sterilization** has become an increasingly popular method of birth control for both men and women, it is not a method recommended for teenagers, except in some medical emergencies, with some genetic conditions, and for those who already have several children. Sterilization is a medical procedure done to eliminate the possibility of ever having children. It is included in this book to familiarize you with the fact that this will be one alternative after you enter adulthood. Sterilization requires surgery and can be performed on either a male or a female.

In women, sterilization is referred to as a **tubal ligation**. In this procedure, the surgeon makes an incision in the woman's abdomen, and then cuts the fallopian tubes. This prevents the egg from moving to the uterus and any sperm from joining the egg in the fallopian tube. Attempts to reverse this operation are *sometimes* successful.

Sterilization of a man is called a **vasectomy**, and can be performed in a doctor's office. In this surgical procedure, a small incision is made in the scrotum in order to reach the vas deferens. The vas is then cut and the ends sealed to prevent sperm from getting through. Consequently, when the man ejaculates, he ejects only seminal fluid without any sperm (it looks exactly the same, except under a microscope). If the man changes his mind later in life and decides that he wishes to have children, the operation can *sometimes* be reversed.

Deciding Which Contraceptive Method Is Best for You

Unfortunately, an absolutely perfect method of birth control has yet to be invented and each of the available methods have various advantages and disadvantages. They vary in effectiveness, convenience, risk to health, whether or not they need to be prescribed by a physician, and many other factors.[7]

Now that you've learned something about the contraceptive methods that exist, take eight pieces of paper and on each piece of paper place one of the following headings: Birth Control Pills; Condoms; IUD; Foam or Spermicidal Suppository; Cervical Cap; Diaphragm; Contraceptive Sponge; and Natural Methods. Now read through the following ten questions, using them to evaluate each of these methods as they were just discussed. Use your sheets of paper to write down notes about each method.

See if you can narrow down your choices to one or two. At that point, it would be best to talk over the advantages and disadvantages of the chosen methods with a parent, a physician, or another professional at a family planning clinic. Some of these clinics are able to provide their services and a contraceptive device without a fee or for a minimal charge. Even if you decide to make your choice without consulting anyone, use the following evaluation questions to make an educated, informed decision.

1. Is there anything in my medical history that would make this method dangerous? With both the pill and the IUD there are women with certain medical conditions or symptoms who should avoid these methods. These conditions are usually listed as "contraindications" on pill packets. Before obtaining either of these contraceptives, a health care practitioner will need to take a complete medical history from you and perform a physical exam. This is for your protection and is very important.

2. What are the general health risks of this method? Unfortunately, the contraceptive methods that are the most effective tend to have more safety problems. On the other hand, health care experts tell us that most of the serious problems associated with contraceptives could be avoided if women paid strict attention to the known contraindications and if women heeded the early warning signs of problems. *Usually*, when your body is in trouble, it will let you know. Common warning signs associated with the various contraceptives were discussed for each method earlier in this chapter. If you have even the slightest thought that your body may be giving you a warning sign, seek medical advice.

3. How effective is this method? It is important to remember that effectiveness always depends on proper and consistent use. The diaphragm can be very effective if used conscientiously, while the pill can be ineffective if you forget to take it. You will notice that the various methods have different effectiveness rates for preventing pregnancy. In fact, there are usually two separate effectiveness rates published for each method. One rate is the "theoretical effectiveness rate," which is how good the method would be if no one ever made any mistakes using it and if the product was never defective. "Actual effectiveness" is the rate measured in real-life use by actual human beings. People can mess up the use of contraceptives in a number of ways: inconsistent use, improper use, running out, forgetting, et cetera. Occasionally, there are faulty contraceptives, like weak condoms. Consequently, the actual rates you'll see published are quite a bit lower than theoretical rates. However, you can make the effectiveness of any method much higher than the typical actual rate by learning how to use your method well and then using it consistently.

Both actual and theoretical rates of effectiveness are based on a percent definition. If it says somewhere that the actual effectiveness rate of a method is 80 percent, it means that out of 100 women using that method for a year, 80 did not get pregnant and 20 did. The table at right reports the actual and theoretical effectiveness of various contraceptive techniques.[8]

4. What are the negative side effects of this method? Side effects are changes that the method causes besides the desired effect of reducing the risk of pregnancy. They can range from very minor to ones that bother you so much that you stop using the method. Since these methods affect different women in different ways, you will not know which side effects you will develop until after you try the method. Unfortunately, sometimes girls quit using their contraceptive device when a troublesome side effect occurs without replacing it with another form of birth control. For this reason, it is important to know about more than one method, keeping another in mind as a backup.

Table 1. Effectiveness Rates
of Birth Control Methods

Method	Highest Observed Effectiveness Rate in Women Who Use It Correctly and Consistently (Theoretical)	Effectiveness Rate in Typical Users, Including Those Who Use It Incorrectly and Inconsistently (Actual)
Chance (no method)	10%	10%
Natural methods (fertility awareness)	80–98%	76%
Foams, creams, jellies, and vaginal suppositories	95–97%	82%
Condoms	98%	90%
Cervical Cap	98%	87%
Sponge (with spermicide)	89–91%	80–90%
Diaphragm (with spermicide)	98%	81%
IUD	98.5%	95%
Mini-pill	99%	97.5%
Combination pill	99.5%	98%

5. Are there any beneficial side effects to this method?
Happily, not all the side effects of contraceptives are negative. Pill use, for instance, often leads to more regular, lighter, and less painful periods. Condoms are a very effective way to cut down on the risk of catching a sexually transmitted disease. Contraceptive foam is a good sexual lubricant.

6. How convenient is the method and how does that affect how likely I am to remember to use it and to follow through each time? For some of the methods there is more responsibility and work on your part in learning to use them correctly or for not having intercourse if you forget to bring your contraceptive with you. With the diaphragm, for example, you must learn to insert it and make sure you always have it with you when you need it. With the pill, you have to remember to take it each day. In contrast, the IUD doesn't require the same kind of vigilance.

7. How expensive is the method? Actually the prices of all the methods vary greatly depending on where you get them. So, if expense is a problem, it makes sense to shop around. Agencies like Planned Parenthood and community health centers tend to have better prices than private doctors and clinics. In fact, some public agencies may be able to furnish you with contraceptives at little or no cost. On the other hand, some women feel that they get more individual attention and privacy from private doctors and other sources.

8. Is my life-style compatible with this method? The frequency with which you engage in intercourse, whether it occurs on a planned or unplanned basis, and the number of different sexual partners you or your partner have are all life-style issues important to contraceptive choice. Girls who very rarely have intercourse and, therefore, do not require constant protection, may not want to use the higher-risk methods (like the pill and IUD). On the other hand, these methods may be more attractive to girls who know that they have a tendency to have intercourse on an unplanned basis. Because the risk of catching a disease increases greatly if you or your partner have sex with other people, methods that help to prevent the transmission of sexual disease are an *excellent* idea for anyone with multiple partners. Condoms and the contraceptive foams, jellies, and creams help in this regard. In contrast, the IUD seems to be particularly dangerous for women with multiple partners.

9. Does this method require that I feel comfortable in touching my own genitals? Sometimes girls who are very nervous about touching their own bodies rush while inserting a diaphragm, sponge, or foam, and end up doing it wrong. Use of an IUD also requires that you regularly insert your fingers into your vagina to check the placement of the strings.

If you are comfortable with your body it is easy to do the things necessary to use these methods.

10. How do I really feel about this method? Listen to your own emotional reactions to a method. If you feel very negative about it for any reason, you are likely to have problems with it. It is important for you to have a positive attitude about your chosen method.

Preventing pregnancy is not a matter of luck, but of planning. As you have seen, there are many methods of birth control available for the teenage couple. *Before* engaging in intercourse, you should be familiar with all of these methods, along with their advantages and disadvantages. Sex can certainly be fun, but it also involves responsibilities. If you have to worry for a month about whether or not you are pregnant, or have to make a decision between abortion or motherhood, the worry can certainly make the overall sexual experience extremely unpleasant. Being responsible about birth control will only help to make your sexual experiences more enjoyable.

13

SEXUALLY TRANSMITTED DISEASES

If you are like many teenagers, getting a sexually transmitted disease (STD) is one of the farthest things from your mind when you think about intimate physical contact with a boy. You probably wouldn't be all that surprised if you caught a cold or the flu, but the thought of catching an STD may seem beyond imagination. But think about that for a minute. If you can catch a cold or the flu from being close to someone who is ill, why is it strange to think that you could catch an STD from pressing your lips against someone or having a boy place his penis inside your vagina? The fact is that the closer the physical contact you have with people, the easier it is to catch certain diseases.

There is nothing mysterious about gonorrhea, **syphilis**, herpes, or any other sexually transmitted disease (these used to be called venereal diseases). They are illnesses, just like a cold or the flu, with two important differences: (1) They are usually transmitted by heavy petting or sexual intercourse; and (2) Unlike a cold or the flu, they do not usually just run their course and then go away. Sexually transmitted diseases should be treated by a physician; otherwise they can do significant damage to your body, even if the symptoms disappear.[1]

I must admit, there is another difference, one I hope will change as people become more educated about STDs. That difference is that because of distorted stereotypes, many people think of STDs as being one step worse than the Plague. They believe that STDs are caught only by "dirty," "bad," "immoral," or "sexually loose" people. Too often the stigma attached to these diseases can lead someone to put off going in for tests and getting the necessary treatment. Embarrassment also sometimes prevents people from informing their sexual partners that they might have a disease, even though this information is essential and can actually save someone from becoming very sick or even sustaining serious physical damage, such as infertility.

The fact is that STDs are so common in the United States, especially among teenagers and young adults, that some of these diseases have been declared "pandemic" (this means more widespread than an epidemic). According to the Centers for Disease Control in Atlanta, for every 1,000 teenagers in the United States between the ages of fifteen and nineteen, approximately 12 cases of gonorrhea or syphilis were reported.[2] This number includes merely the *reported* cases of only *two* of the many STDs. Many of the fairly common STDs are not even included in these statistics because physicians are not required to report them. In addition, many cases of gonorrhea and syphilis are left out of these statistics. If all actual cases of STDs were included, the rate would certainly be many times higher.

Consequently, if you are a high school student and there are 1,000 students who attend your school, on the average, you might expect that students at your school would experience between 100 and 200 cases of sexually transmitted diseases during the four years you attend. Certainly, the rate at your school may be higher or lower than the national average, but the point is clear: All sexually active teenagers share a significant risk of getting STDs.

The incidence of STDs in teenagers has gotten out of control for several reasons. Two important factors are that more teenagers are sexually active and that they tend to have more partners. A third reason is the decline in the popularity of the condom and spermicides as contraceptive measures. These methods provide some protection against STDs. And, fourth, many people who are without symptoms don't know that they have an STD and unknowingly spread their disease to others.

General Guidelines for Preventing STDs

If you are sexually active, there is no sure-fire way to absolutely prevent getting a sexually transmitted disease. These diseases can be spread by sexual intercourse, kissing, touching, or even just close contact. Consequently, even avoiding intercourse does not completely eliminate the possibility of contracting an STD. There are, however, some procedures that can help reduce the risk.

1. The most effective measure is to limit your possible exposure by not having multiple sexual partners or not having sex with someone else who has multiple partners. Couples who have sex only with each other have a lower rate of STDs than people who have more casual or varied sexual relationships.

2. Don't engage in intercourse with anyone who you know has an STD or who shows any symptoms of an STD. The more familiar you are with these symptoms (as listed below and described with each of the diseases that follow), the better chance you have of avoiding them.

3. Use condoms whenever engaging in intercourse with someone who could possibly have an STD. This would include someone you don't know very well or anyone who has had other sexual contacts. Condoms can decrease the spread of *some* STDs by providing a barrier to the bacteria contained in a male's urethra or on his penis. If you believe your partner sometimes has sex with others, ask him always

to use a "rubber" with them and with you, so that he is less likely to get an STD and bring it back to you.

4. Use contraceptive foams, creams, or jellies, since the spermicides in them kill some bacteria and can help reduce the chances of contracting some STDs.

5. Urinate and wash your genitals after having intercourse. Urination may flush out bacteria before they begin to travel up the urethra, and washing can cleanse away much of the bacteria.

6. Gargle with saltwater after oral sex. This may help to flush STD germs out of the mouth.

7. Maintain good general health and hygiene. Proper rest, nutrition, stress reduction, exercise, and cleanliness are important in maximizing your resistance to infection.

8. If you are having intercourse with different people or with someone who is sexually active with other partners, have a medical examination for STDs at least twice a year. These routine exams are particularly important for females, since women *often* have no early warning signs.

Early Symptoms of STDs

As was just mentioned, one of the aspects of STDs that makes them so difficult to eliminate is that a person may have one of these diseases and have no symptoms at all. This is especially true for females, which is an important reason for sexually active women to have regular medical checkups.

When symptoms are present, they can vary widely. Remember, the term "STDs" does not stand for one disease, but rather is a group of different diseases. You can even have more than one of them at the same time. Below is a list outlining the most common early symptoms of sexually transmitted diseases in both sexes.

Discharge—A white, yellowish, greenish, and/or foul-smelling discharge from the vagina or anus of females, or a clear, yellowish or milky discharge from the penis or anus of males.

Burning urination—A painful burning sensation when urinating.

Sores—Any sores, especially in the genital area, whether painful or painless.

Itching—Itching anywhere in the pubic area, inside the vagina, penis, anus, or in any of the hairy portions of the body.

Rashes—Rashes, particularly in the genital area, chest, on the soles of the feet, or on the palms of the hands.

Warts—Any warts or bumps in the genital or anal area.

Pain in the lower abdomen or pelvic area—This can be a sign of an STD that has spread internally.

Sore throat—A sore throat after engaging in oral sex.

What to Do If You Have Any Symptoms of STDs

If you are aware of having any of the early symptoms of STDs, it is important that you get them checked right away. (The appendix gives information on how and where you can get help.) *Don't wait to see if the symptom persists, and don't try to treat yourself. Many of the early symptoms of STDs disappear completely or go "underground" after the first few weeks while the disease continues to exist in your body, and in fact may be entering a more destructive phase.* Even if the initial symptoms have disappeared, don't assume that it was a false alarm or that your body has rid itself of the disease. *At the first sign of a possibile STD, immediately have yourself checked by a physician.* Not being examined can lead to great physical harm to yourself and others.

You also need to go to a physician if *anyone you have had sex with develops symptoms or is diagnosed* as having an STD.

Very often a girl will only realize that she has an STD when her partner turns up with one.

It is *essential* to follow your doctor's instructions for taking medications and to keep all your return appointments: *Your good health and your ability to ever become pregnant may be at stake.* Don't quit taking the medicine just because the symptoms have disappeared. If you are dissatisfied with the care given by your physician, then get a second opinion. There now exist many agencies that are happy to give sensitive, caring treatment to teenagers for little or no cost.

If you find that you do have a sexually transmitted disease, it is essential that you inform any partners with whom you have had close physical contact. Otherwise, they can become seriously ill, spread the disease to others, and even reinfect you. Also *avoid sexual contact until your treatment is complete,* or if you have herpes, at least until the sores are healed.

Understanding the Diseases

The following is a listing of the most common and dangerous sexually transmitted diseases and information to help you recognize and understand each one. Although many symptoms are listed for each disease, any *one* symptom can be a sign that the disease is present.

Gonorrhea

Gonorrhea (gahn-uh-*ree*-uh) is a bacterial infection. It first causes localized infections in the body organs exposed to it and eventually can spread to many organs throughout the body to become a "systemic" illness. Gonorrhea is so common that it is considered an epidemic in the United States. In 1983 there were more than 900,000 cases *reported*, the vast majority of which occurred among teenagers and young adults.[3] It is estimated that there are probably another 1 to 2 million unreported cases per year in the United States. Many people who get the infection go for long periods of time without symptoms, or with only mild symptoms, and spread the disease unknowingly. These people are called carriers.

Nicknames
Clap, strain, sleet, morning drip, morning dew, hot piss, dose, the whites, GC

How Do You Get or Give It?
Gonorrhea is almost always passed by sexual contact. Since the bacteria live best in warm, moist places, they will usually survive in the vagina, penis, anus, mouth, throat, and occasionally the eyes. Outside the human body, the bacteria cannot survive for long. Consequently, it is nearly impossible to catch this disease from infected toilet seats, doorknobs, or cups, as some people fear.

Symptoms
Many women, maybe as many as 50 percent of those infected, go for long periods of time with the disease but do not show any symptoms. Unless a partner warns her that she might have gonorrhea or it is discovered in a routine screening test, a woman may not realize anything is wrong until the infection has spread to her fallopian tubes. At that point she may experience lower abdominal pain, fever, or discharge from the vagina.

If a woman does develop early symptoms, their form will depend on which parts of the body are infected. Infection of the urethra may lead to burning on urination or a milky or yellowish discharge from the urethra. A woman with a cervical infection might notice increased vaginal discharge and sometimes mild vaginal bleeding, especially after intercourse. Anal discharge and burning, pain during bowel movements, and mild anal bleeding may be symptoms of an anal infection. A sore throat may indicate a gonorrheal infection in the throat, although STD-related throat infections are usually without symptoms. Swelling, pain, and redness on either side of the vaginal opening can be an indication of gonorrhea in one of the Bartholin's glands. Untreated, the infection often spreads to the fallopian tubes, creating pelvic inflammatory disease (PID), a dangerous disease that we'll explain in more detail later in this chapter.

Boys are much more likely to experience early symptoms of gonorrhea than girls. Boys may notice a drip from the penis before the first urination of the day, or a continuous milky discharge during the day. In addition, there may be an itchy feeling inside the penis or a painful burning sensation while urinating. Throat and anal symptoms are similar to those for girls. In boys, the infection can spread to the epididymus (see chapter 7) and cause pain, swelling, and sometimes redness in a testicle.

When the infection has become systemic in either sex, symptoms can include fever, skin rash, and pain and swelling of the joints. These may be the first symptoms of gonorrhea or they can occur after a person ignores earlier, milder symptoms.

When Do the Symptoms First Appear?
Usually, the symptoms appear within two to ten days after exposure to gonorrhea, although it can take as many as thirty days. Remember, however, that in many people there are no early symptoms.

Tests and Diagnosis
In females, samples of cells are taken from the vagina, throat, and/or anus and are tested in the laboratory. This is called taking a "culture." In males, any discharge from the penis is tested and cultures may be taken from the urethra, throat, and anus.

Treatment
Gonorrhea can be cured with appropriate antibiotics. Some resistant strains (so-called Super-Gon) from Southeast Asia

may require special antibiotics, but a cure is almost always possible.

Complications
Infertility can result from infections of the reproductive organs due to the scarring it creates in the narrow tubes. In the advanced systemic stages, infection of the joints, skin, heart, central nervous system, or liver can occur. Babies of mothers who have gonorrhea can contract an infection in their eyes during birth that can lead to blindness if left untreated. Infections in males can cause scarring and narrowing of the urethra, and permanent damage to one or both testicles.

Chlamydia and Related Infections

There are a number of infections in women that resemble gonorrhea but are not caused by the same bacteria. Chlamydia (kluh-*mih*-dee-uh) is the bacterialike organism responsible for a large proportion of these infections. A group of even lesser-understood organisms is thought to account for the remaining proportion. Chlamydia is very similar to gonorrhea in that it commonly causes localized infections in most of the same organs.

Since doctors are not required to report these infections to health authorities, the exact incidence is unknown, but they may be even two to three times more common than gonorrhea.

How Do You Get or Give It?
It is transmitted similarly to gonorrhea—through sexual contact.

Symptoms
Very often there are *no* early symptoms. When symptoms are present, they are similar to those of gonorrhea, but usually are milder.

When Do the Symptoms First Appear?
Usually within one to three weeks after exposure to the bacteria, but they can take longer.

Tests and Diagnosis
The diagnosis is as yet usually done by exclusion—if the tests for gonorrhea are negative, it is probably chlamydia or something similar. Laboratory tests to specifically diagnose chlamydia are now becoming available, however.

Treatment
Antibiotics

Complications
Untreated, these infections can cause PID in women and infections of the epididymus in men. In both cases it can scar these narrow tubes and cause infertility. Scarring and narrowing of the urethra can occur in men. A baby can contract chlamydia in its eyes and lungs from its mother during birth. New research has also suggested that it may be related to miscarriage and stillbirth in pregnant women.

Genital Herpes

Genital herpes is a highly infectious disease caused by a virus rather than by bacteria. The common cold sore is also caused by a type of herpes virus. There are approximately 300,000 physician visits per year in the United States for genital herpes. Many of these are new cases, while others represent recurrent infections.[4] Although it is difficult to estimate, it is probably safe to say that at least 20 million Americans have been infected with the genital herpes virus, and many of these persons have recurrent outbreaks. When the new and recurrent cases are added up, genital herpes is far more common than gonorrhea, syphilis, and chlamydia combined.

How Do You Get It or Give It?

The virus is typically passed by direct contact with a herpes sore on someone's mouth, genitals, or anus. You can also infect different parts of your own body by touching infected areas.

Most people think you can only get herpes by contact with herpes sores, but this is not entirely true. Even in the absence of current sores, a person who has herpes can occasionally pass it on to others by a process called shedding. When the infection occurs, the virus travels up the nerve cells and remains in a person's body. The virus later travels back down the nerve cells, sometimes resulting in another outbreak of sores, which are highly contagious. At other times, no new sores erupt, but the virus is "shed" from mucous membranes and semen and can potentially infect another person.

It is believed to be possible to pick up herpes from inanimate objects, such as towels and toilet seats, that have been used recently by an infected person. However, this means of transmission has not been conclusively proven and is probably uncommon.

Symptoms

First symptoms for someone initially contracting herpes are flulike in nature, including achiness, headache, fever, and swollen glands. In about a quarter of the cases there is itching and aching in the genital area, followed by an eruption of a painful group of small, fluid-filled blisters. The blisters gradually break and become open sores, then drain and crust over. Healing takes two to three weeks. Girls and women may not be aware of the sores if they are located inside the vagina or on the cervix. They may notice instead a vaginal discharge. All sores are potentially contagious until completely healed.

After the initial outbreak, a rough estimate is that about 50 to 60 percent of people go on to have recurrent herpes, or repeated periodic outbreaks of sores, particularly at times of physical and emotional stress. Although the attacks tend to become progressively less severe, there is no proven way at the present time to completely eliminate them. Other people remain in a latent (nonactive) stage indefinitely.

When Do the Symptoms First Appear?
Symptoms of the initial infection usually show up within two to twelve days, with seven days being typical. Some people, however, have no visible sores during the initial infection and do not even realize that they have it until sores show up during a later outbreak, sometimes many years later.

Tests and Diagnosis
Diagnosis is generally made from a description of the symptoms and observation of the sores, along with a viral culture.

Treatment
Currently there is no proven treatment that will cure herpes, although many medications and vaccines are being researched. One medication (acyclovir) may be helpful in shortening the primary infections. It may also reduce the severity and frequency of recurrent sores.

The following are a few recommendations that may help minimize the spread and the duration of the infection:

1. Try to minimize the physical and emotional stress on your body by eating a balanced diet, sleeping regularly, and dealing effectively with emotional turmoil.

2. Keep the infection from spreading by keeping the sores dry and clean. Blot the sores carefully after bathing, using a separate area of a clean towel for each area you blot dry.

3. Ice in an ice bag can numb the pain somewhat, and may keep the sores from erupting. Do not apply ice directly, as the wetness may spread the infection. Some local anesthetics may also be useful in relieving pain.

4. If the sores do not disappear within two weeks have them looked at by a physician. Sometimes they can become infected with bacteria.

5. Avoid any sexual activity from the time you feel the attack first coming on until the sores are completely gone. Even masturbation should be avoided, so that the infection is not spread.

Complications

Since genital herpes is as yet essentially incurable, some of the greatest complications are emotional rather than physical. Herpes victims often experience guilt about the danger of spreading the disease to partners and fear telling others about their condition. They may find themselves avoiding social contact rather than having to risk rejection. Support groups, reading materials, and resource centers have been developed to help people deal realistically with herpes. The Herpes Resource Center publishes an excellent newsletter giving up-to-date information about herpes. See appendix A for further information. If you have herpes, there is no need to feel alone or think that your sex life is over.

There are also several physical complications associated with herpes. A link may exist between genital herpes and cervical cancer in women. Therefore, women with herpes should probably have Pap smears done twice a year. It is possible for you to spread herpes to the eyes, which is very dangerous. A baby born to a woman who has an active outbreak of genital herpes at the time of delivery has a high likelihood of acquiring an infection. This can result in brain damage or death to the infant. Consequently, it is very important that the physician know when a pregnant woman has herpes. If she has an outbreak near the time of labor, the baby will be delivered by cesarean section (see chapter 8).

Pelvic Inflammatory Disease—PID

Pelvic inflammatory disease, or PID, is an infection of the fallopian tubes, which may also involve the uterus and abdominal cavity. The source of the infection is often gonorrhea or chlamydia, but it can also be caused by organisms that haven't been transmitted sexually. It is estimated that there are about 1 million cases of PID per year in the United States and that the incidence is increasing. Women and girls with multiple sexual partners are four to six times more likely to acquire PID than those who only have one sexual partner or who are not sexually active. About one in eight sexually active adolescent girls gets PID. Women who have had it once also seem to be at higher risk for getting it again. Use of an IUD as a birth control method also increases the risk of developing PID by three to five times.

Symptoms
The key symptom of PID is persistent pain in the lower abdomen. This pain may also be accompanied by a variety of other symptoms: fever, chills, vaginal discharge, abnormal vaginal bleeding, nausea, and/or vomiting.

When Do the Symptoms First Appear?
The length of time between when a girl first gets some type of infection and when she feels the symptoms of PID can vary greatly. As mentioned in the sections on gonorrhea and chlamydia, the symptoms of PID may be the *first* signs that she has anything wrong at all.

Tests and Diagnosis
The diagnosis of PID is made after a pelvic exam that reveals tender fallopian tubes. If PID is found, tests for specific causes of the infection, such as for gonorrhea, are made.

Treatment
Antibiotics are used to clear up the infection. Sometimes the infection has progressed to the point that pain medication and even hospitalization are required to adequately treat it. If a woman has an IUD, it is usually necessary to remove it for the treatment to be effective. You should also advise your sexual partner(s) to get treatment if the cause of your PID turns out to be gonorrhea or chlamydia.

Complications

An infection in the narrow fallopian tubes can cause scarring inside. This scarring can have two negative results. First, it can reduce your fertility because it can close off the tubes and thus prevent fertilization of the egg. Second, it can increase the risk (by about eight times) of having a **tubal** or **ectopic pregnancy**, in which the egg is fertilized, but is blocked from traveling to the uterus. The fallopian tube can burst during a tubal pregnancy and become a life-threatening situation.

Trichomoniasis

A one-celled animal causes the infection called trichomoniasis (trik-uh-muh-*ni*-uh-sis). It is so prevalent that it may affect as many as a quarter of the sexually active female population.

Nicknames

Trich (pronounced *trick*), TV

How Do You Get or Give It?

The infection is almost always passed through sexual contact. Since the animal that causes it can stay alive outside the body for several hours, some experts believe that it may be possible (though unlikely) to pick up the infection from contact with moist objects used by an infected person (like washcloths or towels).

Symptoms

Females with "trich" usually notice a heavy, smelly, gray or yellow-green discharge from their vaginas. The area around the vulva may get red, sore, and itchy. Usually males experience no symptoms, although some feel a tickling or itching inside the penis and have a discharge. Because of the typical lack of symptoms in males, they can carry and pass "trich" without knowing it.

When Do Symptoms First Appear?

The first symptoms can be expected from four to twenty days after the first exposure.

Tests and Diagnosis

When an infection is suspected, secretions from the vagina or penis are inspected under a microscope and the one-celled animal can be seen. Many times the diagnosis is made after the organism is noticed during a routine urine analysis.

Treatment

Despite the absence of symptoms in the male, *both* the woman and her partner need to be treated. Otherwise, he can reinfect her. Metronidazole (brand name Flagyl) is the medication usually prescribed.

Complications

For females, "trich" can result in an inflammation of the urethra and cervix. In males it can cause infections of the urethra, prostate, and epididymis.

Syphilis

Syphilis (*sif*-uh-lis) is a bacterial infection caused by a spiral-shaped bacteria. As with gonorrhea, the infection starts out localized in one part of the body, but will spread throughout the body to become systemic if left untreated. It is estimated that there are about 100,000 cases per year in the United States, with homosexual males making up about 50 percent of these cases. This century has seen a large overall decline in the incidence of syphilis due to the availability of antibiotics and to the vigorous effort made by public health departments in tracing potential cases. Currently, it is much less common than gonorrhea, herpes, or chlamydia, but the serious nature of syphilis still makes it a significant threat.

Nicknames
Syph, pox, lues, bad blood, haircut, old joe

How Do You Get or Give It?
As with gonorrhea, it would be extremely rare for syphilis to be spread by contact with inanimate objects such as toilet seats or damp towels. The bacteria can live only a very short time when away from a warm, moist environment. Therefore, it is almost always transmitted by sexual contact.

Symptoms/Stages
The symptoms vary with the stage of the disease: primary, secondary, latent, or late (tertiary).

Primary: The first sign of syphilis is usually the appearance of one or more **chancres**. A chancre (*shan*-ker) is a painless sore that starts out as a round, firm bump, then eventually breaks down into a small ulcer with highly contagious secretions. Chancres are usually located on the external genitals, but can also be on hands, mouth, anus, or virtually any other part of the body where contact has occured with the infection. Healing of the sores takes about four to six weeks and may be accompanied by swelling of the glands in the groin.

Secondary: If untreated, the bacteria spread throughout the bloodstream. About six weeks after the chancre heals, a skin rash appears. The rash can take on many different forms and is highly contagious. The rash lasts about two to six weeks and then fades. Other symptoms in the secondary stage can include swollen lymph glands, fever, and a headache. Sometimes the primary stage does not occur, and the rash of the secondary stage is the first sign of syphilis.

Latent: If still untreated, the symptoms disappear and the bacteria quietly reproduce in the body. Although not contagious, the disease can be transmitted to the fetus of a pregnant woman in this stage. The latent stage can last for many years.

Late (tertiary): Eventually, untreated syphilis can lead to a disease that wastes away the skin, nervous system, blood vessels, and other important organs in the body and may ultimately result in death. Again, although not usually contagious during this stage, it may be possible to pass from mother to fetus. It is unusual in the United States for syphilis to reach this stage.

When Do the Symptoms First Appear?
Usually in ten to sixty days after exposure, with twenty-one days being about average.

Diagnosis
Bacteria taken from a chancre or rash can be identified under a special microscope. A blood test, known as the VDRL, can diagnose syphilis after it has spread sufficiently (which may take six to twelve weeks). A test taken too soon may give a "false negative" and convince you that you don't have the disease, when you actually do have it. Consequently, the test should be repeated at a later time.

Treatment
Syphilis can be cured with appropriate antibiotics. The earlier the diagnosis is made and treatment begun, the easier and faster the cure. In order to ensure that the bacteria have been wiped out, blood tests are sometimes repeated periodically for years. In late syphilis the infection can be eliminated by antibiotics, but any damage done to the organs of the body is usually irreversible.

Complications
In late syphilis, the disease may lead to brain damage, heart disease, kidney damage, deafness, paralysis, insanity, muscle incoordination, blindness, damage to blood vessels, and death. Infection of babies during a pregnancy can lead to birth defects or stillbirth.

Pubic Lice

Pubic lice, or **"crabs,"** are small parasites that infest the pubic area. They can move to other sites where there is body hair or can be moved by your scratching the infested areas and then touching other parts of your body. Pubic lice look like small brown scabs at the base of the pubic hairs. Their eggs, small white bumps, are sometimes also visible. When viewed under a microscope, the lice look very similar to crabs, having claws and legs.

Nicknames
Crabs, cooties

How Do You Get or Give Them?
Pubic lice are highly contagious. They can be passed from one person to another by close physical contact, or they can be picked up from inanimate objects, such as infested bedding, clothing, towels, or furniture.

Symptoms
Usually there is intense itching in the pubic area. You may find the crabs in your pubic hair.

When Do the Symptoms First Appear?
Symptoms appear up to five weeks after contact with the lice.

Diagnosis
Diagnosis is made by locating the lice or their eggs.

Treatment
There are both prescription and nonprescription medications available. Pyrinate and Kwell are the most common. These liquid or lotion solutions are shampooed or spread over the body. Since the treatment kills the lice themselves, but not their eggs, it should be repeated a week later when the eggs hatch. Besides treating the body, all clothes, bedding, and

blankets must be thoroughly washed in hot water or sprayed with appropriate disinfectants.

Venereal Warts

Venereal warts are small warts occurring in the genital area that are caused by a virus.

How Do You Get or Give Them?
They are most commonly passed by contact with a wart on another person during sexual contact. However, nonsexual transmission may occur also.

Symptoms
Venereal warts are usually painless, and are either pinkish and soft with a cauliflowerlike appearance or yellow-gray and hard. The bottom part of the vagina and labia (lips) are the most common sites in women, but they can also be found inside the vagina, on the cervix, anus, and area between the genitals and the anus. The most common site in males is the penis, but anywhere on the genitals, urethra, or anus is possible.

When Do the Symptoms First Appear?
Symptoms generally appear about three months after the initial contact.

Diagnosis
This condition is diagnosed by examination of the warts.

Treatment
The warts can be removed by treating them chemically, by freezing them, by burning them, or by surgical removal.

Complications
If not removed, the condition can become worse and can be spread to others. If passed to a child during labor, they can sometimes cause growths around the larynx (voice box).

Hepatitis

Hepatitis is a disease of the liver caused by a virus. Actually, there are at least three separate types of viral hepatitis, some of which can be transmitted sexually: hepatitis A (infectious hepatitis); hepatitis B (serum hepatitis); and non-A, non-B hepatitis.

How Do You Get It or Give It?
Hepatitis A is often passed by anal intercourse, oral-anal contact, or other types of contact with feces. It can also be passed by contaminated water or certain types of contaminated foods.

Hepatitis B can be passed by mouth-to-mouth contact, genital-to-mouth contact, mouth-to-anus contact, or through intercourse. It can also be passed by puncturing the skin with contaminated instruments, such as needles used for piercing ears or for injecting street drugs such as heroin.

Non-A, non-B hepatitis is usually passed by blood transfusions, but sexual transmission is possible.

Symptoms
The symptoms are flulike at first. They include achiness, headaches, fatigue, fever, loss of appetite, dizziness, and nausea. Other possible symptoms are a yellowing of the skin and the whites of the eyes (jaundice), darkening of the urine, lighter-colored stool, and tenderness in the abdominal area.

When Do the Symptoms First Appear?
They appear two weeks to six months after exposure.

Diagnosis
Blood tests can help to diagnose this disease.

Treatment
Treatment for this disease involves waiting it out. Rest and a healthy diet are essential, along with lots of fluids. Alcoholic beverages should be avoided. Physical and emotional stress

should be minimized. There should be absolutely no sexual contact until blood tests confirm the disease has passed.

Complications
Some forms of hepatitis may result in liver damage, possibly to the point of causing death.

AIDS—Acquired Immune Deficiency Syndrome

AIDS (Acquired Immune Deficiency Syndrome) is a newly discovered STD, first documented in 1981. It is caused by the HTLV-III virus. However, many people who contract the HTLV-III virus don't develop AIDS. The immune system of a person with AIDS doesn't work properly and doesn't protect the body from infections as it is supposed to. Because of this, an AIDS victim is very susceptible to a variety of rare and fatal diseases, including rare forms of cancer and pneumonia. AIDS is particularly frightening because no cure has been found and people with AIDS usually die within two to three years of being diagnosed.

Although the incidence of AIDS is still relatively small as compared to other STDs, it is increasing. Currently, the majority of AIDS victims in the United States are homosexual or bisexual men or intravenous-drug users (both men and women). However, other women, heterosexual men, and even children have been victims of this disease as well. In most cases, the few women who have contracted AIDS were either sexual partners of bisexual men, intravenous-drug users, or had received a blood transfusion. Consequently, the chances for most teenage girls of getting AIDS are still slight at this time.

How Do You Get or Give It?
The seriousness of AIDS has led to some myths and misconceptions about how one gets it. At one extreme some people believe that only homosexuals can get AIDS. At the other end

are people who are so frightened of AIDS that they believe it is possible to get it from just being in the same room with an AIDS victim. Both extreme views are false. It has been documented that AIDS can be transmitted in the following ways:

1. Through both heterosexual and homosexual sexual practices;
2. Through the use of contaminated needles when sharing street drugs;
3. By receiving a transfusion of infected blood;
4. And, possibly, from pregnant mother to unborn child.

AIDS is not passed on by casual, nonintimate contact.

Symptoms
The exact symptoms developed depend upon which infection preys upon the person's weakened immune system. The most characteristic ones include unexplained and persistent weight loss, an unexplained persistent cough, persistent fever, night sweats, swollen lymph glands, and reddish-purple coin-sized skin blotches.

When Do the Symptoms First Appear?
It may take more than a year for any symptoms to appear after AIDS has been contracted. Unfortunately, during this long symptom-free time period, the person may unknowingly pass AIDS on to others.

Diagnosis
Diagnosis is made by the presence of certain otherwise rare infections and by a blood test. A person can now tell whether or not he or she has been exposed to the HTLV-III virus through a widely available blood test. A positive test result does *not* necessarily mean that the person will go on to develop AIDS, however, only that he or she is infected by the virus that *causes* AIDS.

Treatment

No cure for AIDS has been developed so far. Research scientists are still investigating potential ways to treat it and to prevent one from getting the infection.

Prevention

A number of organizations have developed hot lines, newsletters, pamphlets, and workshops on how to reduce the risk of contracting AIDS. Most of this information is aimed at gay men, who are the highest risk group. Appendix A lists some of these resources.

Some Uncommon Diseases

There are a few tropical diseases that are generally uncommon in the United States: granuloma inguinale; lymphogranuloma venereum; and chancroid. They all have genital pimples or sores as the primary early symptoms and are spread by contact with the infected areas (the sores). As with all STDs, early treatment is important. Ignoring the symptoms, even when painless, can result in permanent scarring and tissue destruction in your body. Antibiotics are used in treating these diseases.

14

SEXUAL DIFFERENCES

I am sure that there are times when you worry whether there is something wrong with you or if somehow you are different from your friends. All teenagers do. The truth is *you are different*. You are not exactly the same as anyone else. Just look in a mirror. Do you know anyone who looks just like you? Certainly you may have some features that resemble your parents' or you may look similar to a brother or sister, but when you come right down to it, you are unique.

Sexually, too, you are unique. Your feelings, your beliefs, your thoughts, and your values are unlike anyone else's. Your body looks and responds somewhat differently from that of other girls.

However, being different sexually does not mean that you are weird, abnormal, bad, or immoral. Certainly these are terms that you will hear frequently when people describe varying aspects of a person's sexuality. However, these terms are often misused and abused.

Normal is a statistical term meaning "usual." It is "normal" for most women to put one stocking on each foot and then to put on both shoes, but occasionally someone likes to put on her left stocking and shoe, followed by her right stocking and shoe. Even though this person might be considered "abnormal" because she doesn't do what is usual for most people, it does not mean that she is sick, crazy, or weird. It means she has her own way of doing things. Just because you don't conform to what most people do, doesn't mean there is something wrong with you.

Sometimes words are misused in a different way. When people are uncomfortable about something, they sometimes refer to it as "abnormal," "wrong," "bad," "unhealthy," or use some similar term. For example, it is not uncommon to hear people talk about masturbation as being "abnormal." However, since surveys have shown that more than 80 percent of women masturbate at some time during their lives, that behavior is certainly statistically "normal." What these people mean to say is that they don't approve of masturbation. This certainly is their privilege. However, that has nothing to do with abnormal, normal, right, or wrong. What it shows is their personal beliefs.

The power of other people's opinions can be enormous. Just think of what your reaction would be if suddenly a number of influential people in your life labeled you "abnormal" or "weird" because of the way you laugh. And, every time you laughed, your parents, friends, and grandparents would make fun of you. Chances are after a while you would identify your laugh as strange, and maybe begin to think of yourself as strange. You might even begin to avoid laughing for fear of being ridiculed. It is in this same way that many sexual problems originate.

How Different Are You?

If you want to find out if you are of average height, it certainly is easy enough. Simply compare your height to that of other girls your age. The same goes for weight. Comparing weight and height are simple because there are standard units of measure for height and weight that our society has agreed upon. Everyone can be measured in inches or weighed in pounds.

When it comes to sex, however, there is no standard unit of measurement. We don't measure sex in inches, pounds, degrees, or any other unit of measurement. You can't measure that your sexuality is twenty-four and your friend's is twenty-one, making you more sexual than she. You can't decide if you feel okay sexually by comparing yourself to other people. If you are looking for a yardstick to judge yourself sexually, all you will find is confusion.

The following section includes a discussion of a number of sexual differences. For some women these differences are healthily accepted with comfort or even pride as part of the normal variety with which nature provides us. For others, they are experienced as peculiarities or abnormalities and may be associated with such feelings as discomfort, anxiety, guilt, or shame. If one of these differences does cause you serious emotional upset, suggestions are included to assist you in getting help. In addition, the appendix has more detailed information about getting help with these problems.

Differences in Sexual Orientation: Heterosexuality and Homosexuality

What Is Homosexuality?

Homosexuality is one aspect of sexual differences that gets a great deal of attention among teenagers. Yet, it is one of the least understood. Teenagers often throw around words like "gay," "queer," "homo," "dyke," "butch," and "fag" as a way of teasing, hurting, playing, or emphasizing that someone appears different. However, the way that they use these slang terms for homosexual usually demonstrates their lack of knowledge about this sexual life-style.

A homosexual is a person whose primary sexual interest is with people of his or her own sex. Although the term *homosexual* can apply to both males and females, many females prefer to call themselves **lesbians**. Because the label *homo-*

sexual has become associated with unnecessary feelings of shame and ridicule, many homosexuals of both sexes now prefer the term **gay**, which carries with it feelings of pride and fulfillment. In contrast to homosexuals, those people whose primary sexual interest is in someone of the opposite sex are referred to as heterosexual or "straight."

You probably already knew that homosexuality has something to do with being sexual with someone of the same sex. However, it also applies to more than just sexual behavior. Just as heterosexuals can experience strong emotional and romantic attractions toward people of the opposite sex, homosexuals experience similar romantic and emotional attractions to people of their own sex.

Many adolescents are confused about the distinction between homosexuality and other aspects of sexual differences. Homosexuality does not describe how masculine or feminine a person is. Although there is a stereotype that gay men act or dress in a very feminine way and that lesbians act very tough and masculine, for the most part this is not true. Certainly there are some gays who act or dress flamboyantly, but then again there are many straights whose actions are just as distinctive. Most homosexuals do not look, dress, or talk differently from heterosexuals. In addition, being a homosexual is also not the same as being a **transsexual** or a **transvestite**, both of which are discussed later in this chapter.

People often talk as if homosexuality is an all-or-nothing state; as if you are entirely homosexual or entirely heterosexual. This is misleading. Actually, classifying people as gay or straight is like trying to categorize your friends as short or tall. Some are clearly short and others are clearly tall, but many fit somewhere in between. Some women who are primarily straight engage in homosexual acts, and some lesbians enjoy sexual relationships with men. In addition, there are some people who are referred to as **bisexual**, who can equally enjoy sexual relationships with both males and females. A famous researcher in sexuality, Alfred Kinsey, shocked the public in the early 1950s, when he published his findings that

37 percent of men[1] and 13 percent of women[2] interviewed reported that they had previously had sexual experiences with someone of the same sex.

Attitudes, Myths, and Stereotypes

For many teenagers, homosexuality is a confusing and scary topic. Rarely is homosexuality talked about seriously between girls. When it *is* talked about, it is often in the form of a joke or a negative remark. Consequently, a great deal of misinformation has developed as to what homosexuality is all about.

One common attitude about homosexuality is that it is an indication that a person has some serious psychological problem, or is in some way sick or perverted. However, most psychologists, psychiatrists, and other mental health professionals now agree that homosexuality is not a mental disorder. Being gay does not mean that someone is a sick or bad person. Homosexuals are simply people who have different sexual preferences than heterosexuals.

What often complicates a gay person's adjustment is the anticipation of being treated with condemnation. A lesbian may lead a secret life of fear and anxiety while trying to conceal her sexual orientation from friends, family, employers, and co-workers. Also, because gay people have learned the same destructive stereotypes about homosexuality as the rest of society, they often experience sadness and guilt about their own sexual feelings. In fact, since our society has not yet learned to accept homosexuals as equals, those who openly identify themselves as gay often do face forms of discrimination. Like any minority struggling for acceptance in a rejecting society, many gays do experience some degree of additional stress.

One particularly destructive myth about homosexuals is that they are dangerous or will try to seduce you if you are the same sex. Just by listening to the news or reading a newspaper, you hear about sex crimes against both children and adults. However, there is no indication that homosexuals are any more likely to commit these crimes than are heterosexuals. In fact, research indicates that most child molesters are heterosexual males.[3] Unfortunately, we live in a society where sex crimes have increased over the past few years. It is a good idea for all children and teenagers to stay away from any situation that would place them alone with any stranger or even a familiar person who might attempt to pressure them into any sexual activity—homosexual or heterosexual.

"Am I Gay?"

There are no easy answers for the teenager who is struggling with the question of whether she or he is gay. Some people become confident of their sexual preference at an early age, while for others discovery comes only after carefully sifting through many feelings and experiences.

Some of the things that you might believe are proof that you are lesbian really are not. For example, even if you are not sexually involved with boys or you do not enjoy sex, this does not necessarily mean that you are a lesbian. For every person, interest in sex develops at a different pace. Many girls delay their dating contact with boys for various reasons. They may be shy, scared to date, or simply more interested in other aspects of their lives. Also, it is not unusual for a girl to find sexual involvement with a boy dull or even somewhat distasteful.

It is also untrue that any female who engages in sexual activity with another female, or even fantasizes about it, is a lesbian. Many girls engage in sex play with other girls during their growing years. This kind of experimentation is common among children and adolescents. However, because of fear and lack of understanding, for many adolescents this type of experience leads to unnecessary guilt and self-doubt. Likewise, having fantasies or dreams about homosexual experiences will often cause even people who are confident about their heterosexuality to question their sexual preference. Interestingly, studies have found that it is common for straights to have sexual fantasies about people of their own sex, and that gays also have fantasies about the opposite sex.[4]

Still, your sexual fantasies and your feelings about sexual experimentation can provide clues to your sexual orientation. As they mature, some girls find that they prefer sexual experiences with other girls more than being with boys and find that all their crushes are on females rather than males. As explained in *A Way of Love, A Way of Life*, an excellent book for adolescents about homosexuality, "If most of a person's pleasurable sexual fantasies center on imagining sex with another of the same gender, this *may* be an indication of being gay."[5] In any case, if you just give yourself time and allow yourself to be honest about your emotions and feelings of attraction, your orientation will eventually become clear.

Dealing with Fears and Feelings About Homosexuality

Some experts estimate that as many as one in ten people are homosexual. This means that it is very likely that you have some gay friends or relatives, even though you may not be aware of their sexual orientation. Understanding what it means to be gay can help you to be a good friend to a confused acquaintance, as well as help you deal with any of your own fears and misconceptions about homosexuality.

Gay teenagers are often isolated by their fears, especially the anticipation that if they reveal their homosexual feelings they will be ridiculed. Whereas most teenagers turn to family and friends for support when they face serious problems, those with concerns about homosexuality frequently conceal their fears and confusion, either because they fear hurting those closest to them, or because they fear being rejected.

If you think about all the love stories in literature, movies, or TV, you will realize that there are few about gay relationships. Consequently, there is little to help gay and lesbian teenagers understand what they are going through, emotionally or sexually. Likewise, most gay adolescents do not know where to turn for information or where to go to meet other gays. All of these factors can lead to a feeling of being very different or even bad.

Most teenagers have occasional concerns about whether or not they have homosexual feelings. Yet, after they mature, most realize that their concerns were merely part of the confusion associated with growing up. Others realize that they are gay and go on to lead fulfilling lives that include their sexual orientation. On the other hand, some teenagers and adults go through tremendous fears about whether or not they are gay. These worries can be equally upsetting to those who are gay and to those who are not. If this is a serious concern to you, *A Way of Love, A Way of Life* suggests three steps that can be helpful in resolving your confusion and fears.[6] First, take time to get a handle on your feelings. You don't have to decide what to do all at once. Second, get information. There are many excellent books written about homosexuality, some of which are listed in appendix A. Third, find someone with whom you can talk openly. These same three steps can also be helpful in sorting out your emotions if you find out that a close friend is gay.

Unfortunately, many parents, and even many counselors and psychologists, are not very comfortable in discussing homosexuality. If you do find someone to talk with, it is important that it is someone who is willing to explore both your homosexual and your heterosexual feelings. If you find that the person with whom you are sharing your feelings seems to be strongly pushing you in one direction or another, or, if you feel that she or he avoids the topic, you probably need to find someone else to talk with. Choose someone who you feel can be open and honest with you and who is not biased in one way or the other.

There are a number of gay organizations, switchboards, and hotlines usually listed in the yellow pages of your phone book, as well as in the appendix of this book. These can be excellent sources of information, but again, follow the same cautions mentioned above. If you are looking to them for counseling in order to sort out a confused sexual identity, make sure your counselor is unbiased.

Coming Out

"Coming out" is the phrase used to describe the process of publicly acknowledging one's homosexuality. For many gay and lesbian adults the experience ultimately relieves the strain of leading a double life. It lets them have more honest relationships and feel better about themselves. For an adolescent, coming out can be a more complicated decision. Both hiding your feelings and being open can be very painful.

Certainly honesty and openness make for better relationships in most cases. However, the negative attitudes people have been taught about homosexuality mean that being yourself carries real risks. Some sound advice from *A Way of Life, A Way of Love* follows: "If you are thinking of telling your parents, it might be wise to put yourself in their shoes and imagine some of the fears and concerns that they might have. Fear, guilt, shame, and a sense of failure are common emotions which parents first feel when they learn of their child's homosexuality. They often ask themselves where they went wrong. They fear what all this might mean for your life and future happiness. They may worry about what other family members or friends may think. Those who are rigidly traditional may have a value system which insists that your homosexuality be condemned unquestioningly."[7] Friends you tell may worry that they will get labeled as gay if they remain your friend. They might also worry about what your intentions toward them are.

The sad reality is that no one can give any gay or lesbian teenager the right answer as to whether to be open. Many gay teenagers have found parents and friends to be supportive and loving. Others have had their worst fears realized: Parents have disowned them; a trusted friend has spread their secret all over school, where they were teased and avoided. Each person must weigh the possible risks and potential gains after evaluating her or his own family, friends, and school. The decision doesn't need to be all or none. Some close, trusted, or more accepting people can be confided in, while others cannot be. Many gays find it easier to come out publicly after they feel stronger and more comfortable themselves about their orientation. They are then less vulnerable to the negative reactions of others and know where to get support. Furthermore, even though some people's initial reaction to a friend's or relative's gayness might be to pull away or criticize, with time many come to accept it and are able to build more intimacy.

Although facing issues of homosexuality is often confusing and frightening, eventually it can feel very rewarding. Certainly, the process is not impossible. Some wise reassurance is also offered in *A Way of Love, A Way of Life*: "Gays have a special task in coming to terms with their sexual orientation, but the process is similar to what all adolescents go through. Coming out means learning to love yourself as you are, not as others would wish or expect you to be."[8]

Transsexuality

A condition that many people confuse with homosexuality is transsexuality. Transsexuals are people who feel as if they are trapped inside a body of the wrong sex. Unlike a lesbian, who identifies herself as being female but prefers sex with other females, a female transsexual actually feels as if she is a male trapped inside the body of a female. Transsexuals can now be treated with a combination of surgery, hormones, and psychological counseling, so that they can appear and function as a member of the opposite sex.

Since very few professionals know much about dealing with transsexuals, it may be difficult to find a professional who can competently treat this problem. If you do have concerns about transsexuality, call or write the Janus Information Facility (see appendix A). They can refer you to a qualified professional.

Transvestism

Transvestism is also often mistaken for homosexuality. Transvestites, or **cross-dressers** (as they are sometimes called), are people who feel some sexual satisfaction from dressing as someone of the opposite sex. Cross-dressers do not feel as though they are actually members of the opposite sex, as do transsexuals, and most are not homosexuals. An overwhelmingly large percentage of cross-dressers are male.

Transvestism also should not be confused with the typical experimentation that children often go through in dressing up in parents' clothes, or with the fun of dressing up as the opposite sex for a costume party. If you have concerns about transvestism, a psychologist or other counselor may be helpful.

Differences in Sexual Response

Just as there are some people who desire more or less food than others, there are people with greater or lesser sexual appetites. At one extreme, some teenagers seem almost preoccupied with sex, while at the other extreme, some have little or no interest in sex. Actually, since your sexual cravings are determined by a host of physical and environmental factors, you may have little conscious control over how sexual you feel. You are, in a sense, a victim of your mind and body.

Differences in Sexual Desire

Many girls, faced with a flood of hormones within their bodies along with the resulting rapid maturation, are suddenly confronted with a host of very alien sexual feelings. For some girls this is an exciting new experience, while others find themselves trapped with feelings they do not feel comfortable expressing or even having. Like being in any other trap, feeling all alone with these intense sexual feelings can be frustrating and scary.

On the other hand, many young women who do have a somewhat lower sex drive, or those who compare themselves to the inflated exaggerations of their friends or the media, may experience fears that they are abnormally undersexed. In reality, there is a tremendous range of sexual feelings that are considered normal in both women and men. There are even differences that certain women experience during the varying phases of their menstrual cycles. Some find that they feel very sexual at certain points every month and relatively uninterested in sex during other phases of their cycles. In addition, sexual feelings develop at varying ages in different girls, so it is highly unlikely that you and your girlfriends would begin to experience these feelings at precisely the same age.

Another factor that tragically affects many girls is that of sexual trauma. Many victims of rape, incest, or any type of sexual abuse (see chapter 17) find their adolescent and adult sexual desire affected in one way or another. Some turn off their sexuality, others seek sex without intimacy, and some develop other kinds of sexual problems.

Sexual desire also seems to vary considerably between males and females during different stages of the life cycle. Many teenage boys seem to be extremely preoccupied with sex, whereas most teenage girls are interested, but not quite so desperately. It has been speculated that boys' higher interest in sex is due to a higher level of male hormones in their bodies. It may also be related to the fact that girls are often taught more self-restraint regarding sex. In any case, these differences seem to even out as life goes on, with women becoming more comfortable about expressing their sexuality as they get older, while the male sex drive seems to diminish somewhat.

Differences in Sexual Arousal

Simply put, some women just do not seem to get aroused quite as easily or to the same intense degree as do other women.

On both an emotional and a physical level, sexual excitement may be experienced quite differently from one woman to another.

In a sense, men carry around a "yardstick" to measure how sexually aroused they are. Of course, it is an exaggeration to call the male penis a measuring stick, because many other factors do affect erections besides arousal. However, the fact remains that for men, the hardness of the penis is often a visible gauge of their excitement level. Often difficulties during this phase of sexuality leave males with a feeling that they are unable to have a fulfilling sexual experience with a woman.

For women, variations in arousal appear to be experienced somewhat differently from the way they are in men. In women, these arousal differences take the form of varying levels of emotional excitement or, in some cases, a decrease in the level of vaginal lubrication. In its resting state, the vagina is not a highly lubricated organ. However, when a woman becomes aroused, the vagina will usually lubricate itself to prepare for the penis to be inserted. Just as there are variations in all other phases of the sexual experience, there seem to be significant differences in lubrication. Some find themselves lubricating easily or in great quantity, while others find little lubrication. Difficulty in lubrication can often be due to insufficient foreplay or inadequate stimulation. Young males tend to become aroused more quickly than young females, and often couples begin to have intercourse when only the male is ready. If the couple would simply exercise a little patience in giving the female sufficient time to become fully aroused, lubrication would usually follow. For those who find that this is not the answer, artificial lubricants such as Lubrin are available at most pharmacies.

Differences in Orgasm

One of the most obvious sexual differences that concerns young women is that some experience orgasm and some don't. Although inability to reach orgasm is listed in chapter 15 as a sexual problem, for most teenage girls this is not quite the case. It is quite common for sexually active teenage girls not to experience orgasm at all, or at least with little consistency. Aaron Hass in his survey of teenagers found that among those girls who reported having had sexual intercourse, 27 percent said they had never experienced an orgasm, and only 6 percent reported having an orgasm every time. The other 67 percent reported having occasional orgasms.

Even more reflective of the differences that young women experience in orgasm are the results of another survey question that Hass posed to all of the young women whether they had ever had intercourse or not. All of the girls were asked simply, "Have you ever had an orgasm?" Interestingly, 42 percent indicated that they had, 25 percent said they had not, and *33 percent indicated that they were not sure.* Hass speculates that there are two reasons for this lack of awareness. First, girls do not have the obvious indicator of ejaculation that boys do, and second, girls often experience sexual conflicts that may "inhibit their awareness." In addition, he notes that many of the young women "had no idea what it was supposed to feel like."[9]

Perhaps another reason that girls have so much difficulty in understanding whether or not they have had an orgasm is because the emotional and physical reactions of orgasm vary tremendously from one female to another, particularly during their early sexual experiences. Some women experience their orgasms as slight or barely noticeable genital reactions, while others experience them as fantastically intense reactions of the entire body. Many women have orgasms of different intensity depending on their mood, partner, time during their menstrual cycle, and various other factors.

One very common factor that seems to affect the intensity and regularity of orgasms is the source of the sexual stimulation. Orgasms that occur as a result of masturbation or direct petting of the genitals tend to be more intense and to occur with more consistency than those resulting from intercourse. Again, however, this varies from one female to another. The one thing that you can be certain of is that your pattern of having orgasms will not be identical to those of anyone else.

Women also differ from males as to how easily or frequently they have orgasms. Young teenage men almost always have orgasms. However, orgasms are less common for adolescent girls. In many instances, a woman will experience her first orgasm as an adult, after she becomes more comfortable with her own sexuality and when she feels trust toward her partner.

When Sexual Differences Become Problems

If you find that the frustrations or fear caused by feeling sexually different become overwhelming, sharing your feelings with a parent or an adult you trust can make a big difference. In most cases, just a little factual information may be enough to set your mind at ease. If sharing these feelings doesn't relieve your anxiety or if you have no one with whom you feel comfortable talking, then it may be helpful to seek counseling. A psychologist or counselor who works with adolescents, or a counselor from one of the agencies listed in appendix A, can be of great help.

15

SEXUAL PROBLEMS

No one is perfect. That's just the way it is. Very likely, at some point in your life you will encounter a sexual problem. It may last for only a short period of time, or it may plague you throughout many of your sexual experiences. It may occur only with a single partner, or it may occur with more than one partner. However, the fact is that most people eventually experience some sexual difficulties. It has been estimated that at least 50 percent of married couples experience a sexual problem severe enough to cause serious marital difficulties.[1]

If as you read through this chapter you do suspect that you suffer from any of the problems listed, be sure to finish reading this chapter and then to read through chapter 14 on sexual differences, if you have not already done so. Many of the things that people think of as sexual problems are actually normal, ordinary differences in sexuality. Also, before you panic and conclude that you have a serious problem with sex, take into account your age and experience. What you may be labeling as a dysfunction may merely be inexperience and nervousness. Mixed feelings about having sex can easily interfere with sexual response. If you still feel that a problem does exist, learning more about sexual response through reading or talking to a parent or another trusted adult is often all that is needed. Another option would be to talk to your gynecologist, especially if you are having one of the types of problems that sometimes has medical roots, such as vaginismus. Finally, if none of these suggestions brings a solution to your problem, you can seek out the advice of a certified sex therapist.

For many years it was believed that most sexual difficulties were the result of very deep emotional problems. Consequently, the only treatment available for the sexually dysfunctional person was to undergo years of psychotherapy, often with poor results. Luckily, however, thanks to the pioneering work of Dr. William Masters and Virginia Johnson,[2] many successful treatment programs have been developed for the various types of sexual dysfunctions. Today there are thousands of trained sex therapists throughout the nation with the knowledge and expertise necessary to assist people experiencing problems. For information about licensed, certified sex therapists in your area, write to AASECT (American Association of Sex Educators, Counselors, and Therapists). You will find the full address in appendix A.

Avoiding Sexual Problems

As you read through the remainder of this chapter you will find that there are numerous potential causes of a variety of sexual dysfunctions. Some of the more common reasons include the following:

1. Having sex when you really don't want to.
2. Feeling guilty about having sex.
3. Believing the various myths about sexuality, which lead to exaggerated expectations or unnecessary fears.
4. Fears about performing well.
5. Not receiving adequate stimulation.

6. Not communicating your needs adequately to your partner and/or his not communicating his needs to you.

7. Holding in anger or resentment toward your partner.

8. Medical reasons.

9. Emotional conflicts about sexuality due to sexual trauma (rape, molestation, etc.).

Consequently, by following a few suggestions you can avoid most of these common pitfalls and significantly reduce the chances that you will encounter future sexual problems.

1. Go at your own pace sexually. Be only as sexual as *you* want to be. Do not let yourself be pressured into doing something that is not of your own choosing.

2. Accumulate as much factual information about sex as you can, so you will not be as vulnerable to believing false information.

3. Don't expect to live up to the exaggerated images of sexuality painted by the media.

4. Learn how to communicate clearly to your partner. It is important that both of you are able to share your feelings in order to maintain closeness in the relationship. Also, it is important for both of you to clearly indicate what you need from each other, so that neither of you has to guess what is on the other person's mind.

5. If you have any suspicions that you might have a medical problem, check it out with a physician.

In understanding the nature of sexual difficulties, it is important to realize that pointing fingers at each other as to which partner has a sexual problem, or which one caused the problem, is unnecessary. As the following descriptions of the most common sexual dysfunctions indicate, not only do both partners usually share the uncomfortable effects of most sexual problems, but they both often must share the responsibility for causing the problem.

Problems of Desire

As mentioned in chapter 14 about sexual differences, sex drive varies tremendously among people. Consequently, what each of us defines as "too little" sex drive is a matter of personal opinion. For many years, women with a reduced sex drive were labeled "frigid," while men with lower drives were not. In many situations, women were called frigid because their sexual partners believed their lack of sexual drive to be an indication that they were cold. However, in other cases, it was used as a manipulation to make women feel that they had a problem if they were not responsive whenever their partner wanted them to be sexual. If you are not as sexual in your feelings as your partner, this does not necessarily mean that *you* have a problem. Rather it may be an indication that the *relationship* has a problem.

It is true that physical causes such as hormone imbalance or fatigue can lead to a lowered sexual drive. Often, however, the roots of the problem lie either within the relationship or with the pressured or conflicted feelings of one of the partners. If you feel a lack of sexual desire, the worst thing to do is to force yourself to have sex anyway. That will practically guarantee a bad sexual experience and will likely lead to even less desire the next time.

Problems of Arousal

Lack of Arousal or Lubrication

If you do experience a *consistent* lack of arousal or lubrication in a sexual relationship, it is an indication that a problem does exist. However, it is not necessarily an indication that *you* are the dysfunctional partner. Just because you and your partner are sexually motivated does not guarantee that your body will become aroused as quickly as his does, or even that it will respond at all. Often the cause of this problem is simply a lack of clear communication between the two partners as to what their sexual needs are. For instance, young women often prefer prolonged petting and kissing, while their partners may be more interested in getting to intercourse quickly. If poor communication is the issue, then this problem may be resolved by each making their needs more clearly understood (see chapter 11).

Another common block to sexual arousal is tension. This tension may be related to any of a number of feelings: suppressed anger in the relationship, nervousness brought about by the inexperience of one or both partners, sexual guilt (particularly of a religious nature), or fear generated by previous sexual experiences that were physically or emotionally painful. Rarely is this a physical disorder in women, although some medications and illnesses seem to lead to reduced arousal.

Some women seem to accept the idea that it is their lot in life not to experience any sexual arousal and they believe that it is normal for women just to put up with sex in order to please their partners. However, women too have a tremendous potential to find sexual pleasure. There is no reason for women not to enjoy their sexuality just as much as men.

Problems of Erection (Impotence)

Problems of erection, still frequently called **impotence**, usually refer to any difficulties a male has in having an erection sufficient to complete intercourse. Although almost all men will face occasional difficulties in having or maintaining an erection, some men experience these failures throughout almost all of their sexual relations. For these men, impotence can lead to serious psychological problems if left untreated.

Likewise, impotence can lead to great frustration for the female partners. Often, when faced with their boyfriends' or husbands' constant inability to have or maintain an erection, women are left confused and hurt. Many blame themselves for not being "sexy" enough or fear that their partners no longer love them. A woman may find herself in a no-win situation. If she shows any frustration or anger, her partner becomes even more anxious and has even more difficulty obtaining an erection. If she doesn't express her feelings, her resentment grows and the relationship deteriorates. In addition, partners of impotent men often become very focused on trying to "work" at giving their partners an erection. The unfortunate result of this "work" is to decrease their own sexual enjoyment and to cause the male to become even more anxious as he feels pressured to perform.

Causes of erectile problems may be medical, psychological, or a combination of the two. When the cause is psychological, impotence can be reversed about 70 percent of the time. When the cause is medical, the possibility of reversal depends on the nature of the physical disorder. Two of the most common and most easily reversed physical causes of impotence are the side effects of medications and excessive use of alcohol.

If other means of treating a male's erectile problem are unsuccessful, the problem can now be remedied surgically by implanting a device called a **prosthesis** inside the penis. This device inflates the penis (in a way similar to blowing up a long balloon), using a tiny pump.

Problems of Orgasm

Not Reaching Orgasm

As was mentioned in the chapter on sexual differences, women experience considerably more variability than men do in their ease and consistency at reaching orgasm. Consequently, whereas not reaching orgasm is a fairly uncommon experience for young men, it is not as unusual for women, especially young women. One of the primary reasons that women experience difficulty in this area is that they feel pressured either by their own feelings of inadequacy or those of their partner, and falsely believe that without orgasm they cannot enjoy sex.

Certainly, women enjoy the orgasmic experience and prefer to have the same complete satisfaction and release that men do. However, many women do enjoy sex tremendously even when they do not reach orgasm. There is no way to force yourself to achieve orgasm. The harder you "work" toward that, the more pressure you will experience, resulting in *less* arousal. Orgasm is a *reflex* that occurs when you reach a certain level of excitement. If you bring down that level by pressuring yourself, orgasm will be impossible.

Many times teenage girls do not receive the stimulation necessary for orgasm to occur. This problem is often related to the male ejaculating too quickly or failure of the couple to engage in sufficient petting of the genitals either before or after intercourse. Another frequent cause of this problem among teens is the pressure they put on themselves to perform up to expectations, either their own or those of their partner. These problems can be reduced in two ways: First, by knowing what you want (including when you want to be with a partner and when you don't); and second, by taking more time for foreplay and not rushing things along too quickly.

Again, rarely is this problem physical in nature. Most women who have difficulty reaching orgasm do so because of the self-imposed pressures previously mentioned. Other causes for this dysfunction include guilt, fear of losing control of their feelings, anger with their partner, and poor communication as to sexual needs.

Treatment for this problem can be very successful. However, all of the treatment programs seem to have one thing in common. That is that you need to be familiar with your own body. Masturbation is the easiest way for most women to learn to have orgasms. Consequently, before seeking any treatment, reread chapter 5, which deals with familiarizing yourself with the feelings of your body, and again do the exercises suggested. One type of treatment that has been very successful is the use of special therapy groups that deal specifically with women's orgasmic problems. These groups, however, can be difficult to locate. More traditional, couple-oriented sex therapy can also be a very successful form of treatment.

Premature Ejaculation

When a male and a female engage in sex it is unusual for both partners to reach orgasm at the same time. Usually, young males will tend to "come" somewhat before the female. With some males, however, this point of ejaculation is reached either before or shortly after entering the vagina, not allowing the sexual encounter enough time to develop into a satisfying event for both partners. If this occurs on a fairly consistent basis, the couple is likely to be having problems with **premature ejaculation**.

Ironically, although premature ejaculation is usually listed as a male sexual problem, it is often the female who is the most frustrated by this disorder. Sometimes males, particularly younger males, are able to become aroused again shortly after ejaculating, and are then able to sustain a mutually satisfying sexual encounter. However, the ability for a male to have multiple sexual encounters usually diminishes with age, often leaving the female partner in a state of sexual frustration. Premature ejaculation is almost never due to a physical problem. Rather, it is usually a learned pattern, often associated with anxiety the male has about the quality of his sexual performance or is due to his failure to learn to recognize the sensations in his body that could allow him to have some control over his orgasms.

It should be noted that it is not uncommon for sexual experiences with a new partner to result in quick ejaculations. Therefore, this is usually only considered to be a sexual problem if these rapid ejaculations continue even after the relationship has continued for a while.

Premature ejaculation can often cause serious problems for a sexual relationship. However, it can be reversed almost 100 percent of the time with the help of a qualified sex therapist.

On the other hand, home remedies, such as special creams or the use of condoms to lessen the amount of sensation, or methods by which the male distracts himself, often have little success. Usually these remedies decrease the enjoyment of the sexual experience and sometimes lead to problems that are even more difficult to treat.

Vaginismus

Vaginismus is an involuntary spasm of the muscles that surround the vaginal opening. During these spasms the vagina feels as if it has locked tight, and no penetration is possible. Sometimes the spasms only occur with attempts at intercourse, but in some women the spasms may be so severe as to not even allow for a vaginal exam by a physician.

This problem usually develops when the woman associates intercourse with an experience that is, physically or psychologically, extremely painful. With some women it may result from sexual trauma, such as rape or incest. Others experience vaginismus as a result of sexual experiences with an overly aggressive partner or from continuously having intercourse either without sufficient lubrication or while they had a vaginal infection. On occasion, vaginismus can even stem from severe anxiety caused by guilt or fear of pregnancy.

It is important that both the woman with vaginismus and her partner recognize that these muscle spasms are an involuntary reflex, and that trying to force intercourse when the muscles are "locked" will only make the situation worse. Sometimes, in less severe cases, after the woman relaxes, a mutually satisfying sexual encounter is possible.

Treatment for vaginismus is almost always successful if both partners are cooperative, although, in cases of severe emotional trauma, psychotherapy may be necessary in addition to the treatment by a sex therapist.

Painful Intercourse

Dyspareunia is the technical name that doctors use to refer to painful intercourse, but not every pain is dyspareunia. It is not uncommon, on occasion, for a woman to get into an awkward position or to experience some vaginal irritation during intercourse. Dyspareunia exists only when this pain becomes persistent enough that it interferes with the frequency or the consistent enjoyment of intercourse.

It is important that any consistent pain during intercourse be checked out for at least two reasons: First, in some instances, the pain may be caused by serious physical problems; and second, painful intercourse can lead to vaginismus (see above).

Not Satisfying Your Partner

Many sexual partners worry far too much about whether they are satisfying their partners. Although it certainly makes sense that partners try to please each other, being overly concerned may cause serious performance fears and interfere with enjoyment. If your partner is not feeling sexually satisfied, it is a shared responsibility. First of all, it is his responsibility to share what his needs are. Secondly, it is *your* responsibility to listen to him. That does not mean that you need to do everything he requests. It simply means that you should try to understand what he is telling you. At the same time, you should be sharing your needs with him, and he should listen to you. It is much easier for couples to enjoy each other when they are aware of each other's preferences and desires.

Actually, concentrating too intently on satisfying your partner's needs can be a very unsuccessful way of approaching a sexual encounter. Not only does it put pressure on your partner (as if he is on stage), but it may also prevent you from expressing your own sexual preferences.

16

DEALING WITH AN UNPLANNED PREGNANCY

Whether or not you ever face an unwanted pregnancy, this is an important chapter. Like the alarm on your clock that rings in the morning, this chapter is here to get your attention. Its message is "Wake up! Sex is not a game!" Sex may be fun and it may be exciting; it may make you feel like an adult, but it is definitely not a game. This chapter underscores the fact that whenever you are sexually active with a male, the stakes are very, very high. The risk of pregnancy is an extremely serious responsibility that should not be taken lightly. *Before* you become sexually involved, consider the possible consequences of an "accidental" pregnancy. That way you will be more likely to take responsible actions to prevent it from occurring.

Actually, most "accidental" pregnancies are not accidental at all. Eight out of ten teenagers who have an unwanted pregnancy were not using any form of contraception when they became pregnant.[1] As the following experiences of two young girls illustrate, most teenage pregnancies occur because the couple lacks adequate knowledge about birth control, because they feel that pregnancy is something that happens to "other people," or because they avoid talking about what they are going to do to prevent it. One teenage girl said,

> I never thought about contraception, mainly because I was really never informed about it. The fact that I could get pregnant did not even cross my mind. About a month later I found out I was pregnant. I didn't know what to do; I was afraid to tell anyone. I never thought anything so awful could happen to me. I was eighteen years old and in my senior year of high school; the last thing I wanted was a newborn baby. After I told my boyfriend I was pregnant, we decided the best thing for me to do was to get an abortion. During this time our relationship started to fall apart. I blamed him for getting me pregnant and he blamed me for not using contraception. My whole life was affected; I experienced so much tension and had so many mixed feelings that I could not even think straight. After it was all over I was relieved, but had a lot of guilty feelings. I kept saying to myself, "if I only would have used contraception, this never would have happened to me."

Another teenager said,

> I remember waking up suddenly. It was really early—maybe four A.M.—and the realization that I hadn't had my period for at least seven weeks hit me like a ton of bricks. The thought came from nowhere. I hadn't been worried. In fact, I had never counted the days between my periods. It was a sudden, jolting awareness. I was sure—positive—that I was pregnant.
>
> I was seventeen. My boyfriend and I had been quite serious for over a year. Our lovemaking was warm and satisfying. We were equally committed. We didn't use any method of birth control. Somehow, I was afraid that using contraceptives would ruin the spontaneity of our sex life. So we learned—the hard way—that *every time you make love without effective birth control methods, you are making the decision to get pregnant.*

Pregnancy is not something that happens only to other people. It can very well happen to you. No matter which method of birth control you choose, there is some risk of getting pregnant. As you remember from chapter 12 on contraception, even teenagers who use the best available contraceptive methods sometimes get pregnant—usually because they incorrectly or inconsistently use the method. However, *if you use no contraception at all, the chances of becoming pregnant are about nine out of ten over a one-year period.*[2]

Even if you are lucky enough never to have to face the pain and anxiety of dealing with an accidental pregnancy yourself, it is likely that you will know a number of girls and boys who will do so as you go through your high school years. From recent statistics, it is estimated that more than 1 million teenage girls in this country will become pregnant this year.[3] By reading this chapter, you will better understand the confusion and pain that these teenagers experience, and, in addition, you may even prevent yourself from getting into a similar predicament.

Teenagers tend to think of pregnancy as a girl's problem, and certainly in most cases it is the girl who faces the most serious physical and emotional risks from a pregnancy. However, boys also face serious consequences, emotional and legal, that can affect them for the rest of their lives. For example, if you have a child, your partner is legally its father. This means that a court of law can require him to contribute to the support of the child. It is best if you and your male partner talk about the possibility of a pregnancy and if each of you shares your feelings about how you would prefer to handle that unwanted event *before* it actually happens. The turmoil you will feel if you do become pregnant will be great enough without adding any unnecessary conflicts about what to do or how much responsibility the young man should assume.

"Am I Pregnant?"

As you learned in chapter 8, the first sign that a girl is pregnant is when she misses her regular period or when she has one that is much shorter or lighter than what is normal for her. Because this is such a key indicator, it is important that you keep an accurate chart that shows the first and last day of each period. This may someday help you to figure out whether or not you are pregnant. Other, somewhat later, signs are tenderness in the breasts, frequent urination, a feeling of nausea (especially in the morning), and unusual tiredness. However, even if you find that you have missed a period and have some or all of the other symptoms, it is possible that you are not pregnant. Because periods during adolescence tend to be so irregular and because of all the physical and psychological factors that can delay the beginning of a period, pregnancy scares among teenagers are fairly common.

The last words that any teenage girl wants to hear are: "You're pregnant." Yet, despite how afraid you might be, or how much you may want to avoid knowing, it is terribly important for you to confirm as soon as possible whether or not you are pregnant. First, you'll need time to consider all of your choices in order to make the decisions that are best for you. Second, an early decision may be critical in affecting the outcome of your pregnancy. If you ultimately make the decision to continue the pregnancy, good nutrition and medical care early in the pregnancy will be essential to your health as well as the baby's. If you eventually decide to abort the pregnancy, this can be done much more safely and easily during the early months.

If your period is more than two weeks late and you have had sexual relations, you should immediately have a laboratory test performed either by a private physician or by an agency such as Planned Parenthood. This is the only way you can be certain. Do-it-yourself pregnancy tests currently available at most drugstores tend not to be sufficiently reliable with teenagers. These home tests must be used *exactly* as directed. This includes storing them in a refrigerator. Since teenagers often vary the directions somewhat for fear that their parents will find the test, these test results can get fouled up.

If you have the initial test done by an agency or physician and the results do suggest that you are not pregnant, you will still need to return for follow-up testing until your period starts. Since the test works by measuring the amount of a certain hormone (HCG) produced in the body during a pregnancy, a negative test result may merely mean that it is too early in the pregnancy for this hormone to be detected. Ask the person who gives you the test when you should come back to be rechecked.

If You Are Pregnant

If you do find out that you are pregnant, it is likely that you will experience a period of intense emotions. Such emotions as fear, sadness, confusion, anger, anxiety, and aloneness may overwhelm you. These emotions are very normal at a time when you face so many critical decisions. The following is a discussion of some of the more important decisions that will have to be made.

Decision 1: Should I Tell My Partner?
One of the first things you must decide is how involved in the decision-making process you want your partner to become. You can either include him in the process or you can assume all of the responsibility yourself. It did, in fact, take both of you to create a pregnancy, so half of the responsibility is really his. Ideally, he could provide emotional support and help you with practical matters, such as accompanying you to counseling and medical offices, and by helping you pay for needed services. However, you must decide whether his input will actually be helpful and supportive to you. Ultimately, it is you who has the power to decide what the fate will be of the embryo

in your body. If you choose not to tell the father, or if he doesn't offer you any support, it is still important that you get that support from somewhere.

Decision 2: How Long Can I Postpone My Decision?

When it comes to making critical decisions, many people seem either to make an instant decision so they can remove the problem from their mind, or to postpone the decision in the hope that the problem will disappear. With an unplanned pregnancy, both of these are poor ways of handling the problem.

There are too many important considerations with an unplanned pregnancy for you to make an instant decision. First, consider all of the facts and feelings and look carefully at each of the choices. Having considered ahead of time what you would do if faced with this situation is a real advantage.

This is also not a problem that will go away all by itself. With a pregnancy, the decisions don't become any easier if you put them off. As a matter of fact, some of your choices, such as abortion (which will be discussed later in this chapter), become riskier and sometimes impossible later in the pregnancy.

Take enough time to look carefully at all of the choices, but do not avoid making the necessary decisions.

Decision 3: Where Can I Go for Guidance?

Another serious consideration for you is whether you want outside guidance in looking at all the complicated aspects of this problem. Serious consideration should be given to sharing the problem with your parents or with a trained counselor.

Since everyone's situation is different, it is impossible to say whether or not you should include your parents in the discussions about resolving an unplanned pregnancy. This is a decision that you will have to make, based upon your own knowledge about your parents. If you choose to terminate the pregnancy with an abortion, this can often be done without your parents' knowledge and consent. However, you may be depriving yourself of some reassuring support during a very rough time.

Whether or not you decide to include your parents, a trained professional counselor can still help you evaluate all of the complicated choices. If you have some doubts about telling your parents or partner, a counselor can assist you in weighing all the advantages and disadvantages.

You really have nothing to lose by going to a professional counselor, and you may have a great deal to gain. If you feel that your counselor is overly biased toward one choice, go to another counselor instead. You are still the one who makes the final decision, not the counselor. Some of the agencies listed in the appendix (such as Planned Parenthood) can provide you with such counseling or can refer you to a qualified counselor.

Decision 4: What Do I Do About the Pregnancy?
This is a very complicated decision. Basically, there are three choices to consider. One is for the pregnancy to be ended by means of an abortion. A second possibility is that after the child is born, one or both of the parents can raise the child. Marriage is often a consideration that goes with this second choice. The third choice is for the pregnancy to continue and, after the birth, the child is given up for adoption or to foster care. As the following subsections of this chapter indicate, all of these choices involve some very complicated decisions. There are no easy answers.

Considering an Abortion

For most girls the thought of going through an **abortion** is extremely frightening. This is especially true if their parents do not know about the pregnancy. Frequently, they will experience fears of dying, concerns about never again being able to have children, fears of killing an unborn child, or feelings of guilt brought on by religious beliefs. Making the decision to go through an abortion can be extremely upsetting.

In reality, an abortion done during the first three months of pregnancy by a trained and licensed professional is a very safe procedure. In fact, it involves less physical risk than a pregnancy does.[4] The actual medical procedure takes only a few minutes, although the whole process generally takes from three to four hours when admission, counseling, medical testing, and waiting in the recovery room are included. During these first three months of pregnancy, the most popular form of abortion is the **vacuum aspiration**, or suction, method. In this method, a small tube is inserted through the cervix, and the contents of the uterus are pumped out. This procedure can usually be perfomed with only local anesthetic in a clinic or a doctor's office.

Abortions performed after the first three months become more complicated and require more time under medical care. The procedure used in middle pregnancies, during the fourth and fifth months, is referred to as a **D & E (dilation and evacuation)**. Because the fetus has grown, a larger suction tube and other instruments are needed to completely remove the contents of the uterus. General anesthesia and hospitalization may be required for this type of abortion. A similar procedure, called a **D & C (dilation and curettage)** is used infrequently. In this procedure, a small, long spoon is used to scrape away the tissue inside the uterus.

The longer a pregnancy is allowed to continue, the more complicated and difficult an abortion becomes. Later-stage abortions involve actually having to expel the fetus in a process similar to labor and delivery. In this type of process, chemicals are injected that cause the uterus to contract strongly and expel the fetus. Late-abortion procedures can require hospitalization for up to two or three days. They are more risky than the early procedures and tend to be more emotionally upsetting.

Abortions are legal for adult women throughout the United States up to the twenty-fourth week of pregnancy, although it may be difficult to find a doctor willing to do one after twenty weeks. Many states have tried to require parental permission for teenage girls to have abortions, however. Since the Supreme Court has ruled that a minor " 'mature enough' to understand the nature and consequences of treatment" may give her own consent for an abortion[5], you will probably be able to obtain one without your parents' permission unless you need to have a late abortion, which involves hospitalization. Individual states have the right to outlaw abortions after the twenty-fourth week of pregnancy unless the mother's life or health is endangered.

Many girls experience relief after having an abortion and have little or no doubt that they made the best decision. For others, an abortion can create serious emotional trauma. Most young women heal quickly from the medical aspects of an abortion, but sometimes the emotional scars mend more slowly. After an abortion, some girls find that they have strong reactions toward seeing babies, or start to experience a deep sadness. Sometimes these reactions may not be immediate but, rather, may be delayed until a later time such as the anniversary of the abortion. Whether or not a young woman seems to be handling an abortion well, she will need considerable support from her partner, parents, or friends. If she continues to experience considerable emotional pain, then she should seek professional help.

Sometimes, in desperation, girls attempt to abort a pregnancy by themselves. They may be afraid that their parents will find out or they may think they cannot afford the cost of a medically supervised abortion. Home abortions are *extremely dangerous*; they are also usually *ineffective*. They can result in death, disfigurement, and sterility. Ironically, due to the medical complications from these self-attempts, the parents do find out, and the financial and emotional costs to the family and girl are considerably higher. *Under no circumstances should you attempt to abort a pregnancy by yourself.*

If abortion is the solution you choose, it should be done under the supervision of an experienced, qualified physician.

To find out about the abortion facilities nearest to you, call one of the agencies listed in appendix A, such as Planned Parenthood or Abortion Service.

Becoming a Mother

A second choice that many teenage girls who are faced with an unplanned pregnancy consider is having the child and becoming a mother. However, like having an abortion, this choice is not as simple as it may seem. Due to poor prenatal care and incomplete biological maturation, teen pregnancies have more physical risks for both the mother and the infant.[6] For example, one study reported that the children born to girls under the age of fifteen were twice as likely to have neurological defects and mental retardation than children of mothers in their twenties.[7]

Likewise, there are significant emotional and social consequences of becoming a young mother. Certainly, having a child can be a wonderful experience for the woman who is prepared for it. However, for a young person unprepared for the responsibilities of parenthood, a child can be a terrible burden. Children can be a great deal of fun to play with or to babysit, but parenting involves much more than just enjoying a child. Teenage mothers usually drop out of school, cutting short their education. This leaves them with little money to support a family and few skills to improve their financial situation in the future. Consequently, many end up dependent upon public welfare. Typically, they don't have the time to learn about the world nor do they enjoy the same amount of freedom that their friends have. It appears that many teenage mothers are unable to establish a stable family life and frequently lack the maturity to adequately guide and discipline their children. This may explain the higher rates of psychological problems in the children of adolescent mothers.[8]

Before you decide whether or not parenthood is the answer for you, evaluate the following questions. Write down the answers and discuss them with an adult, so that you can fully explore your readiness for being a mother.

1. Can I earn or receive enough money to support the child?
2. How much time will I have to devote to work in order to support the child?
3. How much time will this leave me to give the child the amount of love and attention he or she will need?
4. How much time does that leave me to pursue the other plans for my future (school, career, personal plans)?
5. What plans for the future will I have to eliminate or postpone for a long time?
6. Can I be the parent that I would like to be and that would be best for the child?
7. How much financial, emotional, and other support will my family give in helping me raise the child?

If, after serious consideration, you do decide to have the child, good prenatal care is essential. Classes on parenting skills are also an extremely good idea. Refer to chapter 8 on pregnancy and childbirth.

Marriage

Another consideration that often goes with having a child is whether or not to get married. This is not the same as deciding whether or not to have the child. You do not have to get married just because you make a decision to have the baby. Marriage may be a way to share some of the responsibilities of supporting and raising a child, but it is not the only way. The father may voluntarily provide financial assistance for the child or he can be required to do so by a court order, even if you do not marry him.

If pregnancy is your only reason for getting married, then it is not likely that the marriage will turn out well. If, on the other hand, there are strong emotional ties between you and your partner, the chances of a good marriage are better. In any case, be aware that the divorce rate for teenage marriages is extremely high. The Sex Information and Education Council of the United States reports an *80 percent divorce rate* within five years for couples who marry before the age of eighteen.[9] All marriages require a great deal of work and are faced with day-to-day conflicts. The additional financial and emotional stresses placed on teenage marriages are usually more than the young couple can resolve. It is difficult to stay close when you are each under pressure. Love is not enough to make a marriage survive.

Before you and your partner make a decision to get married, make the same evaluation you did for having a child. Evaluate how much time you will need to devote to your new marriage and how much this will alter your personal goals. Consider whether you and your partner really want to be together out of mutual caring and respect, or whether you feel rushed or forced into marriage. Having a child and getting married are two very different decisions. Before you decide on either, try to evaluate how the rest of your life might be affected.

Adoption and Foster Care

The third choice is to give the baby up to be cared for by others. This can be done either through adoption or foster care. In adoption, another couple permanently becomes the child's parents and you no longer will have any legal rights to the child. Foster care is a temporary situation, in which the child is given to the foster parents to care for until you or the father is ready to permanently care for the child. Foster care is usually only recommended if you will be able to take over the care of the baby within a short period of time.

Many couples who can't conceive children of their own desperately want to become adoptive parents. They are usually screened very carefully by adoption agencies for their emotional stability and their ability to adequately support a child.

They can make wonderfully loving parents. Allowing her child to be adopted is one way a girl can provide a good home for her baby. However, giving up a child might not be emotionally easy for the teenage mother. The maternal feelings that a girl has after giving birth are often very strong, and turning her child over to others may feel like a difficult sacrifice. She may even feel a period of mourning at the time and may wonder periodically throughout her life how her child is doing.

In some instances, another member of the girl's or boy's family may raise the child. The girl may then still have contact with the child without having to assume the responsibilities of motherhood for which she might not be ready.

A list of local and private agencies dealing in adoption and foster care can be obtained by contacting an agency such as the Florence Crittenton Association or Planned Parenthood (both are listed in appendix A).

17

SEXUAL EXPLOITATION

Sexual exploitation is a sad but very stark reality in our society. Ideally, sex should only be a warm, joyous, and exciting part of our lives, but unfortunately far too often it can be mixed with violence and coercion (pressure, force, or threat). Probably many of our confused emotions about sex stem from its association with the various forms of exploitation, which include **sexual molestation, incest, rape, sexual assault, acquaintance** or **date rape**, and **sexual harassment**.

The purpose of including a chapter on sexual exploitation is not to scare you, but to help you think about these misuses of sex so that you can better take care of yourself. One survey of college women found that more than half had experienced sexual aggression at some time in their lives and that one in eight had actually been raped.[1] Other studies find even higher incidences of rape. When you add the number of women who have been sexually harassed at work or at school, it increases the likelihood that you will face some sort of sexual exploitation during your life. I hope that by being aware of its forms and where to go for help you will be able to reduce the impact of exploitation on your life and on those of your friends, too.

Girls are not the only ones who are the victims of sexual

abuse. Boys and men are also sometimes molested, raped, and harassed. However, females are exploited more often than males, and they tend to be raised in ways that make it harder for them to protect themselves from unwanted sexual advances.

Rape and Sexual Assault

Rape and other forms of sexual assault have reached epidemic proportions in the United States. Of course, rates of assault are higher in some states and cities than in others, but the numbers are still staggering. Rape is an aggressive act in which one person forces or coerces another into having sex. Surprisingly, however, the motivation behind rape is not primarily sexual. It is to dominate, control, and humiliate the victim. To make the victim submit, the rapist may use physical force or violence, or may instead threaten to hurt her or to retaliate against her at a later time. Sometimes a rapist will even threaten to hurt the children or family members of the victim, if she resists.

Many women and girls who are raped never report the crime to the police, often because they are afraid of being further humiliated, not believed, or even blamed. Their reluctance may stem, in part, from the myths surrounding rape that have existed in our society. Below are some of the prevalent myths and the actual facts about rape published by the Rape Awareness and Education Program at the University of California at Irvine.[2]

Myth: Rape is a nonviolent crime.
Reality: Rape is a violent crime, usually committed under the threat of bodily injury or death. The FBI states there are four violent crimes: Murder, Assault, Robbery, Rape. Rape is the most frequently committed violent crime in the U.S. today.

Myth: It could never happen to me.

Reality: Every female is a potential victim, regardless of age, race, class, or appearance. Victims range in age from under a year to over 90.

Myth: The primary motive for rape is sexual, and rapists are sick and sex-starved men motivated by uncontrollable sexual desires.

Reality: Aggression, not sex, is the motivation for rape. . . . Two-thirds of all rapists have available sexual relationships. Two-thirds of all rapes are planned. . . . Rapists come from all walks of life, all socioeconomic classes. Only about 3 percent of rapists are psychotic.

Myth: All women secretly want to be raped.

Reality: Women enjoy consensual [mutually desired] sexual relationships. However, rape is not sexual and certainly not consensual. Women do not enjoy attacks, intimidation, injury, abuse, humiliation, threats, or degradation. It is important to realize that when individuals have any type of fantasy, they are in charge of that fantasy. Rape is a situation where control is taken away from the victim.

Myth: Women who are raped are asking for it.

Reality: Rape is not related to a woman's provocative dress or manner, evidenced by the fact that babies in diapers and fully clothed grandmothers are victims of rape. Forty percent of all rapes occur in a woman's home. . . . When a woman goes out of her way to be attractive, she is asking for acceptance, not to be raped.

Myth: Rape is impossible without a woman's consent and she is only hurt if she is beaten.

Reality: Anyone can be immobilized by fear, violent threats, or the threat of death. Eighty-five percent of rapists use physical force, 23 percent use a weapon. The long-lasting emotional pain does not fit the myth that she is only hurt if she is beaten. A number of rapes result in a sexually transmitted disease and pregnancy.

Suggestions for Self-Protection and Facing an Attack

It is impossible to completely prevent yourself from being sexually assaulted, but there are a number of ways you can help to protect yourself and reduce the risk. The first step is to admit that you are in danger of sexual assault. Once you realize this fact, you can be more alert, take more precautions against it, and prepare potential strategies for facing a would-be attacker.

Important suggestions for self-protection have been published by the Crime Prevention Center of the California Department of Justice[3], as well as by the Rape Awareness and Prevention Program of the University of California at Irvine.[4] These suggestions are reprinted in appendix B of this book. Be sure to read them carefully. For some of the suggestions, such as those about home security, it will be important for you to share the ideas with your parents so that they can discuss possible changes that would make your home more safe. Many police departments have officers who will visit your home and advise you and your parents on needed security changes. Speakers on self-protection are also available to schools, clubs, and religious groups. Ask your school counselor, a favorite teacher, or a club sponsor to help organize such a program for you, your friends, and classmates.

Rape is a horrifying experience and one that you'd probably rather not even think about. Yet, experts say that it is wise to think ahead of time about how you might respond if faced with an attack. Unfortunately, there is no one "right way" to respond or any particular tactic that is certain to stop the attack. You must protect yourself as best you can and in any way that you are able. California's Crime Prevention Center discusses the various considerations in choosing three possible options: submitting to the attack, passive resistance, and active resistance. These can be found in appendix C.

Many rape prevention centers now stress active resistance as a very important and effective option. They say that your odds of escaping an attack are much greater if you resist immediately. Since many rapists expect a girl to be passive, they may be thrown off guard by screams or struggling. Self-defense classes that focus on how to fight off or escape an attack may give you some added hints and very helpful practice.

If You Are Assaulted

Since no precautions can completely guarantee that you'll be able to avoid an attack, every female should have information on what to do if it happens to her. You will need both emotional support, from someone you can trust, and medical attention right away. You'll also need to decide whether to report it to the police. Because women fear the reaction of the police or the further trauma of a rape trial, many will never report the crime. It is, of course, your personal decision. However, police authorities stress that their only chance of stopping the rapist from striking again is with the help of the victims. In many areas, the police have now received training to help make them sensitive to the feelings and needs of the rape victim. They are less likely to blame her and more likely to treat her with support. Many states have also now passed laws that do not allow the victim's past sexual experience to be used against her in court. So as not to destroy possible evidence, do not change your clothes, bathe, or douche until after you have contacted the police and have been taken to the hospital and examined by a physician.

An important alternative to calling the police is to phone a rape crisis center. They are usually listed in the front of your phone book and have counselors on call twenty-four hours a day. These counselors can provide emotional support and give you information on what to do next, including helping you to decide whether to report your rape to the police. They can let you know about the training and reputation of your local police with regard to dealing with rape victims. Services at these centers are confidential in almost all cases.

Whether or not you decide to call the police or a rape crisis center, get some help. Far too many women and girls have held in their pain and fears and have tried to pretend that they haven't been profoundly hurt. There is no need for anyone to go through this alone.

Acquaintance Rape

Experts now estimate that perhaps more than 50 percent of sexual assaults are committed by someone the woman knows. One group of researchers stated that in their interviews with 300 women, one-fifth reported having been forced into some form of unwanted sexual activity on a date or at a party.[5] Other surveys found that even higher percentages, ranging from 50 to 80 percent, of women have experienced this type of sexual coercion.[6]

Few women have been aware of the high risk of being assaulted by someone they know because this type of rape is seldom reported to the police. A girl who has been victimized may feel too embarrassed or believe that people will think she made it up, possibly because of the myth that girls frequently "cry rape" whenever they are angry with a boy. Others don't report attacks because they think people will say they were "asking for it" by being alone with the boy. Some girls even blame themselves for the incident, feeling that in some way their behavior provoked the assault. Many girls don't even realize that what they have experienced is rape. When someone forces you to have sex against your wishes, you have been sexually assaulted, regardless of whether the person is a friend, a relative, or a date. Acquaintance rape is *illegal*, just as if you'd been attacked by a stranger. It is true that it is sometimes harder to prove in court that you did not consent, but the behavior is still wrong and it is against the law.

People are now trying to understand why teenage girls are so vulnerable to this type of sexual assault and why teenage boys are willing to force a girl into having sex. A strong influence seems to be the media, which often makes it look as if women desire sex even when they say no. Scenes abound in which a female resists initially, but then responds with great passion as a man overcomes her with kisses and embraces. Many media descriptions fail to make a clear distinction between seduction and rape. These scenes may teach some boys to push ahead despite their date's protests.

Another influence may be the different ways girls and boys are socialized. Boys in our society are taught to strive aggressively for what they want and they are also taught that sexual experience, even conquests, are a sign of manhood. Girls, in contrast, are often taught to be fairly passive, even submissive, and to try to be popular and to please others. Hence, a young woman may not adequately protect her personal rights or say no as vehemently as is necessary for the boy to believe her. Unless she is screaming rape at the top of her lungs and kicking and punching, some boys don't believe that she is really unwilling.

A third reason that acquaintance rape is so common among teenagers may be that boys and girls seem to differ in what they perceive as sexual behavior. Recent studies with teenagers found that boys were more likely to conclude that if a girl dressed "sexily," went to a secluded or private place with a boy, or even said certain phrases, then she was interested in having sex and was inviting sexual advances. A majority of teenage boys said that a boy has a right to expect sex under some circumstances: when a girl accepts a date with a guy who has a reputation for having sex with a lot of girls, or when a boy has a date with a girl who has a "tarnished" reputation.[7]

Probably the most shocking finding of this series of interviews with teenagers was that many boys and girls said that there were conditions under which it was acceptable for a boy to hold a girl down and force her to have sexual intercourse. Boys were much more likely to approve of forced sex than were girls, but even some of the girls felt force was justified. The young men saw forced sex as okay when the boy is so turned on he can't stop (36 percent); he spends a lot of money on her (39 percent); she has had intercourse with other boys (39 percent); she is stoned or drunk (39 percent); they have dated a long time (43 percent); she gets him sexually excited (51 percent); she's led him on (54 percent); and when she says she's going to have sex with him, then changes her mind (54 percent).[8] Clearly, not all boys believe rape is okay, but enough do so that girls should be aware of these expectations. The fact is that under no circumstances are you *obligated* to have sex.

The purpose of writing about acquaintance rape is not to scare you out of dating boys. Dating can be a lot of fun as well as an important way to learn about and build relationships. The purpose is merely to heighten your awareness so that you can better take care of yourself. Below are some suggestions for dealing with the risk of forced sex.[9]

1. If you feel uncomfortable about going somewhere or being alone with someone, don't go.

2. Be careful of someone who invades your personal space by doing things such as standing or sitting too close, staring at your breasts or crotch, or touching you more than you want. Tell him clearly that you want him to stop what he is doing.

3. Be careful of someone who is too domineering and selfish; who tries to get what he wants even at your expense. You may notice that this kind of person ignores your opinions and wishes or reacts angrily when you don't do what he wants. You may also notice that he lacks sensitivity to other people's feelings and is more concerned with his own gratification.

4. Be careful of someone who participates in delinquent activities, hangs out with a tough crowd, or who gets in trouble with the police. Some of these boys may be pressured by peers to prove themselves or may disregard the consequences of their actions. This caution doesn't mean

that all boys who rape are obvious delinquents or that all delinquents are rapists. In fact, some rapes have been committed by boys who were popular at school and who were star athletes.

5. Be careful at parties with alcohol and drugs. Some boys will interpret your mere presence there as an indication that you want sex. Alcohol and drugs can lower a boy's restraints and at the same time make it hard for you to use good judgment. In fact, group or gang rapes, where several boys rape one girl, are more likely to happen in such settings.

6. Don't accept a ride home or go somewhere alone with someone you've just met.

7. Always have a backup to get a ride home or a way out of a risky situation. Arrange with your parents or friends to be able to call them if you need your own transportation.

8. Be aware that boys may misinterpret your dress or behavior and be prepared to clarify what you do and do not want.

9. Be prepared to deal with pressure to have sex if you date a boy with a reputation for being fast.

10. If you get in a situation in which you are being coerced, pressured, threatened, or forced, *respond quickly and firmly*. Research on attempted but successfully averted date rapes found that the females used three strategies: *fleeing or trying to flee; fighting back; and yelling*. This makes it *clear* that you are not playing hard to get and at the same time alerts anyone in the area that you need help.

Unfortunately, girls who are victims of date or acquaintance rape have as many, or more, negative emotional reactions as those who are assaulted by strangers. They are even more likely to feel guilt, shame, or personal responsibility for the incident. Consequently, they frequently avoid telling anyone and often do not seek the support they need. In addition, they may be continually reminded of the event when they run into the boy at school or in social situations.

If you are assaulted, remember that it is the person who assaulted you who did something wrong, *not you*. Find support for yourself from your parents, friends, teachers, or another adult. Also remember that acquaintance rape is against the law and it can be reported to the police just like any other form of rape.

Incest

Incest is sexual contact between family members. This may include intercourse, but often is confined to touching or fondling. There is a big difference, however, between the sex play and exploration that often occurs among young brothers and sisters of about the same age and sexual abuse. Children often explore each other's bodies and may even kiss and pet. As long as one is not forcing the other into it, it is not really exploitive. Except for potential guilt feelings, this type of family sexuality is usually considered harmless.

Incest is considered sexual abuse when it involves an older and more powerful person (such as a parent, older brother or sister, stepparent, or grandparent) imposing sex on a younger child or adolescent. Sometimes the child is physically forced to have sex, but many times she cooperates because she feels powerless in the situation or is too young to make her own decision. Often the girl is afraid that the family will fall apart if she speaks up or resists. She may also be afraid of losing her family's love or of hurting one of her parents.

Although most girls who have experienced incest feel isolated, alone, and believe that they are different from all other girls, incest turns out to be a disturbingly common part of many girls' lives. It certainly happens much more often than commonly believed. It is impossible to determine exactly how often incest occurs, because many girls and their families try to keep it a secret. However, it has been estimated that somewhere between 5 and 15 percent of children are the victims of sexual abuse and that the majority of these molestations are carried out by a family member.[10] Despite stereotypes that incest occurs only in poor families, it happens in rich and middle-class families and in families of all ethnic and racial backgrounds.

Incest is a confusing and even traumatic experience, with potential lifetime consequences. Many times a girl blames herself or feels that the incest occurred because something was wrong with her. Some girls turn to self-destructive behavior such as drug abuse, prostitution, or suicide. Others find that they distrust men and have trouble developing intimate relationships. Depression and low self-esteem are very common in incest victims. Counseling can help these girls deal with their feelings of hurt, guilt, shame, and anger. It can help them to learn to no longer blame themselves and to rebuild their damaged self-esteem. Group counseling with other girls who have had similar experiences with incest can be especially reassuring.

Previously, there were few, if any, good programs that dealt with the problems of incestuous families, but this situation has changed greatly. Many professionals, such as psychologists, counselors, social workers, psychiatrists, and physicians, have learned to be more aware of sexual abuse within the family. Strategies have been developed for protecting the children while offering constructive guidance for the adults. Most states now have laws designed to help girls or boys who have been sexually abused. Usually the laws require certain people (like teachers, physicians, and counselors) who suspect or know that a child or adolescent is being abused to report it to some sort of child protective agency or to the police. Neighbors, relatives, and friends can and should also contact these agencies.

After a report has been made, the agency will investigate and make recommendations. Because sexual abuse and other forms of physical abuse are illegal, authorities can take the legal steps necessary to protect the children from further exploitation. Usually the parents are required to seek professional counseling, which can later help everyone in the family to learn healthier ways of relating to each other. If the children are still in danger or if the parents are unwilling to cooperate, it may be necessary to separate the family.

If you have questions about how to report incest or how to get help, you can look in the phone book for agencies like the Child Abuse Registry or Child Protective Services. You can also talk to a school counselor, physician, social worker, or psychologist, or visit a community mental health center.

Sexual Molestation of Children

When a child is sexually abused by someone other than a family member, this is generally referred to as **child molestation**. In most cases, the molestation does not include intercourse or physical harm, but is restricted to fondling or undressing. Research indicates that the molester is often a very shy and insecure man who has poor social relationships. He may choose to be sexual with children because he is too afraid to approach women his own age.[11] Unfortunately, some molesters are much more brutal and some outcomes are tragic.

The effects on a child of being molested can vary greatly. In many cases the child is not severely upset by the molestation until the parents, police, or public agencies overreact and scare her. In other cases, where the abuse is violent, prolonged, or the child is threatened, the effects can be extremely damaging. As with rape or incest, self-esteem and trust of others can suffer and the child may experience guilt or an unnecessary feeling of being bad. It is important that the child receive support and reassurance that it was not her fault. This support can come from family and friends or, if necessary, from a professional counselor. Also, it is essential that the victim feel fully reassured that she will be protected from the person who molested her.

Sexual Harassment

"Sexual harassment is any unwanted attention of a sexual nature from someone in the workplace that creates discomfort and/or interferes with the job." (Working Women United Institute, Bartlett)[12] Certainly, this may not sound as scary as being raped or having your life threatened, but sexual harassment can still interfere greatly with your life. For teenage girls, sexual harassment may take place at school or at an after-school or summer job. Any teacher, student, or person with whom you work who continually makes unwanted sexual advances or sexual comments to you is harassing you. One teenager reported to me that a male teacher made the girls stand on their desks and shake their bodies. He also kept her after class and told her how sexy she was. She and the rest of her female classmates were being sexually harassed.

Unfortunately, sexual harassment is very widespread and it can take several forms.[13] A teacher, boss, or supervisor may require sex from a student or an employee if she wants to get a good grade, get hired, keep a job, or get a promotion. A female might be the unwilling recipient of obscenities, dirty pictures, or the target of sexual jokes. Or a woman might be told that she must provide sexual favors to the company's customers or clients. *All* are forms of harassment.

Many girls and women do not realize that sexual harassment is *illegal*. Unless the company you work for or your school takes some action to protect you and to stop the harassment after you report it, they can be held responsible and sued.

The first response you may want to make to someone who is harassing you is to tell him that you don't like it and want him to stop. If this doesn't work, seek out the support of others in the setting, such as other employees or students. Often you are not the only one bothered by the harasser's behavior. Get the help of adults, such as your parents or a school advisor, to report the person to a supervisor. In the event that this doesn't stop the harassment, or if you feel punished or discriminated against for speaking up, you can file a formal complaint with an appropriate agency. Possibilities are the Human Rights Commission, Fair Employment Practices Agency, or the Equal Employment Opportunity Commission. You can also check the phone book for a legal-aid society or women's legal service. [14]

APPENDIX A:
FINDING HELP

We all need help now and then. None of us is completely self-sufficient. Yet asking for help can sometimes be a very difficult thing to do. Even admitting that things are serious enough to require help may be difficult.

If you do find yourself in a situation that requires professional advice or assistance, competent help is usually available if you know how to find it. The following section is designed to ease the problems often connected with finding proper professional help. It is divided into two parts.

1. How to find a referral in a phone book.
2. A listing of various agencies that you can write or call (many of them have toll-free numbers) to get information, or the name of a source of help close to your home.

Using the Phone Book to Find Help

Probably the easiest way to find help is to look for the listings of Community Services numbers or the city, county, state, and federal government offices in front (or back) of the white pages of your local phone directory under the word that best describes the service you require. For example, if you are looking for information about pregnancy, look in the white pages under the word *pregnancy*. If you are looking for birth control information, then look under *birth control* or even under *sex*. If you don't find the referral source that you need, look up *Planned Parenthood* or Family Service. Both of these are large national organizations with chapters in many towns and cities. Even if these organizations do not offer the type of service you need, it is likely that they can refer you to a place where you can get appropriate help.

A second way to use the phone book is to look in the yellow pages. The following are a partial list of headings that you might look under in searching for help.

Abuse
Adoptions
Birth Control Information
Child Abuse
Child Protective Services
Children and Family Services
Churches
Clergy
Clinics
Counseling
Crisis Intervention Services
Disabled Services
Family Planning
General Information and Referral
Health
Legal
Marriage Counselors
Mental Health Services
Psychiatrists
Psychologists
Rape
Sexual Assault
Sexually Transmitted Diseases
Social Service Organizations
Venereal Disease

Some yellow pages even offer an index in the back, where you can look up the specific service that you want. Remember, if you call any organization and they do not offer the service that you require, ask them for suggestions as to where you might locate the kind of service you need. Many helping agencies are very aware of what resources may be available in your vicinity.

Organizations

The following is a list of national organizations that might be helpful in answering any questions you might have or in referring you to an agency in your area that can be of assistance.

Abortion

National Abortion Hot Line
(800) 772-9100
Toll-free referral and information services.

Florence Crittenton Association
67 Irving Place, New York, NY 10011
(212) 254-7410
A counseling and referral organization with many affiliates, which explores alternatives to abortion.

National Abortion Rights Action League
1424 K Street, N.W., Washington, DC 20005
A national organization that favors abortion as an alternative.

National Right to Life Committee
419 7th Street, N.W., Washington, DC 20045
A national organization that opposes abortion as an alternative.

AIDS

National AIDS Hot Line
(800) 342-2437
A toll-free national hot line provided by the Public Health

Service, which provides recorded information and additional phone numbers for people wanting a referral or more information about AIDS.

Birth Alternatives

American Society for Prophylaxis in Obstetrics
1523 L Street, N.W., Washington, DC 20005

Nurse-Midwives
American College of Nurse-Midwives
1522 K Street, N.W., Suite 1120, Washington, DC 20005

Breastfeeding

LaLeche International, Inc.
9616 Minneapolis Ave., Franklin Park, IL 60123

Cancer

American Cancer Society
777 Third Avenue, New York, NY 10017

Child Sexual Abuse

Parents United Inc.
P.O. Box 952, San Jose, CA 95108-0952
(408) 280-5055

Counseling and Referrals

Planned Parenthood Federation of America, Inc.
810 Seventh Avenue, New York, NY 10019
(212) 541-7800
  Offers medical, educational, counseling, and referral services for many aspects of sexuality, including the areas of birth control and sexually transmitted diseases. Has hundreds of affiliates throughout the country.

Family Service Association of America
44 East 23rd Street, New York, NY 10010
(212) 674-6100
> *A general counseling service with affiliated agencies through-
> out the United States.*

Disabilities

Sex and Disability Unit, Human Sexuality Program, University
of California
814 Mission Street, San Francisco, CA 94103

Family Planning *(See also "Counseling and Referrals.")*

Zero Population Growth
1346 Connecticut Ave., N.W., Washington, DC 20036

Fertility

American Fertility Foundation
1608 13th Avenue, S., Suite 101, Birmingham, AL 35205

Gay Services

Gay Switchboard
(215) 546-7100
> *A Philadelphia-based hot line providing information and re-
> ferral services nationwide.*

Gay Community Services Center
1213 North Highland, Hollywood, CA 90028
(213) 464-7400

Gayellow Pages
Box 292, Village Station, New York, NY 10014
> *A directory of gay services, organizations, and businesses.*

Parents and Friends of Lesbians and Gays (Parents FLAG)
P.O. Box 24565, Los Angeles, CA 90024

A national organization that provides support and counseling for parents and friends of gays.

Herpes

The Herpes Resource Center
260 Sheridan Avenue, Palo Alto, CA 94306
(415) 328-7710
A comprehensive resource center that provides a newsletter with up-to-date information, counseling, and referral services in regard to herpes.

Hot Lines

Community Sex Information, Inc.
(212) 982-0052
A New York City–based hot line that provides information and referrals nationwide.

Sex Information Hot Line
(213) 653-1123
A Los Angeles–based hot line that provides information and referrals nationwide.

Rape

National Rape Information Clearinghouse
National Center for Control and Prevention of Rape
5600 Fishers Land, Rockville, MD 20857

Sex Education and Therapy

American Association of Sex Educators, Counselors, and Therapists (AASECT)
111 Dupont Circle N.W., Washington, DC 20036
(202) 462-1171
A national professional organization of sex therapists and sex educators with members throughout the United States.

Sex Information and Education Council of the United States
(SEICUS)
80 Fifth Avenue, Suite 801–2, New York, NY 10011
(212) 929-2300
> *A national organization that offers information about sexuality. It provides a recommended reading list on request and also has its own publications regarding sexual information and issues.*

Sexual Harassment

Working Women's Institute
593 Park Ave., New York, NY 10021

Sexually Transmitted Diseases

VD National Hotline (toll-free numbers)
(800) 227-8922 (outside California)
(800) 982-5883 (in California)
> *A toll-free counseling and referral service.*

Transsexuality

J.T.C.P.
P. O. Box 184, San Juan Capistrano, CA 92693
(714) 496-5227
> *An information and referral service for those seeking information about transsexuality.*

Recommended Readings

The following is a list of books and readings that might be useful for expanding upon the information presented in this book. For a child or a parent looking for quality reading material about sex, the array of books available can seem very confusing. The books are listed according to the topic areas they supplement.

Abortion

Corsaro, Maria, and Carole Korzeniowsky. *A Woman's Guide to Safe Abortion*. New York: Holt, Rinehart and Winston, 1983.
A realistic approach to the planning of an abortion. Also includes information on how to avoid future unwanted pregnancies.

Assertiveness Training

Butler, Pamela. *Self-Assertion for Women*. New York: Harper and Row, 1981.

Becoming a Young Parent

Gordon, Sol, and Mina Wollin. *Parenting: A Guide for Young People*. New York: William H. Sadlier, Inc., 1975.
Written for the young person preparing to become a parent.

Fiction

Blume, Judy. *Forever*. Scarsdale, N.Y.: Bradbury Press, 1975.
A novel written for teenagers that gives a realistic view of teenage sexuality.

Health

Boston Women's Health Collective. *Our Bodies, Ourselves*. Rev. 2nd ed. New York: Simon and Schuster, 1976.
A health-oriented book on women's bodies and concerns written by women.

Homosexuality

Fairchild, Betty, and Nancy Howard. *Now That You Know: What Every Parent Should Know About Homosexuality*. New York: Harcourt Brace Jovanovich, 1979.

A book helpful for parents trying to understand their homosexual child.

Hanckel, Frances, and John Cunningham. *A Way of Love, A Way of Life: A Young Person's Introduction to What It Means to Be Gay.* New York: Lothrop, Lee and Shepard (William Morrow), 1979.
A sensitively written book for the teenager trying to understand what it means to be gay.

Jones, Clinton. *Understanding Gay Relatives and Friends.* New York: Seabury Press, 1978.
A very personal book to help the relatives and friends of homosexuals.

Silverstein, Charles. *A Family Matter: A Parent's Guide to Homosexuality.* New York: McGraw-Hill, 1977.
A book to help parents of homosexuals deal with their concerns.

Legal Rights

Sussman, Alan. *The Rights of Young People.* New York: Avon Books, 1977.
A guide for young people about legal rights. Covers several areas of sexuality, such as marriage, contraception, and abortion.

More About Females

Gardner-Loulan, Joann, Bonnie Loppez, and Marcia Quackenbush. *Period.* San Francisco: New Glide Publications, 1979.
A book for preteens that explains in an understanding and supportive way what menstruation is all about. Well illustrated.

Wagenvoord, James, and Peyton Bailey, eds. *Women: A Book for Men.* New York: Avon Books, 1979.

A helpful book for men trying to broaden their understanding of women.

More About Males

Gale, Jay. *A Young Man's Guide to Sex*. New York: Holt, Rinehart and Winston, 1984.
A sensitively written, easily readable book for an adolescent or young adult male trying to gain an understanding about the facts and emotions involved in becoming a sexual person. It is the companion book to A Young Woman's Guide to Sex.

Hite, Shere. *The Hite Report on Male Sexuality*. New York: Alfred A. Knopf, 1981.
Results of a survey of more than 7,000 men, listing and discussing some of the common (and uncommon) fears and sexual preferences of males.

Zilbergeld, Bernie. *Male Sexuality*. Boston: Little, Brown, 1978.
A well-written, easily readable book for the man or woman trying to gain a more complete understanding of the physiology and emotional side of male sexuality.

Rape, Sexual Assault, and Sexual Exploitation

Adams, Caren, and Jennifer Fay. *"Nobody Told Me It Was Rape": A Parent's Guide for Talking with Teenagers about Acquaintance Rape and Sexual Exploitation*. Santa Cruz: Network Publications, 1984.

Bateman, P. *Acquaintance Rape: Awareness and Prevention*. Write: Alternatives to Fear, 1605 17th Avenue, Seattle, WA 98122.
A workbook for teenagers on preventing and coping with acquaintance rape.

Fay, Jennifer, and Billie Jo Flerchinger. *Top Secret: Sexual Assault Information For Teenagers Only*. Write: King County Rape Relief, 304 S. 43rd, Renton, WA 98055.

Crime Prevention Center, California Department of Justice. *Sexual Assault Prevention Handbook.* Write: Office of the Attorney General, 555 Capitol Mall, Suite 290, Sacramento, CA 95814.

Ledray, Linda. *Recovering from Rape.* New York: Henry Holt and Company, 1986.
A comprehensive handbook for survivors of sexual assault, and for their families, lovers, and friends.

Reproduction

Demarest, Robert J., and John J. Sciarra. *Conception, Birth and Contraception: A Visual Presentation.* New York: McGraw-Hill, 1976.
A well-illustrated book for the middle-to-later teen about the process of human reproduction.

Sex for Teens

Gordon, Sol, and Roger Conant. *You! The Teenage Survival Book.* New York: Times Books, 2nd edition, 1984.
A personal book about sexuality and teenage concerns.

Hass, Aaron, Ph.D. *Teenage Sexuality.* New York: Pinnacle Books, 1981.
Results of a survey in which teenagers discuss their attitudes about and their expectations of sex.

Sex for the Disabled

Mooney, Thomas O., Theodore M. Cole, and Richard A. Chilgren. *Sexual Options for Paraplegics and Quadraplegics.* Boston: Little, Brown, 1975.
An excellent source for helping the disabled person reach his or her maximum sexual potential.

Kempton, Winifred, Medora Bass, and Sol Gordon. *Love, Sex and Birth Control for Mentally Retarded: A Guide for Parents.* Planned Parenthood of Southeastern Pennsylvania, 1973.

A guide for parents of mentally handicapped children or adults about educating their child sexually.

Sexually Transmitted Diseases

Corsaro, Maria, and Carole Korzeniowsky. *STD: A Commonsense Guide to Sexually Transmitted Diseases.* New York: Holt, Rinehart and Winston, 1982.

A nonjudgmental, straightforward book for those interested in recognizing and understanding sexually transmitted diseases.

Gordon, Sol. *Facts About VD for Today's Youth.* Rev. ed. Fayetteville, N.Y.: Ed-U Press, 1979.

Information about sexually transmitted diseases; stresses the importance of prevention and early treatment.

APPENDIX B:
SUGGESTIONS FOR
SECURITY

Outside Security

- Stay in well-lighted areas as much as possible.
- Walk confidently and at a steady pace. A rapist looks for someone who appears vulnerable.
- Walk on the side of the street facing traffic.
- Walk close to the curb. Avoid doorways, bushes, and alleys where a rapist can hide.
- If you think you are being followed, walk quickly to areas where there are lights and people. If a car appears to be following you, turn and walk in the opposite direction.
- Be careful when people in cars ask you for directions. Always reply from a distance and never get close to the car.
- If you believe you are in danger, don't be reluctant to scream and run. Consider carrying a whistle or any type of noise-maker. And, if you're in trouble, use it!
- If you are in trouble, attract help in any way you can. Scream, yell for help, yell "Fire!" or break a window. Remember, if a weapon is involved, your choices will be limited.
- Probably the most effective deterrent to any type of attack is to travel with a friend whenever possible.

Home Security

- Make sure all doors and door frames are solid and sturdy. Entry doors should be solid-core wood or metal. Good locks, such as deadbolt locks with 1-inch throws, are a must. Don't rely on chain locks. A person of average size can easily break most chain locks.
- Have your locks changed or rekeyed or a new lock added when you move into a new house or apartment.
- Install a peephole-viewer in your door. And use it! *Never* open your door without knowing who is on the other side.
- Install good exterior lighting around your house.
- Make sure all windows can be locked securely.
- Secure sliding glass doors.
- Be sure to use these door and window locks at all times— when you are out and especially when you are home.
- If you live alone (or without a man in the house), do not advertise it. Use only your initials and last name on your mailbox and telephone listing.
- Always check identification before opening your door. Ask that identification cards of repair or salespeople be slipped under your door for you to check. If there is any question, call the person's office. Any reputable sales agent or repair-person will be glad to have you check.
- If strangers ask to use your telephone in an emergency, offer to make the call yourself. Have them wait outside while you make the call.
- If strangers or repairpersons telephone or come to your door, do not admit that you are alone.
- If you live in an apartment, avoid being in the laundry room or garage by yourself, especially at night. Tell your landlord if security improvements are needed. Better lighting, stronger locks, and night security guards are methods to make a build-ing safer.
- If you come home and find a door or window open or signs of forced entry, do not go inside. Go to the nearest telephone and call the police.

Vehicle Security

- After entering or leaving your car, always lock the door.
- Check the back seat before you get in.
- Keep doors and windows closed and locked while you drive.
- If you think you are being followed, drive to a public place or a police station.
- If your car breaks down, open the hood and attach a white cloth to the car antenna. Then wait inside the car with the doors locked. If someone stops to help, stay in your locked car and ask them to call the police or a garage.

Additional Suggestions

The Rape Awareness and Prevention Program at the University of California at Irvine makes these additional security suggestions:

- In elevators, don't get on or off with someone against your instincts.
- Keep emergency phone numbers handy and money to call.
- Don't hitchhike or pick up hitchhikers.
- Hold your keys between your fingers, ready to unlock your car or home.
- Put emergency numbers by the phone.
- Don't stop for a disabled motorist: Call the police from a phone for them instead.
- If someone signals that something is wrong with your car, drive to the nearest station and check.
- Park in well-lighted areas and away from vans or cars with someone "waiting" in them.

*Information in appendix B was reprinted from *Sexual Assault Handbook*, published in 1982 by the California Attorney General's Office, Crime Prevention Center.

APPENDIX C:
RESPONDING TO
AN ATTACK

Submitting to an Attack

In every rape, the attacker threatens the victim's safety or life. Sometimes a rapist threatens the victim's children or other family members.

If you believe you might get hurt by defending yourself, or if you're afraid to fight back, don't. It is not necessary that you resist. Submitting to a rape out of fear for your own or your family's safety does not mean that you consented. It is still a rape and still a crime, even if you do not have a single cut or bruise. It should be reported to the police. Victims who do not resist should never feel guilty. It is the rapist who committed the crime!

Passive Resistance

Sometimes a victim may want to resist but is afraid to scream or fight back. In these cases, a more passive type of resistance may help to "defuse" the violence of the attacker. With passive resistance you can

- Try to calm the attacker. Talk to him and try to persuade him not to carry out the attack. If you win his confidence,
- you may be able to escape.

- Claim to be sick or pregnant. Tell him you have VD. This may deter the attacker.
- Try to discourage the rapist. Some women pretend to faint, some cry hysterically, others act insane or mentally incapacitated.
- If you're at home, tell the attacker a boyfriend is coming over or that your husband or roommate will be home soon.

Active Resistance

Nobody can tell you whether active resistance—screaming, struggling, fighting back—will be the "right" thing to do. In some cases, it can frighten off or discourage the attacker. But resistance may also lead the rapist to become more violent or increase his desire to subdue the victim.

There are many kinds of active resistance. Here are some pros and cons regarding the most common ones:

- *Screaming*—A scream can surprise or frighten an attacker away if he fears that people will come to help; but screaming won't help in isolated areas.
- *Struggling and fighting back*—A forceful struggle also may discourage the rapist. If you are not afraid to hurt someone, and can land a strong kick or blow, fighting back may give you the opportunity to escape. All blows or kicks must be forceful and should be aimed at vulnerable areas.
- *Martial arts*—Special self-defense courses, such as judo or karate, are very popular in some areas. Many women have taken courses to protect themselves from attack. If you are proficient in these techniques, they can be very effective. But proficiency takes continuous practice.
- *Weapons*—Some women carry weapons, such as guns, knives, or chemical sprays to ward off attackers. Unless you are trained and not afraid to use these weapons, they can be very dangerous. The attacker might be able to turn them against you. In the state of California it is illegal to carry some weapons, including all concealed firearms. To legally carry most chemical sprays, you must complete a training course offered

by a certified agency or organization. . . . *Check with your local law enforcement authorities before you select a weapon.*

In many cities and towns, groups like the police and sheriff's departments' crime-prevention units, YMCAs and YWCAs, women's clubs, rape crisis centers, and local high schools have programs on rape defense and protection. Check with your local groups to see if they offer such help.

*Information in appendix C was reprinted from *Sexual Assault Handbook*, published in 1982 by the California Attorney General's Office, Crime Prevention Center.

GLOSSARY

Abortion—The ending of a pregnancy prematurely. The egg, the embryo, or the fetus (depending upon the stage of pregnancy) is removed or expelled from the uterus.

Acne—Large, deep pimples and blackheads, which are common during adolescence.

Acquaintance rape—Sexual relations forced upon a person by someone he or she knows. It is a form of sexual assault.

Adolescence—The period of time in a young person's life beginning with puberty and ending with adulthood.

Afterbirth—The material made up of the placenta and fetal sacs, which are typically expelled after the fetus has been delivered.

AIDS (Acquired Immune Deficiency Syndrome)—A condition caused by the HTLV-III virus in which the body's immune system no longer works effectively. It can leave the person susceptible to many deadly forms of infection and disease. Gay and bisexual men have been especially vulnerable to catching AIDS.

Amnion—A sac containing fluid, which encloses and protects the fetus within the uterus.

Anal sex (anal intercourse)—A form of sexual intercourse in which the penis is inserted into the partner's rectum.

Anus—The opening of the body leading from the rectum, from which feces are expelled from the body.

Areola—The darker, circular area of the breast that surrounds the nipple.

Artificial insemination—A medical procedure in which semen is mechanically inserted into the vagina or uterus in order to produce a pregnancy.

BBT (basal body temperature) method—A fertility-awareness method that requires a woman to take her body temperature each morning with a special thermometer in order to establish a regular pattern. It often detects a slight drop in temperature just prior to ovulation and a small consistent rise in temperature after ovulation.

Birth control pill—A pill used to ensure that sexual intercourse does not result in pregnancy. Birth control pills are made from artificial hormones.

Bisexual—A person who has an attraction for both males and females and who can engage in sexual activity with both sexes.

Blastocyst—A stage of embryo development that consists of a ball of cells that is produced by cell division of the zygote.

"Boner"—A slang expression for an erection.

Calendar method—See Rhythm method.

Candidiasis—Often called a yeast infection, it is an overgrowth of yeast fungus in the vagina, which causes irritation.

Cervical cap—A contraceptive device that forms a caplike barrier over the cervix, preventing sperm from entering.

Cervix—The narrow necklike portion at the bottom of the uterus, which extends into the vagina.

Cesarean section (C-section)—A childbirth procedure in which the child is delivered through incisions made in the abdomen and uterus.

Chancre—A painless sore, characteristic of the early stages of syphilis. The secretions from the chancre are highly contagious.

"Cherry"—Slang term for hymen.

Child molestation—See Sexual molestation.

Chlamydia—A sexually transmitted disease caused by a bacterialike organism. Its symptoms resemble gonorrhea.

Chorion—A sac of tissue surrounding the amnion and the fetus inside the uterus.

Circumcision—The process in which the foreskin is surgically removed from around the top of the penis.

Clitoral hood—Tissue from the labia minora that forms a hood-like covering over the clitoris.

Clitoris—A small, extremely sensitive female sex organ located immediately in front of the urethra. Stimulation of the clitoris is often involved in the process of a woman reaching orgasm.

Coitus—A medical term for sexual intercourse.

Coitus interruptus—A very ineffective means of birth control in which the penis is withdrawn from the vagina prior to ejaculation.

Combination pill—A type of birth control pill that contains both estrogen and progestin.

"Come"—A slang term that refers to orgasm or to the semen that spurts from the penis as a result of ejaculation.

Conception—The joining of the male sperm and the female ovum to form a fertilized egg.

Condom—Commonly called a "rubber," or prophylactic. A bag-like rubber or membrane covering that is worn on the penis both as a contraceptive device and as a way of protecting against the spread of sexually transmitted diseases.

Contraceptive—Any device used to minimize the possibility of pregnancy as a result of sexual intercourse.

Contraceptive foam— A form of birth control that consists of sperm-killing chemical agents contained in a foamy base. It is inserted into the vagina prior to intercourse.

Contraceptive sponge—A form of birth control that consists of a soft plastic sponge that contains a spermicide, which is placed over the cervix.

Cowper's glands—Two small glands that connect with the urethra in a male, just below the prostate gland. They emit a bit of fluid before ejaculation, which can contain sperm.

"Crabs"—See Pubic lice.

Cross-dresser—Formerly called a transvestite. A person, usually male, who has a strong compulsion to dress in the clothing of the opposite sex.

Cunnilingus—A form of oral sex in which the tongue is used to stimulate a female's vulva.

D & C (dilation and curettage)—A medical procedure in which the cervix is dilated and then the lining and contents of the uterus are scraped away with a metal instrument.

D & E (dilation and evacuation)—A medical procedure commonly used for abortions during the thirteenth to sixteenth week of pregnancy. In this procedure, the cervix is dilated and the contents of the uterus are eliminated through a combination of scraping and suction.

Date rape—Sexual relations forced upon a person by his or her date. It is a form of sexual assault.

DES (Diethylstilbestrol)—A synthetic estrogen that has been linked to potential cancer risks in women and their children. Used by pregnant women in the 1940s and 1950s to prevent miscarriages, the drug is no longer prescribed by doctors for this purpose. However, a small amount of DES is contained in some morning-after pills.

Diaphragm—A contraceptive device made of soft latex, which acts as a cup covering the female's cervix. It should be used in combination with a spermicide.

Douching—Flushing out the vagina with a liquid.

Ducts—Tubelike structures in the body that conduct fluids or secretions.

Dyspareunia—Painful intercourse.

Ectopic pregnancy—A pregnancy in which the fertilized egg implants in a location other than the uterus. Typically, the alternate location is one of the fallopian tubes. This is also called a tubal pregnancy.

Eggs—Another term for ova.

Ejaculation—The sudden shooting out of semen from the penis, which almost always occurs when a male experiences orgasm.

Embryo—The stage of development of an unborn infant from conception through eight weeks.

Epididymis—A long, compactly wound tube in which the newly developed sperm mature inside the scrotum.

Erection—The enlarging and stiffening of the penis as a result of an increased blood flow to that area. Although erections are usually attributed to sexual stimulation, there are other factors that can cause erections.

Estrogen—A hormone that produces female sex characteristics. Estrogens also affect the female's menstrual cycle. "Combination" birth control pills contain synthetic estrogens.

Fallopian tubes—The tubes that transport the eggs from each ovary to the uterus. Conception usually takes place in these tubes.

Fellatio—A form of oral sex in which the mouth makes contact with a male partner's penis.

Female-superior position—A position of sexual intercourse in which the female lies on top of and facing the male.

Fertile—Capable of becoming pregnant.

Fertilization—See Conception.

Fetus—The developing infant inside the mother, from the eighth week of pregnancy until birth. Before the eighth week it is referred to as an embryo.

Forceps—A surgical tonglike instrument that is sometimes used during the delivery of a child to help pull the child through the birth canal.

Foreplay—The beginning stages of sexual play prior to having sexual intercourse.

Foreskin—The fold of skin that covers the tip of a boy's penis at birth. Often it is removed by circumcision.

Gay—A popularly used term for anything having to do with homosexuals.

Genital herpes—A sexually transmitted disease whose primary symptoms include blisters and sores around the genital area. Outbreaks can reoccur repeatedly and, as yet, there is no cure.

Genitals—The external sex organs of both males and females.

Gland—An organ of the body that produces a secretion.

Glans—The head of the penis.

Gonorrhea—A common sexually transmitted disease caused by a bacterial infection. Although dangerous, it often produces no early symptoms in females.

Growth Spurt—The period of time during adolescence when the body increases in size relatively rapidly.

Gynecomastia—A temporary enlarging of the breasts in males. This occurs in about 80 percent of teenage boys going through puberty.

"Hard-on"—A slang term for a male's erection. See Erection.

HCG (human chorionic gonadotrophin)—The female hormone that is measured in order to confirm whether or not a woman is pregnant. It is produced by the developing embryo or placenta during pregnancy.

Health care practitioner—A physician, nurse, or other person qualified and legally authorized to provide certain types of medical care.

Hepatitis—An infection of the liver, which is sometimes transmitted sexually.

Herpes—See Genital herpes.

Heterosexual—A person whose sole or primary sexual attraction is to people of the opposite sex.

Homosexual—A person whose sole or primary sexual attraction is to people of the same sex.

Hormones—Chemical messengers produced by the endocrine glands. They regulate many of the body's activities, including sexual functioning and maturation.

Hygiene—The science of health and practices that promote health.

Hymen—A membrane that covers the entrance to the vagina.

Hypoallergenic—Any substance that is designed not to elicit allergic reactions.

Impotence—A condition in which a male is unable to attain an erection sufficient to engage in sexual intercourse.

Incest—Sexual activity between close relatives.

Inner lips—Another term for the labia minora.

IUD (intrauterine device)—A contraceptive device made of metal or plastic, which is inserted by a physician into a woman's uterus.

Labia—The lips of the female genital area. There are two sets of lips. The labia majora are the larger outer lips, and the labia minora are the smaller inner lips. Both are part of the vulva.

Labor—The process of giving birth to a child.

Lateral position—A position of intercourse in which the couple lies in a side-by-side position, facing each other.

Lesbian—A female homosexual.

Maidenhead—A popular term for the female hymen.

Male-superior position (missionary position)—A position of sexual intercourse in which the male lies on top, facing the female.

Mammary glands—Milk-producing glands contained within the female breasts.

Masturbation—Self-pleasuring by touching one's own genitals to produce sexual excitement and often orgasm.

Menarche—The onset of menstruation in a young woman.

Menopause—The time of life when a woman ceases to menstruate. This will usually occur between the ages of forty-five and fifty-five.

Menstrual cycle—A woman's fertility cycle. For many women this cycle is between twenty-eight and thirty days, but it can vary considerably between women.

Menstrual sponges—Special sponges inserted into the vagina like tampons (see Tampons) in order to catch the menstrual flow before it leaves the body. These sponges have not yet been approved by the federal government because their safety has not been sufficiently proven.

Menstruation—A part of the menstrual cycle in which the inner lining of the uterus, along with a small amount of blood, is eliminated through the vagina. Often referred to as a period.

Mini-pill—A type of birth control pill that contains only a small dose of synthetic progestin rather than both progestin and estrogen as contained in combination pills.

Mittelschmerz—A term meaning "middle pain" in German, it refers to the cramping or slight abdominal pain produced when the egg breaks loose and the ovary bleeds a little during ovulation.

Mons pubis—The "pubic mound." The soft mound of tissue located just above a female's external genitals and covering the pubic bone.

Morning-after pill—Birth control pills, taken the morning after unprotected intercourse, which reduce the chances of becoming pregnant.

Morning sickness—Nausea that is rather typical in women during the early stages of pregnancy and most common in the morning hours.

Mucus—Liquid secretions from the various moist membranes in the body, such as the nose, vagina, and cervix.

Mucus method—A fertility-awareness method in which one learns to recognize changes in cervical mucus at different stages of the menstrual cycle.

Natural methods—Methods of birth control that are based upon trying to predict when a female is fertile. None of these methods is recommended for adolescents.

Nipple—The tip of the breast from which milk is ejected when a woman is nursing.

Nocturnal emission—Ejaculation of semen that occurs on occasion during a male's sleep. Often referred to as a "wet dream."

Nursing—The feeding of a child at the mother's breast.

Oral contraceptive—See Birth control pill.

Oral sex (oral-genital sex)—Any sexual activity that involves contact between the mouth and the genitals. See Cunnilingus and Fellatio.

Orgasm—The peak experience that occurs at the height of sexual excitement, resulting in reflex contractions of the muscles in the pelvic region and a discharge of sexual tension. Often referred to as "coming" or climax.

Outer lips—Another term for the labia majora.

Ovum (*plural*, **ova**)—The egg released by the female's ovary. It is the female reproductive cell.

Ovaries—A pair of sex glands in the female that are responsible for the production of ova (eggs). In addition, they produce female sex hormones. They are located on each side of the upper portion of the uterus.

Ovulation—The process, approximately once each month, of the ovum breaking through the wall of the ovary in order to begin its journey down the fallopian tube.

Pap smear—A test in which cells from the cervix are examined for the presence of abnormalities, in order to detect signs of cancer of the cervix.

Pelvic exam—A medical exam of the female genitals and internal reproductive organs.

Pelvic inflammatory disease (PID)—An inflammation of the fallopian tubes, which may also involve the uterus and the pelvic cavity. It is very dangerous and can lead to sterility.

Penis—The cylindrical male organ used for urination and for sexual activities such as intercourse.

Period—See Menstruation.

Petting—Touching by a partner of any of the sensitive sexual areas of the body.

Placenta—An organ that exchanges oxygen, nutrients, and waste material between the mother and the fetus. It is attached to the inside wall of the uterus.

Pregnancy—The time between conception and childbirth, when the embryo or fetus is developing in the uterus.

Premature ejaculation—A sexual difficulty in men, in which ejaculation occurs too quickly, thus making sexual satisfaction difficult for one or both partners.

Premenstrual syndrome (PMS)—A condition of physical and emotional discomfort that some women experience during the days before menstruation.

Progesterone—One of the female sex hormones. Progesterone causes the lining of the uterus to prepare for implantation of a fertilized egg and helps support the embryo or fetus within the uterus during pregnancy. It is also contained in birth control pills.

Progestin—A synthetic form of progesterone.

Prostate gland—A gland in the male that surrounds the urethra, just below the bladder. This gland is responsible for producing much of the seminal fluid.

Prosthesis (penile)—A permanent implant, surgically placed into the penis of men who are impotent, which then enables them to get an erection.

Puberty—The period during which a boy or girl matures physically and becomes capable of reproduction.

Pubic area—The area of the body just above the external genitals. It becomes covered with pubic hair during puberty.

Pubic bone—The front bone in the group of bones that form the pelvic girdle.

Pubic hair—The hair that covers the area above the vagina in females and penis in males. Pubic hair is one of the first signs of the onset of puberty.

Pubic lice—Small, crab-shaped parasites that can be spread by sexual contact.

Rape—Forced sexual intercourse against a person's will. It is one form of sexual assault.

Refractory period—A period that occurs after orgasm in most men during which the male is incapable of having another erection or ejaculation. This period may last from a few minutes to a few days, depending upon such factors as age, health, and degree of sexual excitement.

Rhythm method—A method of birth control in which sexual intercourse is planned to coincide with times when it is thought that fertilization of the female's egg is unlikely. This tends to be an extremely unreliable form of birth control, especially for teenagers.

"Rubber"—A slang term for a condom.

Sanitary napkins—Sometimes called "feminine pads," they are strips of absorbent material used to collect the menstrual fluid during a female's period.

Scrotum—The pouch of skin in a male that contains the two testes.

Semen—A thick, sticky, whitish liquid that spurts from the penis during ejaculation. It includes a mixture of sperm and seminal fluid.

Seminal vesicles—Two sacklike structures in the male body that produce a secretion that begins the whipping motion of the sperm's tails.

Sex glands—Glands of the endocrine system that are different in the two sexes and produce sex hormones. The male sex glands are the testes and the female sex glands are the ovaries.

Sexual assault—Sexual relations forced upon a person against his or her will. Sexual assault often involves physical force or violence, but also includes sex forced upon someone by the use of threats.

Sexual harassment—Any unwanted attention of a sexual nature from someone in a work or school setting, which creates discomfort or interferes with work performance.

Sexual intercourse—The placement of the male's penis into the female's vagina.

Sexual molestation—Sexual acts that are forced upon a child by an adult whether the child consents to them or not. Also referred to as child molestation.

Sexually transmitted diseases (STDs)—Formerly called venereal diseases. Any of a number of diseases that can be transmitted during the close body contact that occurs with sexual activity. Gonorrhea, herpes, and syphilis are some examples.

Shaft—The longer part (or body) of the clitoris or penis.

69—Mutual oral-genital sexual activity. This term is so called because the positions of the bodies during this type of sexual activity somewhat resemble the figure *69*.

Smegma—A cheesy mixture of secretions and skin cells that can build up under the foreskin of the uncircumcised penis or around the lips of the vulva.

Speculum—A duck-billed medical instrument used to open and view the vagina during a pelvic exam.

Sperm—Microscopic cells that are responsible for fertilizing the female egg (ovum). These reproductive cells are produced by the testes.

Spermicide—A substance used for birth control that, when placed in the female's vagina, kills sperm before they can meet with the ovum. These substances may be in the form of foams, jellies, creams, suppositories, or, in a relatively new method, can be placed in a special sponge. Spermicides are often used along with a condom or a diaphragm to ensure that they work more effectively.

Statutory rape—A legal term for sexual intercourse with any adolescent under the age of consent. Often these laws apply only to females under the age of consent. It does not matter whether or not the intercourse was voluntary on the teenager's part.

STD—See Sexually transmitted diseases.

Sterility—Inability to become pregnant.

Sterilization—Any permanent procedure that causes a male or female to be unable to produce offspring. Common methods of sterilization are vasectomy in the male and tubal ligation in the female.

Syphilis—A highly contagious sexually transmitted disease. One of the common symptoms during the early stages are chancres. These disappear as the disease enters the more dangerous later stages.

Tampons—Absorbent material that is inserted into the vagina during a female's period to catch the menstrual flow before it leaves the body.

Testes—The two male sex glands located in the scrotum. They produce sperm and male sex hormones.

Testicles— Another name for the testes.

Testosterone—The primary male sex hormone. See Androgen.

Toxic shock syndrome (TSS)—A dangerous disease caused by a bacterial infection. In most cases, this disease has occurred in menstruating women. It may be related to the use of tampons.

Transsexual—A person who biologically is born of one gender (sex), but constantly feels that he or she is trapped in the body of the wrong sex. Surgical procedures to change the sex of the person are often performed.

Transvestite—See Cross-dresser.

Trichomoniasis—An irritation or infection of the female genitals caused by a microscopic one-celled animal. Males also contract and transmit "trich," but seldom have symptoms of the disease.

Trimester—A three-month segment of pregnancy. Pregnancy is typically divided into three trimesters.

Tubal ligation—The most common method of surgical sterilization performed on females. In this method, the fallopian tubes are cut so the ova cannot meet the sperm.

Tubal pregnancy—See Ectopic pregnancy.

Umbilical cord—The cord connecting the fetus with the placenta.

Urethra—The tube through which urine is discharged from the body. In the male it is also used to ejaculate the semen.

Uterus—The womb. The organ that holds the growing baby during pregnancy.

Vacuum aspiration—A method of abortion typically used in the first three months of pregnancy in which the contents of the uterus are removed via a vacuum method.

Vagina—The tube that connects the uterus with the vulva. During sexual intercourse, the erect penis is placed into the vagina. During childbirth, the vagina acts as the birth canal through which the newborn child is delivered.

Vaginitis—Any infection or irritation of the vagina.

Vaginismus—A sexual dysfunction in females in which the muscles surrounding the vagina involuntarily go into spasm when penetration is attempted.

Vas deferens—A duct consisting of two narrow tubes that carry sperm in the male from the testes to the urethra.

Vasectomy—Cutting of the vas deferens. This operation is performed on men as a form of birth control. After a vasectomy, the male still ejaculates the seminal fluid, but without the sperm, which are necessary for reproduction.

VCF (Vaginal contraceptive film)—A new contraceptive product consisting of paper-thin, two-inch-square films containing spermicide. The film is inserted into the vagina prior to intercourse.

Venereal warts— Small bumps on or near the genitals, which are caused by a virus. They can be spread by sexual contact.

Vestibule—The indented area of the female vulva between the inner lips. It contains the openings of the vagina and the urethra.

Virgin—A person who has never engaged in sexual intercourse.

Vulva—A term that refers to a woman's external sex organs.

Wet dream—An ejaculation that occurs during a male's sleep. It is also referred to as a nocturnal emission.

Withdrawal—See Coitus interruptus.

Yeast infection—Another term for candidiasis.

Zygote—The single cell that results from the union of an egg and sperm after fertilization.

NOTES

1. BECOMING A SEXUAL PERSON

1. Crowe, Cameron, *Fast Times at Ridgemont High: A True Story* (New York: Simon and Schuster, 1981), 65.

2. LEARNING ABOUT SEX

1. Hass, Aaron, Ph.D., *Teenage Sexuality* (New York: Pinnacle Books, 1981), 210.
2. Crowe, Cameron, *Fast Times at Ridgemont High: A True Story* (New York: Simon and Schuster, 1981), 65–66.

4. THE MENSTRUAL CYCLE

1. U.S. Department of Health and Human Services, Public Health Service, *Toxic Shock Syndrome and Tampons*, HHS Publication No. (FDA)81-4025.

5. BEING COMFORTABLE WITH YOUR BODY

1. Hass, Aaron, Ph.D., *Teenage Sexuality* (New York: Pinnacle Books, 1981), 210.
2. Hite, Shere, *The Hite Report: A Nationwide Study of Female Sexuality* (New York: Dell, 1976).

6. KEEPING YOUR BODY HEALTHY

1. This chapter was prepared with the assistance of Grant Leroy Campbell, M.D.
2. Boston Women's Health Collective, *Our Bodies, Ourselves* (New York: Simon and Schuster, 1976), 137.
3. Ibid., 128.
4. American Cancer Society, *How to Examine Your Breasts*, pamphlet No. 2088-LE.

8. PREGNANCY AND CHILDBIRTH

1. The major reference for this chapter was Pritchard, J. A., and P. C. MacDonald, *Williams Obstetrics* (New York: Appleton-Century-Crofts, 1976).

9. MAKING DECISIONS ABOUT SEX

1. Butler, Pamela, *Self-Assertion For Women* (New York: Harper & Row, 1981).

10. SEX: WHAT IT'S ALL ABOUT

1. Hite, Shere, *The Hite Report: A Nationwide Study of Female Sexuality* (New York: Dell, 1976).
2. Hass, Aaron, Ph.D., *Teenage Sexuality* (New York: Pinnacle Books, 1981), 55.
3. Kaplan, H. S., *Disorders of Sexual Desire* (New York: Brunner/Mazel, 1979).

11. FIRST SEXUAL EXPERIENCES AND CONTINUING SEXUAL RELATIONSHIPS

1. Knox, D., "Sexual Intercourse," chapter in *Human Sexuality: The Search for Understanding* (St. Paul, Minn.: West, 1984).

2. Coles, R., and G. Stokes, *Sex and the American Teenager* (New York: Rolling Stone Press, 1985), 73.
3. Weiss, D. L., "Affective Reactions of Women to Their Initial Experience of Coitus," *Journal of Sex Research*, 1983, 19: 295–306.
4. Coles and Stokes, *Sex and the American Teenager*, 85.
5. Kolodny,R. C., in W. H. Masters, V. E. Johnson, and R. C. Kolodny, *Human Sexuality* (Boston: Little, Brown, 1985), 237.
6. Zellman, G. L., P. B. Johnson, R. Giarrusso, and J. D. Goodchilds, "Adolescent Expectations for Dating Relationships: Consensus and Conflict Between the Sexes." Paper presented at the meeting of the American Psychological Association, New York, September 1979.

12. CONTRACEPTION (OR BIRTH CONTROL)

1. Alan Guttmacher Institute, *11 Million Teenagers* (New York: Planned Parenthood, 1976).
2. The major reference for this chapter is Hatcher, Robert A., Felicia Guest, Felicia Stewart, Gary K. Stewart, James Trussell, Sylvia Cerel, and Willard Cates, *Contraceptive Technology: 1986–1987* (New York: Irvington Publishers, Inc., 1986).
3. Ibid., 107.
4. Ibid., 216.
5. Ibid., 212.
6. Ibid., 155.
7. Ibid., 101–111.
8. Ibid., 102.

13. SEXUALLY TRANSMITTED DISEASES

1. This chapter was prepared with the assistance of Grant Leroy Campbell, M.D.
2. Centers for Disease Control, Division of Venereal Disease Control: STD Statistical Letter, 1982.

3. U.S. Department of Health and Human Services/Public Health Service, *Morbidity and Mortality Weekly Report: Annual Summary 1983*, December 1984, Vol. 32, No. 54, 22–25.
4. Ibid., 91.

14. SEXUAL DIFFERENCES

1. Kinsey, A. C., W. B. Pomeroy, and C. E. Martin, *Sexual Behavior in the Human Male* (Philadelphia: W. B. Saunders, 1948).
2. Kinsey, A. C., W. B. Pomeroy, C. E. Martin, and P. Gebhard, *Sexual Behavior in the Human Female* (Philadelphia: W. B. Saunders, 1953).
3. Crooks, R., and K. Baur, *Our Sexuality* (Menlo Park, Calif.: Benjamin/Cummings, 1983).
4. Masters, W. H., and V. E. Johnson, *Homosexuality in Perspective* (Boston: Little, Brown, 1979).
5. Hanckel, Frances, and John Cunningham, *A Way of Love, A Way of Life: A Young Person's Introduction to What It Means to Be Gay* (New York: Lothrop, Lee and Shepard [William Morrow], 1979), 35.
6. Ibid., 80–81.
7. Ibid., 67.
8. Ibid., 46.
9. Hass, Aaron, Ph.D., *Teenage Sexuality* (New York: Pinnacle Books, 1981).

15. SEXUAL PROBLEMS

1. Masters, W. H., and V. E. Johnson, *Human Sexual Inadequacy* (Boston: Little, Brown, 1970).
2. Ibid.

16. DEALING WITH AN UNPLANNED PREGNANCY

1. Zelnick, M., and J. Kantner, "First Pregnancies to Women Aged 15–19: 1976 and 1971," *Family Planning Perspectives*, 1978, 10–11.

2. Hatcher, R. A., G. Stewart, F. Stewart, F. Guest, N. Josephs and J. Dale, *Contraceptive Technology: 1982–1983* (New York: Irvington, 1982), 5.
3. Gordon, S., P. Scales, and K. Everly, *The Sexual Adolescent: Communicating with Teenagers About Sex* (North Scituate, Mass.: Duxbury Press, 1979), 3.
4. Hatcher, et al., *Contraceptive Technology*, 7.
5. Gordon, et al., *The Sexual Adolescent*, 100.
6. Sex Information and Education Council of the U.S., *Teenage Pregnancy: Prevention and Treatment*, 1971, 5.
7. National Institutes of Health, *The Women and Their Pregnancies: The Collaborative Perinatal Study of the National Institute of Neurological Diseases and Stroke* (Washington, D.C.: GPO, 1972).
8. Gordon, et al., *The Sexual Adolescent*; Oppel, W. and A. Royston, "Teenage Births: Some Social, Psychological, and Physical Sequelae," *American Journal of Public Health*, 1971, Vol. 61(4): 751–56; and Sex Information and Education Council of the U.S., *Teenage Pregnancy*, 6.
9. Sex Information and Education Council of the U.S., *Teenage Pregnancy*, 6.

17. SEXUAL EXPLOITATION

1. *Ms.* Magazine Campus Project on Sexual Assault, funded by the National Center for the Prevention and Control of Rape, in *Ms.*, October 1985, 56.
2. Rape Awareness and Education Program, Women's Resource Center, "Myths—Realities" (University of California at Irvine).
3. Crime Prevention Center, California Department of Justice, *Sexual Assault Handbook*, 1982, 5–7.
4. Rape Awareness and Education Program, Women's Resource Center, "Suggestions for Self-Protection" (University of California at Irvine).
5. Masters, W. H., V. E. Johnson, and R. C. Kolodny, *Human Sexuality* (Boston: Little, Brown, 1985), 467.
6. Wilson, K., and R. Faison, "Victims of Sexual Assault Dur-

ing Courtship," unpublished paper, Dept. of Sociology, Anthropology, and Economics, East Carolina Univ., 1983; Kanin, E. J., "Selected Dyadic Aspects of Male Sex Aggression" in *Journal of Sex Research*, 1969, 5; and *Ms.* Magazine Campus Project on Sexual Assault, funded by the National Center for the Prevention and Control of Rape, in *Ms.*, October 1985, 56.

7. Zellman, G.L., P.B. Johnson, R. Giarrusso, and J.D. Goodchilds, "Adolescent Expectations for Dating Relationships: Consensus and Conflict Between the Sexes," paper presented at the meeting of the American Psychological Association, New York, September 1979.
8. Giarrusso, R., P. Johnson, J. Goodchilds, and G. Zellman, "Adolescents' Cues and Signals: Sex and Assault," paper presented at the Western Psychological Association Meeting, San Diego, April 1979.
9. Adams, C. and J. Fay, *"Nobody Told Me It Was Rape": A Parents' Guide for Talking with Teenagers about Acquaintance Rape and Sexual Exploitation* (Santa Cruz, Calif.: Network, 1984); and Sherman, J., "Acquaintance Rape on Campus," unpublished paper, Rape Awareness and Education Program, University of Calif., Irvine.
10. Justice, B., and R. Justice, *The Broken Taboo: Sex in the Family* (New York: Human Sciences Press, 1979), 16–17.
11. Crooks, R., and K. Baur, *Our Sexuality* (Menlo Park, Calif.: Benjamin/Cummings, 1983), 602–603.
12. Bartlett, K., *The Oregonian*, Feb. 28, 1982, A 22.
13. Bartlett, K., and C. Safran, "What Men Do to Women on the Job: A Shocking Look at Sexual Harassment," *Redbook*, Nov. 1976, 148ff.
14. Crooks and Baur, *Our Sexuality*, 602–603.

INDEX